DIALOGIC: EDUCATION FOR THE INTERNET AGE

Dialogic: Education for the Internet Age argues that despite rapid advances in communications technology, most teaching still relies on traditional approaches to education, built upon the logic of print, and dependent on the notion that there is a single true representation of reality. In practice, the use of the Internet disrupts this traditional logic of education by offering an experience of knowledge as participatory and multiple.

This new logic of education is dialogic and characterizes education as learning to learn, think and thrive in the context of working with multiple perspectives and ultimate uncertainty. The book builds upon the simple contrast between observing dialogue from an outside point of view, and participating in a dialogue from the inside, before pinpointing an essential feature of dialogic: the gap or difference between voices in dialogue which is understood as an irreducible source of meaning. Each chapter of the book applies this dialogic thinking to a specific challenge facing education, rethinking the challenge and revealing a new theory of education.

Areas covered in the book include:

- dialogical learning and cognition
- dialogical learning and emotional intelligence
- educational technology, dialogic 'spaces' and consciousness
- global dialogue and global citizenship
- dialogic theories of science and maths education.

The challenge identified in Wegerif's text is the growing need to develop a new understanding of education that holds the potential to transform educational policy and pedagogy in order to meet the realities of the digital age. *Dialogic: Education for the Internet Age* draws upon the latest research in dialogic theory, creativity and technology, and is essential reading for advanced students and researchers in educational psychology, technology and policy.

Rupert Wegerif is Professor of Education and Director of Research at the Graduate School of Education, University of Exeter, UK.

DIALOGIC: EDUCATION FOR THE INTERNET AGE

Rupert Wegerif

 Routledge
Taylor & Francis Group

LONDON AND NEW YORK

First published 2013
by Routledge
2 Park Square, Milton Park, Abingdon, Oxon OX14 4RN

Simultaneously published in the USA and Canada
by Routledge
711 Third Avenue, New York, NY 10017

Routledge is an imprint of the Taylor & Francis Group, an informa business

British Library Cataloguing in Publication Data
A catalogue record for this book is available from the British Library

Library of Congress Cataloging in Publication Data
Wegerif, Rupert, 1959-
Dialogic : education for the Internet age / Rupert Wegerif.
p. cm.
ISBN 978-0-415-53678-3 (hardback) -- ISBN 978-0-415-53679-0 (paperback) --
ISBN 978-0-203-11122-2 (ebook) 1. Internet in education--Philosophy. 2. Education--
Effect of technological innovations on. 3. Questioning. I. Title.
LB1044.87.W475 2013
371.33'44678--dc23
2012026137

ISBN: 978-0-415-53678-3 (hbk)
ISBN: 978-0-415-53679-0 (pbk)
ISBN: 978-0-203-11122-2 (ebk)

Typeset in Bembo
by Fakenham Prepress Solutions, Fakenham, Norfolk NR21 8NN

Printed and bound in Great Britain by
TJ International Ltd, Padstow, Cornwall

To Danny, who has taught me so much

CONTENTS

ACKNOWLEDGEMENTS

I would like to thank my wife Julieta for her love and support. Thanks are also due to Exeter University for providing some study leave to help with this book. The projects described involved the work and ideas of a large number of people. I would particularly like to thank Yang Yang and Ruth Gwernan-Jones for giving feedback on early drafts and Keith Postlethwaite for substantial help with the chapter on science education. Two projects described in the book are funded by the European Union under their FP7 programme: 'Metafora' (ICT 257872) and Science Education for Diversity (SED) (SiS 244717). All the members of these two project teams need to be thanked. I am also grateful to Dr John Raven who holds the copyright for Raven's Reasoning Tests for preparing a parallel problem to Raven's B12 for use by the 'Thinking Together' research team in publications.

1

THE CHALLENGE

The Internet has changed everything. Although it has been around for a while now we are only just beginning to explore the many ways in which it can enable us to do things differently. The Internet has obvious potential for education. But the kind of education that it supports is not exactly the same as the kind of education found in schools. In fact there seems to be some tension between the concept of education that emerges from engagement with the Internet and the concept of education that lies behind schooling. The concept of education afforded by print is a form of monologic which can be summarized as the transmission of true representations. The concept of education afforded by the Internet is a form of dialogic which can be summarized as participation in ongoing enquiry in an unbounded context. Understanding the shift from print to the Internet as a shift of underlying ways of thinking from monologic to dialogic can help us understand what is really happening to us now, which can help us to design the future together.

What is happening to us?

The Internet has been with us for a while now but we are still just at the beginning of understanding how best to work with it and to live with it. Various attempts have already been made to rethink education through the experience of the Internet. I think that most of them fail to understand the emerging new logic of the Internet Age. The problem is that we are trying to understand the future in terms of ways of thinking that helped to guide us in the past. In this book I uncover the logic of the Internet Age and I apply this new logic – a form of dialogic – to understand education.

The obvious affordances of the Internet for education are becoming a commonplace experience for many of us. Recently I heard my 12-year-old son talking to someone while sitting in front of his laptop. I looked over his shoulder and saw the face of his slightly older cousin on the top right hand side of his screen while on the left of the screen was a website. His cousin was talking him through a complicated procedure. It turned out my son had decided to try to build a music collection by stripping the music tracks out of his favourite YouTube music videos. He had got stuck and so he video-Skyped his cousin who talked him through how to do the job. I wondered if this was legal, but I was impressed at this collaborative problem solving.

When my son was about 8 years old he became really frustrated with a stage in a stand-alone video game, I think it was Lego Batman. Seeing him practically crying on the sofa I wanted to help. I recalled how I usually managed to solve computer problems by Googling the obscure error messages that pop up on my screen when something goes wrong. This kind of search often led me to an online discussion forum where people offer each other advice on what the error message means and how to solve the error. I therefore suggested this strategy to my son. Together we Googled his video game problem using an initially vague search question like 'stuck on lego-batman stage three, how do you get the door open?' We soon found detailed 'walk-through' videos of how to get through every challenge in the video game. These 'walk-through' videos had been made and uploaded by other young players just to help out. I was impressed. It struck me that these children had taken a lot of trouble to help people that they did not even know. I wondered what motivated them. On reflection I thought that it might be the same sort of motivation that leads me to want to share my own passions and discoveries with others by writing articles and books.

Thinking and writing with the Internet now is a very different experience for me than the kind of thinking and writing that I remember from before the Internet. In those days when I had the glimmer of an idea that I wanted to follow up, I searched the library catalogues to find relevant books, I went to the place on the shelves indicated and when this proved fruitless, as it often did, I had to order articles from the British Library or recall books that were out with another reader and I then had to wait for days or weeks for them to arrive. When they did arrive they often proved disappointing or no longer relevant as my ideas had already moved on. Now, whenever I have an idea that I think might be fruitful, I Google it to see if others have tackled this same problem before, or just to find out what other people have to say. Yesterday, for example, I tried to find out about the impact of print on ways of thinking in China and I found a bibliography on the web of studies of the history of literacy in China that will help me approach this topic. I felt grateful that someone was prepared to offer such a useful service for me in this way. In return I try to make sure that my educational research is available for free on the web for anyone who might find it useful. My son has not put up any walkthroughs to video games in order to help others yet but I think that he will one day soon.

Surveys of Internet behaviour show that these kinds of informal educational experiences online are common now for everyone who is connected to the Internet, regardless of age. My mother, who is 80, shares tips on her family tree with others who are searching to construct their own family tree. She also shares the beautiful paintings that she has made throughout her life but which, up until now, have had only a very limited audience. Facebook, which began in 2004 in Mark Zuckerberg's student dorm, now, as I write in 2012, has 1 billion users and is still growing. It essentially consists of creating and sharing online resources many of which include the sort of thoughts and tips that others can and do learn from. As people learn about each other in social networks like Facebook they also learn about music, films, books, politics and places worth visiting.

Informal educational activity using the Internet has become so normal now that we perhaps think that it does not imply a need for any new educational theory. I do not agree. It is interesting that the one place children are not connected to the Internet is the school classroom.[1] New businesses have arisen because of the Internet, old businesses have been transformed by the Internet, but one major human activity which remains largely unaffected by the Internet is formal education. This may be because of a deep-level incompatibility. If we think through the kind of education that is happening now on the Internet it embodies a quite different educational logic from the logic that lies behind formal education systems.

The Internet will not go away. All the signs are that the Internet will continue growing in bandwidth, in number of users and in associated technologies giving access in more situations. This means more new uses, more compelling interfaces and more immersive experiences. It is important that we take the trouble to step back and think through the implications of what is happening to us now. Understanding what is happening to us might enable us to be less reactive to change in the future and more proactive in response to the opportunities that the Internet Age offers. We need a new theory of education that understands the Internet in order to be able to design a better future.

From print to Internet: from monologic to dialogic

In this book I argue that the Internet is a disruptive technology for education. It cannot simply be incorporated into existing formal education systems without changing them. This is because existing formal education systems are built around the logic of print and the Internet has a different inner logic. Print can be used in many ways, of course, but the formal schooling system has been built around its affordance for monologic and serves to reinforce the monologic potential of print. Monologic assumes that there is one correct version of reality and one correct method of thinking. The correct version of reality is represented in the books that are selected as the core curriculum and schools transmit these representations into the minds of students. Despite some variations and experiments, on the whole the model of schooling is remarkably similar all around the world.[2]

One distinctive new affordance of the Internet, in contrast to print and most other mass-media, is that it is intrinsically participatory. Like print, the Internet can be used in many ways but unlike print, it affords dialogic. Dialogic, as opposed to monologic, assumes that there is always more than one voice. More than this, dialogic assumes that meaning is never singular but always emerges in the play of different voices in dialogue together. An implication of this, which I bring out later, is that a certain kind of infinity or unbounded potential is opened onto by dialogic, an infinity of possible meaning which monologic tries to close down or to ignore. The point of dialogic education, is therefore, not so much transmission of representations, but drawing students into participation in dialogues in an ultimately unbounded context. In other words, as well as having to learn how to dialogue with this or that specific other and this or that carefully bounded cultural voice, students need to learn how to dialogue with the Infinite Other, an other that they cannot know in advance or pin down or even ever fully understand.

I will bring out the nature of dialogic education in more detail in the next two chapters but before that, to preempt a possible misunderstanding, I want to say that it is not simply the same thing as student-centred education or constructivism. If one wants to join a dialogue it is wise not to butt in too abruptly. It is best to take time initially just listening to what people are talking about and learning how they are talking about it. Dialogic education is not only about joining in dialogues with our peers in the present time, say, for example, getting children to talk together in a classroom, but more essentially it is also about engaging in the longer-term dialogue of the culture. This implies dialogue with absent cultural voices. In other words drawing children and students into dialogue with the voices of wisdom and experience from our past is a key function of education and is part of helping them to find their own voice. Teachers therefore have an essential role in summing up the dialogue so far and guiding newcomers in how to participate in it. Dialogic education is neither student-centred nor teacher-centred, or, rather, it is both student-centred and teacher-centred, because it is *dialogue*-centred.

Dialogic space

Although many aspects of dialogic education make it compatible with both social-constructivism[3] and situated learning theory,[4] there is an important difference with both that makes it useful as a distinct way to understand education for the Internet age. This difference is the underlying dialogic gap, a gap which manifests in experience as dialogic space. The dialogic gap is the gap between perspectives in a dialogue.

When we think of dialogues we probably think of empirical dialogues that occur at a certain place and time between particular people, three children talking together in a classroom for example. In doing this we are looking at dialogues as if from the outside. But dialogues also have an inside. On the inside of the dialogue we might be talking about people who are not present, distant places and past or future events. From the outside dialogues are always situated in space and time but when lived from the inside, dialogues establish their own space and time. This is what distinguishes a dialogue from an interaction. Robots can interact but their interactions remain in external space. When humans enter into dialogue there is a new space of meaning that opens up between them and includes them within it. The external 'objective' view that locates things in their proper place is always 'monologic' because it assumes a single fixed perspective. The internal view that takes the other seriously is 'dialogic' because, when experienced from inside dialogues, meaning always assumes at least two perspectives held together in creative tension. Without this creative tension over a gap of difference there would be no experience of meaning.

Social constructivism and connectionism and networked learning theory and other theories that claim to be responding to the new educational needs of the Internet Age often seem to assume only an external view and do not go beyond this. Yes, it is quite true, as connectivism and networked learning claims, that people can be looked at from the outside as if they are nodes in a network, but unlike machines they also have an inside perspective which enables them to transcend the network and to rethink the network.[5]

The space of the Internet that is sometimes called 'cyberspace', is not an external space that can be measured in terms of servers and fibre-optic cables: it is a dialogic space supporting the interplay of billions of voices. Yes, as social constructivism says, people do construct meanings together in dialogues, but dialogic education is not only concerned with the quality of what they construct but, more importantly, it is concerned with the quality of the space within which they construct and with the quality of the educational dialogues through which they construct. Good education is not just about making things, even if we label these things 'meanings' or 'cultural artefacts', but it is also, more importantly, about expanding the capacity to participate in dialogue.

Re-wiring our brains?

The increasing use of the Internet has led to educational concerns often focusing on the danger of brains being wired differently. Nicholas Carr argued, in his influential book, *The Shallows*, that the use of the Internet has inevitably distracting effects leading to brains with short attention spans incapable of deep reflection.[6] His main contrast is between the multi-tasking and short-term kind of attention of new technology use by the typical teenager with the experience of thinking gained through longer and more contemplative activities like reading books. In the UK the distinguished neuro-physiologist, Baroness Susan Greenfield appeared to lend support to this argument with various talks and interviews about the danger of minds being damaged. She told a House of Lords enquiry, for example, that children's experiences on social networking sites

> are devoid of cohesive narrative and long-term significance. As a consequence, the mid-21st century mind might almost be infantilised, characterised by short attention spans, sensationalism, inability to empathise and a shaky sense of identity.[7]

These are dramatic claims that point to an important topic for research. However, I suspect that it is a little too soon to pass judgement on the Internet. It is noteworthy that perhaps the best known dialogic educational thinker, Socrates, is reported by Plato in his dialogue, the *Phaedrus*, to have made some remarkably similar claims about the infantilizing effects of the then new information technology of writing. Writing, Socrates said, will lead to a loss of memory, as people can now just look things up instead of having to learn everything by heart. It is easy to give the impression of being clever by copying other people's speeches, Socrates continued, but a text cannot answer back. Writing therefore encourages people to be superficial and does not support learning to reason in dialogue with others which is the true source of intelligence. Socrates' implication is that by living in a world of written words one can avoid the face-to-face accountability for one's own proper words, which is essential for moral development.[8]

What if Socrates was right? Carr and Greenfield's arguments point to the interesting fact that our use of communications technologies shapes the way our brains work and the kind of thoughts that we are capable of having. Drawing attention to the new brain-shaping impact of Internet use also makes us aware, retrospectively, of how print-based education must have shaped the brains of generations of children. Print-based education probably has some positive benefits or it would not have arisen and spread to become almost universal. But what if it also has limitations that impact negatively on the potential for human development and for collective well-being?

Before mass print-based education, culture everywhere was largely oral and thinking was mostly understood in terms of dialogues. According to Toulmin, the tradition of thinking about thinking as a type of dialogue was maintained up to the sixteenth century by humanist writers such as Erasmus and Montaigne.[9] Toulmin points out that there was a major shift in Europe in the seventeenth century with thinkers such as Descartes, Leibniz and Newton. This new generation of thinkers at the beginning of what became called the Enlightenment, replaced the image of arguments as utterances in dialogues with the image of arguments as propositions in proofs.

The shift in the dominant means of communication that we are now undergoing is bigger than the shift introduced by Gutenberg's printing press but is in fact closer in significance to the shift from oracy to literacy that Socrates lived through. The Internet, like oracy, is a medium that affords participation and dialogue. It is not surprising, therefore, that some of the changes that are occurring now might seem like a return to the experiences and ways of thinking of oral societies. However, the Internet is also much more than a return to oracy. Like print, it can support dialogue at a distance, both distance of space and distance in time. And like print, ideas that flow through the Internet remain after they have been expressed, carried in a form that enables them to be reflected upon and improved. In this way the Internet continues to support print-based ways of thinking, but it locates this kind of thinking more clearly than before in a larger context, the context of the long-term living dialogue of humanity. Calling this dialogue 'living' is another way of saying that it is unpredictable and unbounded in its potential because nobody can get outside of it and tell you where it will go or what its limits are.

For the last 400 years or so, theory has been dominated by a powerful and dangerous delusion, the delusion of monologism. This delusion has been maintained and even enforced by educational practices associated with print technology. The Internet, now emerging as the new dominant means of communication from within the age of print, opens up new possibilities for thinking and for being human. Perhaps partly because of the rise of the Internet, many are now able to see the dangers and distortions of monologism as if for the first time. But, despite regular critiques of monological assumptions, we still in fact remain largely in the grip of monologic ways of thinking and monologic ways of being because monologic is built into many of the structures we inhabit, the education system in particular, and it is implicit in many of the tools that we use to help us think.

Monologic is not imposed by writing and by print but it is imposed by the way that writing and print are used within formal education systems to establish authority. Like writing and print, the Internet can be used in many ways and so has many possibilities for shaping our brains. In this book I argue that some of these new possibilities for brain-shaping brought in by the Internet could correct the distortions of the monologic illusion sustained by print-based education and so could be very positive, even liberating, for the future of humanity. Whether or not we realize this positive potential of the Internet does not depend upon the technology alone but it depends much more upon what we do with the technology. The advent of the Internet raises a challenge for educators to think about how we will use the Internet in education.

Neuroscience as a useful lens

The assertion that print-based education shapes our brains so that reality is experienced in a limited way may sound extreme to some readers but it is just another way of saying something quite simple that I think we probably all already know. When you recognize something and respond to it, a word on this page for example, your brain is following a route laid down at some point in your educational history. There are now techniques that can track this brain activity to some extent using scanning machines and brain caps that detect blood flow and changes in electrical potential.[10] One clear and simple message relevant to education from this neuroscience research is often expressed in the aphorism: 'neurons that fire together, wire together'. As you are reading this text now you are not really looking at each letter, assembling them into words and then decoding them, at least I hope not, as that approach to reading would be very slow. I expect it is more likely that as you read you move in a world of meaning that depends upon a complex hierarchy of automatic neural processes laid down during your past educational experience. In other words neurons that fired together in the past as you learnt to read have now wired together enabling a relatively smooth and automatic experience of reading that moves straight into a virtual world of meanings evoked by the letters.

I will give a very simple example that I hope will bring home the relevance of this neuroscience perspective to education. Newborn babies can both hear and produce the full range of sound distinctions used in all human language.[11] People around them direct their attention by showing interest in some sounds and not in others. In this way the initial multitude of neural responses is reduced, meaning that the initially vast number of synaptical links between neurons becomes pruned. By the age of just ten months it is no longer possible for most English babies to hear some of the key sounds used as distinctions in any of the spoken varieties of Chinese such as the difference between the 'chi' and 'qi' sounds. It is similarly impossible for most Chinese babies to even hear key distinctions in English such as the difference between the 'l' and the 'r'.

Some educationalists resist the use of neuroscience language claiming that it adds nothing to what we already know and implies reductionism. I choose to refer to neuroscience in this book because I think that the language of neurons and neural pathways can help us to think more clearly about what education is and what it does. It is not at all reductionist to claim that everything we experience implies correlated neural activity. In my view this is an 'expansionist' claim since it offers us a new way of looking at familiar things. I find it illuminating to think about aspects of education in terms of neural routes laid down over time such that the more we make certain connections the stronger the route becomes. The way children learn the spoken language of their culture, as we have seen, shows that the routes involved are not hard-wired from birth. However, such neural pathways can easily come to seem hard-wired after only about ten months of constant practice. This closing down of neural patterns is not an absolute law. There are always things that we can do to keep the mind open for longer. Interestingly, for example, the window of time during which children are most open to learning to hear and to produce new words sounds (phonemes) is increased significantly in bilingual households. This is because children in bi-lingual households have two different sets of sounds to learn and so are less quick to dismiss new sounds as being irrelevant.[12]

Research on people recovering from brain damage reveals, against the consensus view held during most of the last century, that the brain is remarkably plastic. This means that we are capable of learning almost anything at almost any age. Plasticity in the sense of the ease of forging new neural pathways, does fall off as people get older. This is especially true for sensory discrimination such as the example I gave of learning the new sounds of a foreign language. However, this falling off in plasticity just means that more effort is needed to dig up established routes and re-wire them.[13] While the easy learning of new phonemes in early childhood has a short time window for most people, learning to think does not have any similar time limitations. There is no evidence that the activity we normally call thinking, talking to others and talking to ourselves, needs to become fixed in established routes as we get older. This is a shocking finding. It contradicts the evidence of experience that in fact most people seem to get more fixed in their thinking as they get older.

How literacy changes the brain

That the brain changes whenever we learn new skills is hardly surprising. While any given neural pathway may enable a particular way of experiencing or way of thinking it will inevitably limit other possible ways of experiencing or ways of thinking. Learning to read and write can happen at any age but when it does happen it has an impact on the structure of the brain. Literates do not only hear words, but they also have the option of 'seeing them'. We know this from experience but also because when literates listen to spoken words activity is often found in the parts of their brain that process vision.[14] Non-literates cannot see words but can only hear them as they are spoken. This shift from only hearing words to also seeing words is very significant for thought, giving the impression that we can pin down and analyse meanings themselves simply by holding words in our inner visual attention. This literate potential to see words as well as hear them provides essential support for the monologic illusion that meanings can be objectified and treated as if they were things independent of any dialogue.

Neuroscientist Stanislaus Dehaene conducted ground-breaking research comparing literates, illiterates and ex-illiterates on various tasks with FMRI (Functional Magnetic Resonance Imaging) brain scans. These scans offered clear evidence for differences in brain structure between these groups.[15] Because word recognition colonizes functions in the visual cortex, there are some losses associated with becoming literate. Dehaene found reduced function in the recognition of faces, for example, and that literates lost some of their capacity for holistic perception while gaining a greater capacity for analytic perception. This effect was most marked in those taught literacy from their infancy. Research in comparative psychology, ethnography and communications studies suggest that these findings reflect quite important distinctions in the ways of thinking found in oral cultures, like that of Socrates, compared with contemporary literate cultures.[16] The big question that this research raises is: what will be the impact on ways of seeing, thinking and being of those now engaged in Internet use from birth onwards?

From truth to dialogue

Bakhtin, a classical scholar much influenced by Socrates, relates the contrast between monologic and dialogic to the difference between an authoritative voice and a persuasive voice. The authoritative voice remains outside of me, he writes, and orders me to do something in a way that forces me to accept or reject it without engaging with it, whereas the words of the persuasive voice enter into the realm of my own words and change them from within.[17] This contrast has obvious implications for education. Are we educating only for the transmission of truths backed up by authority or for the capacity for thinking and learning together?

I still sometimes overhear my university colleagues warning students against using Wikipedia as, so they say, it is 'not reliable' since, 'anyone can change anything'. I guess that is true, but I find it useful to find out what other people have to say about topics that interest me. In fact a recent study found that Wikipedia, the collaboratively constructed encyclopaedia of the Internet, is not only more up to date than *Encyclopaedia Britannica*, which one would expect, but also more accurate when it comes to checkable factual errors.[18] But such comparisons miss the point. Wikipedia is an altogether different kind of text than a print encyclopaedia. Print is a one-to-many medium with the authority, which is also to say, the authorship, controlled by the centre. Wikis are collaborative and participatory. This means that the reader needs to be critically aware and to cross-check with other sources. Using Wikipedia effectively requires a shift in attitude from being a passive consumer of other people's version of the 'truth' to becoming an active participant in the process through which we construct useful but always fallible shared knowledge. It is also worth noting that for using Wikipedia effectively some prior education into how to question, triangulate and learn together with others, might be valuable.

Those who compare Wikipedia to print encyclopaedias and find Wikipedia wanting often reveal an underlying monological or print-based conception of knowledge. The same assumption can be seen behind the consternation expressed by newspapers and politicians when websites and email trails reveal that scientists have different views on matters such as whether global warming is man-made or the harmful side-effects of vaccinations. The Print Age supported by formal print-based education encouraged the illusion revealed by Socrates as the danger inherent in writing. This is the idea of unsituated Truth that is not part of any dialogue, like written down speeches that, as he put it, look good but cannot answer back when questioned. The Internet Age brings into focus the reality that truth is only found within real dialogues in which there are real differences of perspective. Print texts are often seen as representations of truth. The Internet, by contrast, carries the dialogue within which truths emerge as fallible insights within a never-ending process of enquiry.

According to the logic of print, education is the transmission of true knowledge through reading the right books.[19] The logic of the Internet Age returns us to Socrates' original insight that intelligence lies in dialogues and not in books. The essence of Wikipedia knowledge is not the passive representation of true knowledge but the active participation in dialogues that construct and deconstruct knowledge. At its best, Wikipedia consists of the intelligent words that Socrates valued, words that can be questioned, that answer back, and so that participate in the development of understanding.

A Copernican shift in consciousness: the virtuality of the real and the reality of the virtual

Recently someone shared with me a link to a remarkable YouTube video.[20] It consisted of a virtual choir, two thousand voices, each face visible, each singing a different part of the whole composition. The result is beautiful both visually and as a piece of music. I looked into the process and learnt that, composer Eric Whitacre, had sent out the individual parts to volunteer participants from twelve different countries and they had then recorded their pieces sitting in their living rooms or bedrooms or offices and uploaded the resulting video for Eric to 'compose' again into a multi-media experience on the Internet. The anecdotes on the website suggested that this was a significant experience of connectedness for many of the participants. One woman in Alaska, who claimed to live 400 miles from the nearest town, had found it particularly life-changing to participate in this way in a public event on the Internet.

This illustrates an interesting reversal in ways of thinking about reality. Once music was always clearly bound to particular spaces and particular times. In fact, if you listen closely, you will find that music always generates its own invisible space and time, which is not quite the same as the visible physical space and time that musicians appear to play in. However, this special space and time of musical experience was always assumed to be located and contained within a physical space and time; perhaps people drumming around a fire on the savannah in the evening or in the Royal Albert Hall in London on the last night of the proms. With print notation musical compositions could be sent through the post to other countries and reproduced. With recordings on gramophone records and then with the radio, this general sharing of musical experiences expanded and became global. However, it was always clear that the music listened to around the world was a copy of a situated musical event. On the one hand there was the real original live musical event in a place and at a time and then there was its virtual reflection mediated by transistors and radiowaves.

With Eric Whitacre's virtual choir this relationship between reality and virtuality is reversed. The live musical event was not located in any one place at any one time but on the Internet. It is always here and now every time anyone clicks the play icon on the YouTube web-page. The causal chain here is not from physically located real events to a virtual reflection of those events but from the virtual reflection retro-causing the real events. Individuals recorded their lone voices in their own spaces motivated by the thought of participation in an Internet interaction. The real Internet event or interaction that we now participate in as an audience is the causal driver explaining why so many people sat in front of cameras and microphones and recorded their pieces. Here physically situated experience is an incomplete fragment of a more real event situated on the Internet, which is to say, situated everywhere and nowhere or not really situated at all.

The Internet challenges default assumptions about what is 'real' and what is 'virtual' by changing our everyday experience. An ordinary working day for me as an academic could include swooping down the spiral staircase of a hotel in Hong Kong, because I am thinking of booking a room to attend a conference, and then talking, via Skype, face-to-face with a research colleague seated in the front room of her house in Jerusalem. Many of the children I know spend many hours, if they can, absorbed in virtual reality worlds where they assume an avatar form and run around with an array of weapons mostly chasing and killing, or being chased by and being killed by, other avatars of other children in a realistic 3D environment.[21] Because most of the many games they play allow for interaction, forming alliances, trading and giving and getting advice etc, some of these other children become friends even though they only know each other through their avatars.[22] Despite being mediated by the screen and speakers of a laptop, this world of experience seems to be very vivid and very engaging for the children I talk to. Where these other children exist in the real world, or where this game space exists in the real world, is simply not an issue for them. For many this virtual game space is a real world because it is a world in which interesting events happen about which stories can be told.

For more than a century now physics has made it clear that the world that we experience bears little relation to the world as it is in itself. From the point of view of physics and neuroscience it appears that the external world that we actually experience, the world of solid objects, smells and colours, is a convenient fiction created by our species to aide survival in the context of natural selection.[23]

When Bishop Berkeley argued in the eighteenth century, that the world is an illusion sustained in the mind of God, Dr Johnson responded by kicking a stone and saying 'I refute him thus!'[24] Technology means that this argument is no longer available to those who want to defend the solidity of the really real. There are already immersive reality games in which the solidity of objects is simulated through cyber gloves that are programmed to resist solid-objects. Cyber-boots are not in such common use but it would be easy enough to adapt the gloves to be used by feet in order to give users the same experience of kicking stones that Dr Johnson had when he thought he was refuting Bishop Berkeley.[25]

As computer processing power increases the quality of experience gained through being an avatar in virtual reality will become harder to distinguish from experience gained through the mediation of the flesh. As to the reality-in-itself, it appears to be constructed out of particles that do not simply exist where we see them but are everywhere in the universe all at the same time.[26] In other words, far from being the solid kickable material stuff imagined by Dr Johnson and other physicalist true believers, a much more plausible metaphor for reality is something rather like the code of an advanced video game.

Recent surveys show that young people spend on average nearly eight hours a day with electronic media, that is all the time they have when they are not asleep or in school.[27] Increasingly these devices enable them to inhabit a shared dialogic space, keeping in touch with a global community and participating in global events. It is possible that we are just at the beginning of a Copernican shift in our understanding and experience of reality. This is the shift from thinking of dialogic space as always secondary to, and somehow contained within physical space, to experiencing physical space as just one more space within the many dialogic spaces that we generate together.[28] Dialogues that carry learning might appear to be contained physically within the walls of the classroom but actually they participate within a global dialogue of humanity. The Internet is significant in embodying the deeper reality of global dialogue and bringing this reality into the classroom and into apparently private lives in a way that has the potential to dissolve the illusion of physical separation.

Structure of this book

The rest of this book develops the dialogic theory education that I have briefly introduced here and then applies this theory to understanding some key challenges for education. Although the main contribution of this book is to the theory of education each chapter contains illustrations connecting this theory to practice. Chapter 2, 'Educating dialogue', begins with a critical review of some of the key thinkers behind dialogic education and some of the recent successful practices of dialogic education. This leads to an initial outline of key principles for a dialogic theory of education. Chapter 3, 'Educating reason', investigates how children first learn to think through being drawn into dialogic relationships with real voices and with virtual voices. This dialogic account of how reason develops is continued through evidence from classroom experience and through a phenomenological analysis of our experience as thinkers. The implications of this dialogic account of learning to think for how we should teach for thinking are drawn out. Chapter 4, 'Educating creativity', looks at how thinking developed and continues to evolve in the life of the species as a whole. The latest research in the area of consciousness studies points to the importance of intersubjectivity or feeling how others feel, to the development of distinctively human ways of thinking. Creative thinking appears to involve a dynamic tension between older metaphorical ways of experiencing and the more recent intentional consciousness carried by dialogues. Chapter 5, 'Educating technology', focuses on the role of communications technologies in combination with educational practices in order to argue that the way in which we educate children to use communications technology has proved key to the emergence of different forms of collective thinking. This offers a challenge for the future. The chapter ends with a suggested framework for the design of education with technology in order to develop and support a more global form of consciousness.

Chapters 6 and 7 apply the dialogic theory of education developed in the preceding chapters to offer a way forward in the two areas of science education and citizenship education. The chapter on science education, Chapter 6, 'Educating science', draws on material from a large international study of science education, *Science Education for Diversity*. A discussion of the nature of science concludes with a focus on the communicative virtues that inform scientific debate: virtues like listening with respect to alternative views, responding to challenges with reasoning and a search for evidence, being patient, persevering, and brave in pursuing insights and so on. The evidence suggests that developing complex conceptual knowledge of the kind that can be flexibly adapted to new situations requires engagement in shared enquiry. Chapter 7, 'Educating the planet', begins with a brief review of the impact of communications technologies on the formation of different kinds of identities in order to put forward the view that the Internet has the potential to support a new kind of self-identity which is at the same time a new kind of citizenship: this is a dialogic identity characterized by responsibility towards the other even when that other is not known personally and is not a member of one's tribe or language group. In the second half of the chapter, I outline a proposed design framework for education into global dialogue and offer illustrations of how this can be done.

In the concluding chapter, Chapter 8, 'Education into dialogue', I summarize once more the main themes and contents of the book and provide a fuller account of a dialogic theory of education for the Internet Age and the implications that this has for the design and implementation of a global democratic future.

2

EDUCATING DIALOGUE

This chapter offers an initial answer to the question: what is dialogic education? It briefly looks at contemporary dialogic education in schools and reviews some of the sources that have inspired this approach to pedagogy. This review of sources leads to the articulation of some key features of dialogic education. In practice the term 'dialogic education' is used to refer to education *for* dialogue and not simply education *through* dialogue. The concept of *dialogic* is explored and distinguished from *monologic* and also from *dialectic*. A key philosophic feature is that from a dialogic perspective, difference is seen as a necessary condition of meaning rather than as something to be overcome. The important corollary of this is that there is an unbounded openness at the heart of dialogue; an openness can be expressed metaphorically as a relationship with the Infinite Other. This chapter ends with a specification of a dialogic theory of education.

Some dialogic approaches in classrooms

Robin Alexander compared talk in primary classrooms in five countries, England, France, India, Russia and the United States and found many similarities. There was rote, recitation, instruction, exposition and some discussion in the classrooms of every country. However, the kind of talk that he found was most effective for promoting thinking, while at the same time supporting learning, was a kind of talk that he called *dialogue*. In calling this kind of talk dialogue he was influenced by Bakhtin. Bakhtin distinguished dialogue from other kinds of conversation with the claim that in dialogue there is a chain of questions and answers and each answer gives rise to another question. In other words dialogue is shared enquiry and shared thinking rather than simply, for example, just sharing feelings or sharing information. Alexander found this kind of dialogue more in Russian classrooms than elsewhere. In Russia dialogue was a common feature of the way that the teacher spoke to members of the class, engaging individual students in thinking through issues in public and supporting them in long sequences of authentic questions and answers.[1] This observation inspired him to develop an approach to primary teaching in the UK which he called Dialogic Teaching.[2] In Dialogic Teaching:

1   Questions are carefully framed to encourage reflection and good answers.
2   Answers are not end points but a stimulus for further questions in a long chain of dialogue.
3   The teacher's role is to weave contributions into a coherent whole, leading children to find meaning and helping them think of further questions.[3]

Alexander's approach is just one approach to structuring talk in primary classrooms that can claim to have been successful in improving the thinking and learning of students. It is interesting because it contrasts to the assumption held by many that dialogic pedagogy is about talk in small groups. In Alexander's approach dialogic education often takes the form of whole class teacher-student talk. However it is true that other approaches that some call dialogic focus more on student-to-student talk. Philosophy for Children (P4C) for example, a worldwide movement that began in the USA, promotes the kind of dialogue Bakhtin referred to between children discussing issues of meaning in a broadly 'philosophical' manner. In P4C this approach to education is not called dialogic but is referred to as the 'community of enquiry' method, revealing that the intellectual influence behind P4C was from Dewey rather than from Bakhtin.[4]

The specific pedagogy for dialogic education that I have been most involved in is called 'Thinking Together'. This was developed by Neil Mercer, Lyn Dawes and myself in the early 1990s as a way to improve the educational effectiveness of small group work in any area of the curriculum. Originally we developed this approach to improve the quality of the talk of small groups of children working together around computers.[5] We created a series of lessons or educational activities to raise students' awareness of the importance of the way in which they talked together and then to guide them towards a set of shared expectations or social 'ground rules' for talking together. In theory these expectations or set of assumptions guiding the interactions were meant to emerge from the students awareness of what works and what does not work for them and to be different in each context and to develop over time.[6] Our initial set of 'ground rules', or guiding assumptions that we hoped would help group thinking and learning around computers included the expectation that they would reach agreement about the group decision before anyone clicked the mouse, that they would take shared responsibility for these decisions, that they would expect any claims to be questioned or challenged with counter claims and that they would always seek reasons in response to challenges.

I have written extensively about the 'Thinking Together' programme elsewhere so I will not say too much here.[7] But I will mention that it works. A number of studies around the world have shown that this approach, when pursued by committed teachers, can change the way that children talk together in groups, improve their ability to think together as a group, and improve learning in a number of areas including maths, science, citizenship and creative writing tasks.[8]

Why does the 'Thinking Together' programme work? Our initial idea, influenced by Vygotskian theory, was that it gives children language strategies that act like tools to help them think together.[9] However, I have since argued that, while the way that they use language is important, it reflects something even more important which is the dialogic quality of the relationships in the groups. Successful groups seem to shift their attitudes towards each other and towards the shared problem or task. They become more engaged and more open, asking for help, listening to the others, changing their minds, happy to take on each others' words and voices.[10] The argument that the cause of the improved thinking and learning is the shift to more dialogic relationships, has been supported by a recent study using the same 'Thinking Together' approach in China. In China the initial ways of talking together in the classroom were rather different from those observed in the UK and in Mexico. The lessons teaching or promoting 'Exploratory Talk', or what we now called 'Dialogic Talk',[11] had the same positive impact on group thinking that had been observed elsewhere. However there was not much change in the way of talking together in groups. Rather, the programme seemed to provoke a shift in the roles of the children within the groups. From initially supporting the group leader in solving the problems as quickly and efficiently as possible the groups shifted to each child participating more because they recognized the importance of their own voice in the group and how this taking up of their voice served to improve the quality of group thinking.[12]

Alexander's Dialogic Teaching, Philosophy for Children and Thinking Together share something which is common to all approaches to education which have been called dialogic, including those of Nystrand,[13] Wells[14] and Matusov:[15] this is teaching *for* dialogue as well as through dialogue. Each approach has, as one of its aims, the promotion of students' ability to ask questions and to engage in productive dialogue. This is very significant in the light of the new cognitive demands of the Internet Age. One of the criticisms of the Internet's effects on thinking made by Carr and others, is that it leads to distraction and superficiality. Teaching children and young people how to critically examine information, how to ask good questions that will make the best of the vast resources of the Internet and how to work together to deepen shared enquiry, is an educational response to the needs of the new Internet Age.

In Chapter 5, 'Educating technology', I introduce the concept of Learning to Learn Together (L2L2). Dialogic approaches to teaching and learning all promote this complex competence that is essential to making effective use of resources of the Internet. Although distraction and superficiality is one possible effect of the Internet, it is not essential. Those who know how to learn effectively together with others can convert the multiplicity of voices and vast quantities of information on the Internet into focused learning and deep understanding.

The successful practice of specific forms of dialogic education raises the question of what exactly 'dialogic' is? Where does it come from and how does it work to improve the quality of group thinking? Answering these more theoretical questions might help us achieve a more general understanding that could be applied to education as a whole and help in designing educational activities, environments and curricula. With that end in mind I will now look briefly at some of the intellectual sources for understanding what we mean by the term 'dialogic'.

Socrates and the essential dialogic distinction

I mentioned above that Alexander found dialogic teaching in Russia and was influenced by Bakhtin in the way in which he described this. Bakhtin was a classical scholar influenced by Socrates whom he often refers to as the inspiration for his dialogic ideas.[16] As I mentioned in the Introduction, Socrates was an oral thinker who lived and taught at a time of transition in communications technologies. In his lifetime the use of the new technology of alphabetic writing was spreading throughout Greece. This new technology was changing the nature of education in a way that troubled Socrates. Perhaps ironically we only know this because his student, Plato, wrote down Socrates' reflections on writing in the dialogue with Phaedrus.

Socrates is concerned that writing down words threatens a loss of their meaning. He uses a range of metaphors to make this point, referring to written words as being like bastard children, like orphans, like ghosts and finally as like seeds planted on flagstones in the sun. His main point, repeated many times, is that they may appear to have meaning but this meaning is a superficial illusion because there is no intelligence behind the words to back them up:

> You would imagine that they had intelligence, but if you want to know anything and put a question to one of them, the speaker always gives one unvarying answer. And when they have been once written down they are tumbled about anywhere among those who may or may not understand them, and know not to whom they should reply, to whom not: and, if they are maltreated or abused, they have no parent to protect them; and they cannot protect or defend themselves.[17]

After some discussion Socrates and Phaedrus agree about the superiority of words spoken in dialogue over words written down:

Socrates: I mean an intelligent word graven in the soul of the learner, which can defend itself, and knows when to speak and when to be silent.
Phaedrus: You mean the living word of knowledge which has a soul, and of which the written word is properly no more than an image?[18]

The neuroscience research on the difference between the literate and the non-literate brain which I referred to in the Introduction gives a helpful context to the strong contrast that Socrates makes between words as meanings (when spoken) and words as things (when written). It may seem obvious to us as literates who are able to see words in front of us as well as to hear them, that words can be separated from the contexts in which they are spoken.[19] Non-literates like Socrates experience the meanings of words differently, not as things but as part of a living relationship with others and with otherness. For example, the term 'philosophy' applied to Socrates' work was not merely a concept word or 'tool to get things done', but indicated his close relationship (philos) with the goddess Sophia. As literates we inevitably think of the goddess Sophia as a personification of the concept of wisdom. From a fully oral point of view it might be more appropriate to think of the abstract concept of wisdom as a depersonification of the goddess Sophia.[20]

Writing did not, of course, replace oracy in ancient Greece, it merely augmented it to a modest extent. Oral dialogues remained the main medium of education in Plato's academy. Oral reasoning was taught in medieval universities. In the sixteenth century Montaigne, in his essay 'On Education', quotes many classical sources in support of his case for the importance of learning through dialogue not only with tutors but also with as many different people as possible so as to learn how to think for oneself.[21] In fact the large majority of people remained illiterate everywhere until the advent of mass education systems in the nineteenth century. In elite universities such as Oxford and Cambridge in the UK the tutorial system preserves the importance of oral dialogue between professors and students, although this is always oral dialogue in the context of written texts.

It would be foolish to oppose literacy to oracy in general, since literacy is almost always combined with oracy. Nonetheless Socrates is making an important point about the potential of literacy to impact not only on how we think but also on how we think about thinking. In a fascinating study of the shift from the warm and multi-voiced thinking of Montaigne to some of the narrower and more abstract thinking that shaped the modern age, Toulmin argues that Socrates' fear that writing had the potential to depersonalize meaning proved in some respects prophetic.[22] Socrates was however wrong to claim that writing could never carry real dialogic intelligence. Bakhtin's dialogism is based on an analysis of the way in which texts, particularly the written characters in Dostoevsky's novels, enter into dialogic relations which illuminate what he refers to as 'infinite' spaces of 'contextual meaning'.[23] But, overlooking this error of exaggeration, Socrates was profoundly right when he pointed to the difference between a living meaning within a dialogue and the dead mere form of meaning when words are treated as meanings-in-themselves outside of any dialogue. It is this crucial, but still largely overlooked, distinction between the inside of dialogues and the outside of dialogues that is the basis for the contemporary dialogic critique of much educational practice.

Is Socratic education dialogic?

Socrates himself is sometimes referred to as the father of dialogic education. This attribution probably stems from the way in which he practiced philosophy as the pursuit of truth through dialogues in which all claims are tested and his own ignorance is discovered along with the ignorance of his interlocutors. He claimed to be the wisest man in Athens, a title bestowed upon him by the oracle at Delphi, not because he knew more than others but because he alone knew his own ignorance whereas all others believed in their claims to knowledge. His method was often to question others in a way that brought to light the contradictions in their beliefs and so made them reflect. His aim or teaching objective was not the transmission of knowledge, nor even collaborative knowledge construction, so much as teaching critical thinking and through this expanding awareness. To put this same point in another way, the focus of his teaching was not on finding answers so much as on improving the quality of questions. Socrates was never happier than when moving people from shallow knowledge, the assumption that they knew something, to profound ignorance, the realization that they did not know and still needed to try to find out. This approach is brought out clearly in the *Meno* in the context of a discussion about virtue, when Meno accuses Socrates of being like a torpedo fish whose touch leaves people both stunned and confused. Socrates is happy with the idea of leaving people confused but does not accept that he is like the fish since he is as confused as anyone else:

> I myself do not have the answers when I perplex others but I am more perplexed than anyone when I cause perplexity in others. So now I do not know what virtue is; perhaps you knew before you contacted me, but now you are certainly like one who does not know. Nevertheless I want to examine and seek with you what it may be.[24]

This little speech touches on several aspects of dialogic education; it appears to be a serious shared enquiry into truth following genuine questions where there is equal respect for each of the different voices in the dialogue. Here respect for the voices of others is not presented as a moral stance but as a pragmatic necessity stemming from the humility of acknowledged ignorance coupled with a desire to learn.

However, reading the dialogues gives the impression that Socrates' educational practice was often very different from his educational theory. It is hard, for example, to read the dialogue between Socrates the slave boy in the *Meno* as anything other than intellectual bullying. Matuzov has conducted a detailed analysis of all Socrates' dialogues as reported by Plato. He concludes that:

> I did not find any evidence of Socrates seeking truth and learning something new himself from participation in these dialogues. Rather he tried to bring other participants to something he already knew.[25]

Dialogic versus dialectic

Socrates often argues by examining the claims that others make in order to draw out a contradiction. This may or may not lead to a new and better understanding but at least it leads to their awareness of their own ignorance. This approach is sometimes called dialectic and it lies behind the more elaborated dialectic of Hegel in which an initially too abstract claim is tested and challenged by its opposite or its negation in order to develop a more complete or concrete understanding. Hegel's dialectic has been referred to as the movement from the thesis through the antithesis to the synthesis. This sums it up quite well even though these are not the precise terms that Hegel used. Clearly this kind of dialectical reasoning, or reasoning through oppositions, emerges out of dialogues in which different voices confront each other.

However, despite its origins in real dialogues, dialectic is a monological argument presented in the form of a dialogue. In a study of the relationship between dialectic and dialogue, Nikulin writes that dialectic was only possible because of writing and had its origin in the writing down of a dialogue after the event.[26] Because dialectic is dialogic argument written down after the event it loses the multiplicity, contingency, uncertainty and potential creativity of the original dialogue to become a formalized argument written from the perspective of a single voice.

Bakhtin claims that dialectic is trying to make the argument too abstract and so forgets the embodied nature of dialogues and the real personalities behind dialogues.[27] Hegel's dialectic, like the kind of dialectical reasoning often practiced by Socrates, seems to assume that the correct answer or 'synthesis' is predetermined in advance and so will inevitably emerge from the dialogue. Hegel calls this 'the cunning of reason' whereas Socrates in the *Meno* refers to the way that reasoning helps us recall the truth that we know from the beginning. In real dialogues, however, it is not always possible to know what the outcome will be in advance.

The problem with replacing real dialogues (dialogic) with written imitations of dialogues (dialectic) is the loss of creativity and ultimately a loss of meaning. Bakhtin brings out this problem with dialectic in some typically cryptic notes:

> The text lives only by coming into contact with another text (with context). Only at the point of this contact between texts does a light flash, illuminating both the posterior and anterior, joining a given text to a dialogue. We emphasise that this contact is a dialogic contact between texts (utterances) and not a mechanical contact of 'oppositions', which is possible only within a single text (and not between a text and context) among abstract elements (signs within a text), ... Behind this contact is a contact of personalities and not of things. If we transform dialogue into one continuous text, that is, erase the divisions between voices (changes of speaking subjects), which is possible at the extreme (Hegel's monological dialectic), then the deep-seated (in-finite) contextual meaning disappears (we hit the bottom, reach a standstill). Complete maximum reification would inevitably lead to the disappearance of the infinitude and bottomlessness of meaning (any meaning). A thought that, like a fish in an aquarium, knocks against the bottom and the sides and cannot swim farther or deeper. Dogmatic thoughts.[28]

Bakhtin is concerned here that looking at dialogues as if from the outside erases the real difference between voices but it is that real difference that gives rise to meaning in the first place opening up the dialogic space on the inside of dialogues which is, as he says, a space of potentially infinite new meaning.

Perhaps a simpler way to approach the loss of creativity that occurs in the shift from living dialogue to formal dialectic is suggested by Nikulin.[29] Nikulin points out that the dialectic form of argument described by Plato and attributed to Socrates' dialogues, is entirely negative. It can only refute claims but it offers no way to construct or produce anything positive. This renders Plato's claim in the

Republic, that only rigorous dialectical reasoning should be used to reveal the true forms of being, inconsistent and ultimately pointless. Rigorous dialectic reasoning can judge and undermine other people's claims to truth, but it cannot assert any itself or justify any as true. Real dialogue, on the other hand, is always at least as creative as it is critical. New ideas simply keep popping into existence stimulated by what Bakhtin refers to as the 'inter-animation' of different perspectives, especially the inter-animation of text and (infinite) context. Because it cannot be formalized this real creativity of dialogues is lost once dialogues are formalized and converted into dialectical arguments.

Buber

The distinction between taking an external view of dialogues and an internal view is at the heart of all theories that could be called dialogic. Socrates, as we have just seen, distinguishes between living words that are carried on the warm breath of relationships and the dead words of written accounts that are like seeds left on flagstones in the sun.[30] This same distinction is picked up by Paul in the New Testament in a resonant phrase: 'the letter kills but the spirit brings life'.[31] Buber, made this distinction the basis of his philosophy. He defined it as the difference between the attitude of objectification, 'Ich-Es' ('I-it') and the attitude of dialogue 'Ich-Du' ('I-thou'[32]).

The external 'objective' view that locates things in their proper place is 'monologic' because it assumes a single true perspective within which everything can be situated or located. The internal view that takes the other seriously is 'dialogic' because from this perspective meaning always assumes at least two perspectives at once and, as will become clear, the moment there are at least two perspectives then the gap between them opens up the possibility of an infinite number of possible new perspectives and new insights.

Buber celebrated the dialogic attitude, describing how it is possible to take this attitude towards everything, not only in relation to specific others. He describes, for example, the many ways in which we can see a tree, perhaps as an aesthetic image like a painting, or as an organism focusing on its biology, or reducing it to numbers but finally we can also allow the tree to speak to us and we can allow ourselves to be taken over by the tree.[33] Buber's language is poetic but his basic idea that even perception can be dialogic if we allow it to be is supported by the phenomenology of perception.[34]

In addition to talking about the significance of the dialogic orientation to others and the shift from the 'I-it' attitude to the 'I-thou' attitude, Buber also talked about the importance of what he called the space of the 'in-between' or the 'space of meeting'. This is the first clear reference that I am aware of to the real dialogic space that opens up between people in dialogue.

I found the term dialogic space useful in classrooms when trying to answer the question why some groups of children were more successful in solving reasoning test problems than others. The more successful groups seemed to be listening to each other, asking each other for help and changing their minds as a result of seeing the problem as if through the eyes of the others. In less successful groups children related to each other differently, either competing as individuals to see who could get the right answer or not challenging or criticizing each other in order to maintain group solidarity. In the less successful groups they seemed to be identifying with limited images of self in opposition to others or with the group image. I used the term dialogic space to understand what they were identifying with in the more successful groups.[35]

Buber was a committed adult educator. Education for Buber involved drawing students into the space of dialogue. But there was more to it than that: 'Education worthy of the name', Buber wrote, 'is essentially the education of character'. He continued, 'Genuine education of character is genuine education for community'.[36]

> Everything depends on the teacher as a man, as a person. He educates from himself, from his virtues and his faults, through personal example and according to circumstances and conditions. His task is to realise the truth in his personality and to convey this realisation to the pupil.[37]

From Buber's account it seems that the way that a teacher ought to be can be summed up as a dialogic self, both empathetic and critically reflective, listening respectfully to the voice of the other and also listening attentively to the voice of the moment.

Bakhtin

Bakhtin continued the awareness of the essential dialogic distinction between the inside space of dialogue and the outside space. Although Bakhtin did not apply his insights about dialogism directly to education he presented them in forms which educators have found very relevant. His characterization of the essential dialogic distinction in terms of the difference between an authoritative word and a persuasive word has obvious implications for education. The authoritative word, which he explicitly associates with school teachers, remains outside us, he writes, not entering us so that we either have to accept it or reject it. He contrasts this to the 'the internally persuasive word' that

> is half-ours and half-someone else's. Its creativity and productiveness consist precisely in the fact that such a word awakens new and independent words, that it organises masses of our words from within, and does not remain in an isolated and static condition.[38]

This version of the essential dialogic distinction naturally leads to an account of education as drawing children into dialogue. Meaning only exists in the context of a dialogue, specifically as an answer to a question that we have posed either explicitly or implicitly in dialogue together or in dialogue with ourselves.

For Bakhtin dialogues are never simply between people, if these are understood as physical entities, but always also between cultural voices. Cultural voices are embodied in texts and in ways of talking and ways of being. If those voices are authoritative than one either accepts or rejects them but education for creativity and for thinking implies engaging in dialogue with persuasive cultural voices. This is not a question of using cultural voices as tools but about being open to them and allowing oneself to be, at least in part, possessed by them. The ideal of the dialogic self that emerges from Bakhtin is perhaps like that of the author Dostoevsky, who allows the characters in his novels to have independent voices and engage in dialogues with each other and yet maintains the unity of self simply by providing the context within which his characters interact.

There are many powerful ideas for thinking about education in Bakhtin's writing. I refer to some of them throughout this book. His concept of the super-addressee is particularly relevant for rethinking cognitive development dialogically. I will say more about this in the next chapter. The essential idea is that every dialogue generates a third voice or position, that of the witness or the 'super-addressee'. When speakers do not think that their words are being understood by the physical addressees they will orient themselves towards the superaddressee whom they assumes does understand. With some re-working I think that the intersubjective reality of this superaddressee mechanism in dialogues explains how and why we are called forth to justify ourselves and to understand our situation more generally. Invoking the superaddressee or the absent other is a very important strategy for education into thinking.

Vygotsky

Vygotsky is often referred to as a dialogic educationalist. I disagree with this judgement[39] but it is certainly true that his well-known concept of the 'Zone of Proximal Development' or ZPD brings the idea of dialogic relations into education. In the ZPD the teacher has to engage with the perspective of the student and vice-versa in order to connect the development of ideas in the student to the pre-existing culture.[40] The dialogic relation, which can be characterized as 'attunement to the attunement of the other',[41] is certainly implicit in the idea of the ZPD. However, the reason why this concept is not really dialogic is that dialogic space (the ZPD) is invoked by Vygotsky as a temporary tool or scaffold to help in a direction of individual development that is known in advance.

Mercer suggested we turn this ZPD into a more open and multidirectional 'Intermental Development Zone' (IDZ) where 'interthinking' can occur between peers without the necessary assumption of a teacher leading a learner.[42] This is clearly a move in a more dialogic direction, but the idea of dialogic space goes further again in that dialogue is not primarily conceptualized as a 'mediating means' supporting cognitive development but as a medium rather than as a means. Viewed from the outside a dialogic space like a ZPD or an IDZ, can look like a means to achieve purposes that are independent of dialogue, exchanging information for example or learning how to use a specific tool. When experienced from the inside dialogic space is the medium of thought. The point of dialogic education is therefore not only to teach how to use dialogue as a tool in order to achieve something other than dialogue, as notions such as ZPD and perhaps the IDZ imply, but is more essentially focused on teaching how to enter more completely into dialogue.

In his book *Thinking and speech*, Vygotsky presents himself as a dialectical thinker concerned with the development of a capacity for abstract reasoning. Education is presented as education away from the relative chaos of the participatory and more dialogic thinking which Vygotsky claims is naturally found both in children and in people he refers to as 'savages'.[43] In this he reflects the dominant strand of thinking about education in his time and place. As a Marxist in the early Soviet Union it is not surprising that he should be concerned about education for rationality and the creation of a more rational society.

However, in many ways dialogic theories of education have arisen out of and remain within the broad socio-cultural approach to education that has been inspired by Vygotsky. This socio-cultural approach can perhaps be understood as a response to the overly individualistic and unsituated assumptions of what is now referred to as 'classical' cognitive psychology. Vygotsky's claim that good thinking is first found in social interactions and only later 'internalized' or appropriated by individuals is one that a dialogic theory of thinking would also accept. Dialogues are culturally and historically situated and if meaning is located within dialogues then it is reasonable to refer to a dialogic account of meaning as a broadly socio-cultural theory of eduction.

The main way in which a dialogic theory of education departs from socio-cultural assumptions could be understood as a development of socio-cultural theory from within. This is the important addition of the insight that there is always also something unsituated in dialogues explaining their infinite potential for creativity. This claim is not a return to the unsituatedness of abstract logical structures implied by classic cognitivist theory. It is just pointing out that dialogues open up an inner infinity that is not pinned down, or pin-downable, a kind of inner interconnectedness of everything with everything else. This is an idea which I will develop more in the next two chapters. I raise the issue here only to say that although I think a dialogic theory of education needs to criticize aspects of Vygotsky's theory of education it is still reasonable to think of this theory as compatible with the broad church of the socio-cultural movement in educational psychology that Vygotsky has inspired.

Freire

In the second half of the twentieth century Paulo Freire, a Brazilian-born educator, explicitly argued for the need for dialogic education in the context of what he called the 'pedagogy of the oppressed'. Conventional education, Freire claimed, followed what he called a 'banking model' in which knowledge is treated as something to be deposited in the heads of students. Education on the banking model is a way of oppressing people through manipulation in which the words and meanings of the oppressors are inserted into the heads of the oppressed. Dialogic education, by contrast, is about empowering the oppressed to speak their own words and so to name the world in their own way. Freire offers three key elements that can contribute to an understanding of dialogic education: first, the importance of starting with the lived experience of students; secondly, the idea that dialogic education is about making a real difference in the world through empowerment or giving a voice to those initially without a voice and finally the importance of genuine respect and collaboration between educator and student so that meaning can be co-constructed rather than imposed. Freire made an explicit link between a dialogic approach and education for meaning:

> If it is in speaking their word that people, by naming the world, transform it, dialogue imposes itself as the way by which they achieve significance as human beings. [. . .] And since dialogue is the encounter in which the united reflection and action of the dialoguers are addressed to the world which is to be transformed and humanized, this dialogue cannot be reduced to the act of one person's 'depositing' ideas in another; nor can it become a simple exchange of ideas to be 'consumed' by the discussants. [. . .] Because dialogue is an encounter among women and men who name the world, it must not be a situation where some name on behalf of others. It is an act of creation; it must not serve as a crafty instrument for the domination of one person by another.[44]

Freire argued clearly for a kind of dialogic education that did not impose meanings on people. However, he has been accused of doing precisely what he argued against, that is manipulating people into meanings prepared in advance. Freire made it clear in his writings and actions that he was committed to a socialist vision of liberation. This can be seen in his location of education within the dichotomy of oppressor and oppressed. Those who have examined his methods in practice and tried to implement them tend to converge on the conclusion articulated by Mark Smith that:

> what is claimed as liberatory practice may, on close inspection, be rather closer to banking than we would wish. In other words, the practice of Freirian education can involve smuggling in all sorts of ideas and values under the guise of problem-posing.[45]

Matusov argues that Freire's commitment to dialogue as a means to bring social justice overwhelmed his concern with dialogue as a shared enquiry into truth.[46] In a way this is a particular version of the dialectic as opposed to dialogic problem that emerged also from examining Socrates educational practice. The main problem with dialectical thinking is the illicit assumption of an 'above' perspective or master standpoint outside of any dialogue from which one can know in advance how the dialogue should turn out. Freire appeared to accept a broadly Marxist dialectical understanding of history in which the oppressed needed to become conscious of their oppressed state and overthrow it in order to bring about a better world. The opening of dialogue was seen by Freire as a necessary moment within this larger dialectical vision. As with Socrates, Freire's practice was not really as dialogic as his rhetoric.

Oakeshott

Writing in a very similar period to Freire, the English philosopher Michael Oakeshott articulated an essentially dialogic theory of education that is interesting partly because it does not share Freire's socialist political assumptions.[47] Oakeshott did not explicitly use the term dialogic but he applied the metaphor of conversation to education and he linked education to his idea of what he called 'the conversation of Mankind'.

> In conversation, 'facts' appear only to be resolved once more into the possibilities from which they were made; 'certainties' are shown to be combustible, not by being brought in contact with other 'certainties' or with doubts, but by being kindled by the presence of ideas of another order; approximations are revealed between notions normally remote from one another. Thoughts of different species take wing and play round one another, responding to each other's movements and provoking one another to fresh exertions. Nobody asks where they have come from or on what authority they are present; nobody cares what will become of them when they have played their part. There is no symposiarch or arbiter, not even a doorkeeper to examine credentials. Every entrant is taken at its face-value and everything is permitted which can get itself accepted into the flow of speculation. And voices which speak in conversation do not compose a hierarchy. Conversation is not an enterprise designed to yield an extrinsic profit, a contest where a winner gets a prize, not is it an activity of exegesis; it is an unrehearsed intellectual adventure. It is with conversation as with gambling, its significance lies neither in winning nor in losing, but in wagering. Properly speaking, it is impossible in the absence of a diversity of voices: in it different universes of discourse meet, acknowledge each other and enjoy an oblique relationship which neither requires nor forecasts their being assimilated to one another.
> [...] As civilized human beings, we are the inheritors, neither of an inquiry about ourselves and the world, nor of an accumulating body of information, but of a conversation, begun in the primeval forests and extended and made more articulate in the course of centuries. It is a conversation which goes on both in public and within each of ourselves.[48]

I quote this eloquent passage at some length because it offers a clear expression of several key dialogic ideas. Facts are never fixed and final but constructed and deconstructed within dialogues. A diversity of voices is essential for meaning. There is no privileged outside standpoint offering a 'correct' view. Dialogue is an end in itself and not a means to an outside end such as profit or adaptation to the environment. Oakeshott's account of the importance of the 'conversation of Mankind' implies a particular understanding of education as initiating newcomers into this conversation.

This is an account of education that Oakeshott developed in several papers explicitly opposing policies that tried to make education serve the needs of the larger society or what he referred to as the end of 'socialization'. In a way he shared Freire's concern to preserve education from the banking model and a concern that education served the end of intellectual emancipation rather than an economic or productive end. But he would have rejected Freire's assertion that dialogic education should be about transforming society towards greater social justice. For Oakeshott education should be about education. It needed a space separate from economic concerns or political concerns where the distinctively educational freedom to imagine alternatives is protected from the encroachment of outside agendas of every kind.[49]

Oakeshott presented his conversational or dialogic account of education in conservative terms focusing on the need to initiate students into their inheritance of culture from the past. However, it is clear that the goal of education for Oakeshott is a person able to participate in the conversation of humanity and to take it forward. In other words the aim of education is not only an educated person but also a better quality of conversation. Although it is clear that teachers are needed to induct students into conversations from the past, the role of these teachers is also to empower and liberate students to acquire their own voice and be able to speak in order to help shape the shared human world of meaning in the future.

Oakeshott is useful in showing us that dialogic education is not intrinsically radical or intrinsically conservative but that it is, above all, intrinsically educational. Education is a continuation of a dialogue that requires that we preserve voices from the past and deepen our dialogue with them just as much as it requires that we engage in dialogue with the superaddressee positions calling us to different possible futures. For Oakeshott education can only liberate students and help to create a better future (if we understand a better future here simply as 'a more educated future'), through first engaging them within their inherited traditions of thought so that these can be inhabited and developed from within. We can learn from Oakeshott the importance of treating dialogue and dialogic education as ends in themselves and not simply as a means to the end of more knowledge or more productivity or more social justice.

Some key ideas for dialogic education

This critical review of a few of the thinkers behind dialogic education can provide us with a number of key ideas that can contribute towards a dialogic theory of education.

First, what is 'dialogic'?

The everyday meaning of dialogic is 'pertaining to dialogue' and it is often used in this sense in education. But the more specialist meaning, the meaning mediated by the dialogue Bakhtin founded, is not really about actual dialogues anymore so much as about a way of understanding how human beings make meaning in general.[50]

Dialogic theory begins with the claim that meaning is always internal to dialogues – where the term dialogue is understood to refer to dialogues between different voices – and so should not be thought of on the model of fixed external things like objects that we might think that we encounter in the world.

This claim can be justified through an appeal to our common experience. The meaning of the words I use in a dialogue with a friend is not given by their dictionary definitions but depends on the words my friend spoke to me previously that I am now responding to. The meaning of my words is also not exhausted by what I intend them to mean. If my friend responds to my words in a way that I did not intend this does not necessarily mean that they have been misunderstood but it might mean that my friend interprets my words differently from the way that I do and this interpretation leads to reflection and contributes to their meaning. The meaning of any word therefore can never be fixed since at any time a participant in the dialogue might interpret previously spoken words in a new way. This is true not only of small local dialogues such as that between me and my friend but also of the larger dialogues of culture such as the long-term dialogues of science and philosophy which are often global in reach and can last for thousands of years. The meanings of Socrates' words, for example, have evolved over centuries of interpretation and each new reading by a student freshly introduced to Socrates may add to or change this meaning. The true meaning of the words does not exist in itself, or in the intentions Socrates might have had when he spoke his words, but it only exists in the living dialogue.

The claim that the meanings of words are forged in dialogues and only exist within dialogues might seem to be obviously true of our experience but, as I will show, taking this truth seriously has profound implications for education.

Dialogic education is education for dialogue

From the brief survey above of practical approaches to education that have been called dialogic, the approaches of Alexander, Philosophy for Children and 'Thinking Together' and the more theoretical approaches of Socrates, Buber,

Freire and Oakeshott, it has emerged that the key factor in distinguishing dialogic education from other kinds is that one important aim of dialogic education is dialogue itself. Any content whatsoever can be taught through collaborative learning and shared enquiry and often is better for this. But the use of dialogue as an educational means does not make education dialogic. For education to be dialogic it is necessary that dialogue is not only the means of education, as it often is, but is also an end. There are an indefinite number of ways of teaching for dialogue but if their end is to give the student a voice as a participant in a dialogue then they are potentially compatible with a dialogic theory of education.

The dialogic gap or difference between voices is constitutive for meaning

Voice is a term in dialogic theory for a unique perspective on the world that is the unit of analysis of a dialogue. Individual humans can speak with many voices. Things can be given voice. Nations and abstract conceptual entities can take on voice. The gap between voices is what constitutes them. There is a dialogue between voices only if they are different. If two voices merge into complete unity then the dialogue between them ceases and so the meaning ceases.

Progress occurs through augmentation not through supersession.

Bakhtin gives the example of how reading the texts of ancient Greece gave him an extra perspective from which to see his situation in twentieth-century Russia in a way that opened up the possibilities of thought in general.[51] Many theories of development and educational progress are monologic, assuming that under-standing progresses in a linear way from A to B, replacing old theories with better theories and old cognitive structures with new cognitive structures. For dialogic, however, the past is always preserved as a voice that we should not ignore. Progress in a dialogue is seldom from simply wrong to simply right but usually from A to both A and B. For example, the voice of the child is still available to adults and allowing that voice to speak can expand and enrich the experience of the adult. Bakhtin hinted at an idea of progress from the narrow time and space of small dialogues concerned with local issues to the great time and space of the dialogue between all voices from all cultures and all times.[52] This does not mean that we should forget our local place and our local time but that, by bringing a larger dialogic awareness of multiple perspectives to bear, we should enrich our experience of our situation .

Dialogic includes monologic

Conceptually we can only understand dialogic by contrasting it with monologic. The danger is that in affirming the importance of dialogic, dialogic education theory appears to be rejecting and dismissing monologic. This raises a paradox. The idea that being dialogic is a good thing and that being monologic is a bad thing is itself not a very dialogic sounding idea. The dialogic principle of progress by augmentation means that the voice of monologic should not be simply rejected but engaged in the dialogue at a higher level. In practice becoming more dialogic, both as an individual and as a society, can and should also mean becoming more monologic.

This apparent paradox can be resolved if we think about the size of utterances in a dialogue. When primary school children learnt how to talk together more effectively in order to solve more Raven's analogical reasoning test problems (see illustration in Chapter 4) one of the clearest indicators of their better dialogic thinking was that the size of their individual utterances increased. In our pre-tests, before the intervention to teach more dialogic ways of talking, their utterances when working on the tests were often very short like 'I think it's that one', 'OK', 'Let's move on to the next one'. Once they were using more dialogic talk they approached the problems quite differently. Utterances expanded because they thought more about what they were saying and tried to give reasons and explain to others who obviously did not always see things the same way. Typical utterances in the more effective dialogic talk were more like: 'I think it is number three, because, look, the circle goes out and the square remains the same, what do you think?', 'I don't agree because it could be number six as well and you have not looked at the way the little cross thingy is moving around'. In fact the length of utterance turned out to be the best single predicator of more successful talk around the reasoning tests, a finding that seems sensible in retrospect but was quite unanticipated at the time.[53] Here, becoming more dialogic in orientation also led these children to become better at monologic in the simple sense their turns at talk got larger because many more of their single utterances managed to express a complex idea in a coherent way.

Dialogues of the kind that lie behind progress in the natural sciences often include utterances of great length. Being able to work alone for long periods developing a coherent understanding of a domain of knowledge in the way that Einstein did, for example, is tremendously useful for the quality of the larger dialogue. But it is useful not for finally finding an ultimate theory of everything that all others will have to accept. It is useful for fashioning more insightful and valuable contributions to the ongoing dialogue of humanity (what Oakeshott referred to as the conversation of mankind). Monological thinking is good for dialogue as long as it does not become conceited and think that it is everything, at which point it becomes the voice of authority and closes down the dialogue. Einstein presented his theories as arising out of a creative dialogue with nature as a whole.[54] There was no incompatibility between his dialogic orientation towards the cosmos and also towards his colleagues and the extraordinarily systematic and rigorous quality of his theories.

The story of how Andrew Wiles solved Fermatt's last theorem, might be helpful to understanding the relationship between apparent monologic and dialogic in the context of an actual dialogue. Andrew read the theorem aged ten and decided to be the first person to solve it. He found he did not know enough maths to solve it so he went away and learnt a lot of maths and then came back to the theorem. He produced what he thought was a proof of the theorem at a conference in Cambridge in 1993. Criticism by other mathematicians revealed a major flaw. He went away and came back with a better proof in 1995. This time all agreed that he really had solved it. Clearly this was a dialogic process even if the 'turn at talk' size in one case looks like two years.[55]

The reason why it is useful to understand that even the most rigorous and systematic kinds of thinking are ultimately dialogic is both ethical and pragmatic. Learning does not progress well if we think we have all the answers and do not need to listen to other perspectives. As Bakhtin says, in dialogues there is never a final word. Even though Andrew Wiles solved the theorem this does not mean that there might not be a more elegant solution in the future or that, at some indefinite point in the future, our understanding of mathematics might change so radically as to cast the theorem and its solution in a new and different light, rather as Cantor's set theory reinterpreted all previous thinking about infinity.

The inside:outside/outside:inside nature of dialogic relations

In any dialogue the person you are speaking to, the 'addressee', is always already there at the beginning of the utterance just as you are there already on the inside when they frame their reply to you. This can be understood easily if you think about where an utterance in a dialogue starts. Let us suppose that my son Danny and I are making 'mini weapons of mass destruction'[56] out of everyday stationary items and he shows me a catapult he has made out of pencils and rubber bands and I say: 'That is pretty cool, but I think it needs something: let's try putting a bar here to stop the arm going too far.' You might think it is obvious that the utterance starts with me saying, 'That is pretty cool,' but even as I framed that utterance my image of Danny was there on the inside because I was speaking for him. The words 'That is pretty cool' came quite naturally but I would not say that if my boss, Sir Steve Smith, the Vice-Chancellor of Exeter University, showed me his latest report on how the university is going to reach its research targets. In any dialogue we do not just address ourselves to the other as a physical object, a body, but we address them from within a relationship in which the words are often as much theirs as ours.[57]

This inside-out and outside-in nature of dialogues explains why education is possible at all. Education, as opposed to training or dressage, always requires what Bakhtin calls the persuasive voice that speaks to us as if from the inside. The addressee enters into the very beginning of an utterance, In a true dialogue, it is no longer always possible to say who is thinking.[58] In dialogic education it is not always possible to say who is learning and who is teaching.

Dialogues are not just with real others but also with cultural voices

Even when the 'other' I address appears to be a physical person standing in front of me I may well be addressing a cultural voice. For example if I am talking to you about the role of research and you use key words that I associate with an Enlightenment view of progress through reason then I might find myself engaged in dialogue with that cultural voice while apparently engaged in dialogue with you, a physically embodied person. Indeed it is not possible for words to have simple, single and located meanings as they always carry with them echoes of all the other voices that have used the same words before in different ways.

In a similar way the historical and cultural contexts of dialogues are not a fixed container but enter into dialogues as if they were voices within the dialogue which the speakers engage with often implicitly.

Dialogues always project virtual superaddressee positions

As well as having perhaps a physically situated addressee and cultural voices, Bakhtin argued that utterances in dialogues also always address a 'superaddressee'.[59] Bakhtin does not spell this out but the 'third' addressee in a dialogue is inevitably present in all dialogues simply because I can hear myself speaking. When I talk and hear my own words it is as if I am another person listening to them and then I naturally assume the position of a witness or 'third' to myself. Bakhtin makes the point that, as well as seeking to persuade you, my immediate addressee, I also seek to engage in dialogue with an ideal listener who could make sense of what I am saying even if you cannot. I think this could be seen as stemming from a projection of the self as another who listens to the words of the self but can understand and judge them as if from an outside position. He points out that in different times this superaddressee is imagined differently, sometimes being God and sometimes 'the future community of scientists' but in every age there is such an ideal as it is an essential part of the nature of dialogue. This elaborated cultural image of the superaddressee is an extension, I would argue, of the witness position in every dialogue that comes from listening to myself speaking as if I was other to myself.

Every dialogue has both an inside and an outside

When we think of dialogues we probably think of empirical dialogues that occur at a certain place and time between particular people. In doing this we are looking at dialogues as if from the outside. But dialogues also have an inside. On the inside of the dialogue we might be talking about people who are not present, distant places and past or future events. From the outside, dialogues always appear to be situated in space and in time but when lived from the inside dialogues establish their own space and time. This is what distinguishes a dialogue from an interaction. Robots can interact but their interactions remains in external space. When humans enter into dialogue there is a new space of meaning that opens up between them and includes them within it.

Dialogic space

Dialogues in education are often discussed in terms of epistemology as a form of 'shared enquiry' and as a way of helping in the 'collaborative construction of knowledge'.[60] I think that it is also useful to think of dialogues in terms of ontology. By using the term ontology I am suggesting that the concept of dialogic space, mentioned earlier in discussion of Buber, is not just an idea constructed within dialogues but is pointing to something real that makes dialogues possible in the first place, a kind of real lack of foundation and a real interconnectedness of all with all in a way which is unbounded and so intrinsically undetermined and undeterminable. I am not sure if this idea should count as ontology because it is not the idea of a foundation outside of dialogue but more the idea of a real lack of foundation outside of dialogue that makes dialogue possible in the first place.[61] Another way to think about dialogic space is to think about the space of the Internet. What is it, where is it, and how is it possible in the first place?

A second way in which the term ontology is useful is to suggest that the aim of education is not simply knowledge or ways of knowing but also ways of being. Dialogic is not simply a way for a subject to know about a world out there beyond the subject but it is also about a way of being in the world.[62] Referring to an ontological interpretation of dialogic is another way of saying that dialogic education is education *for* dialogue as well as *through* dialogue in which dialogue is not only treated as a means to an end but also treated as an end in itself.[63]

A more pragmatic reason for getting ontological about dialogic space is that I think it is useful pedagogically to be able to talk about 'opening dialogic space', through interrupting an activity with a reflective question, for example or 'widening dialogic space' through bringing in new voices or 'deepening dialogic space' through reflection on assumptions.

A preliminary dialogic theory of education in the Internet Age

Outlining some of the key ideas that emerge from taking dialogic theory seriously has already sketched the outlines of a dialogic theory of education. However, most of the dialogic educational practice and theory that I have reviewed in this chapter pre-dates the widespread adoption of the Internet and so is dominated by the image of physically embodied people talking face to face. The theory of dialogic education that emerges from this literature is therefore necessarily preliminary and provisional. In the rest of the book I will argue for ways in which we need to add to and expand this preliminary understanding of dialogic education to build a theory of dialogic education for the Internet Age.

1) Education can be understood as participation in the dialogue of humanity carried both through culture and through individual thoughts

It is possible to talk about a single dialogue of humanity, as Oakeshott does, because all dialogues interconnect. Dialogues reference each other and interpret each other through a kind of universal resonance of ideas on the inside of each apparently separate dialogue. This dialogue of humanity is an end in itself but is also a shared enquiry making sense of the world and learning from the past how best to act in the future. Although ultimately this is one dialogue, its unity is not that of simple identity but is a dialogic unity made up of many voices. As a large river has many eddies so the dialogue of humanity has many smaller dialogues, where more or less specialist dialogues work out responses to particular challenges or understandings in specific domains of experience.

2) Engage in dialogue first and then support students in acquiring the skills and knowledge that they need to participate more productively

Many educational curricula and approaches to instructional design start with teaching the sub-skills and the content knowledge that it has been decided might be required for participation in real dialogues or real problem-solving and knowledge-construction one day. This can mean that students do not know why they are learning whatever it is they are learning and lose intrinsic motivation. Dialogic education takes the opposite approach of always beginning with those questions and challenges that motivate and engage students. If and when it emerges through this engagement in pursuing real inquiries that specific skills are needed, specific mathematical skills for example, or that more knowledge would help with the enquiry, then opportunities need to be available to help students acquire these skills and to learn this knowledge.

3) Dialogic education is about expanding the context through widening and deepening the dialogue

A dialogic vision of education offers a clear direction for progress away from identification with narrow and parochial concerns and towards identification with the unbounded and infinite space of collective dialogue in which all voices can be heard. This expansion in awareness is achieved not through increasing abstraction and generalization so much as through engagement in dialogue with multiple voices, including disembodied cultural voices of the past and superaddressee voices that call us to the future. Ultimately what is being taught here is an expansion not of knowledge so much as of a capacity to respond to otherness and to newness in the moment. Opening, widening and deepening dialogic space(s) is a new way of understanding what it means to teach thinking.

4) Dialogic education is about empowering voices

Participating in dialogue implies acquiring or finding a voice. An individual voice only exists in the context of other voices. Finding one's voice within a dialogue is about knowing when and how to listen as well as about knowing when and how to speak. To acquire voice students do not only need skills and knowledge but also opportunities to speak as well as the motivation to do so. Teaching for voice often involves setting challenges and knowing how much support to give and when to withdraw support.[64]

One aim of dialogic education is the development of dialogic selves. A dialogic self is not just a composite self made up of many 'I-positions' as Hermans seems to imply.[65] More specifically it implies being able to be both on the inside talking and on the outside listening at one and the same time. In other words a dialogic self identifies with the process of dialogue more than with any fixed identity. This in turn implies a capacity to participate convivially and constructively in many relationships without the need either to oppress or to be oppressed.

5) Dialogic teaching implies contingent responsiveness within relationships

The answer to the question of how we should teach, is also dialogue. It is the 'inside-out: outside-in' nature of the dialogic relation that makes teaching and learning possible. In order to teach at all, this relationship needs first to be established and then all teaching needs to be responsive to and build on the voices of learners. Education into dialogue is therefore ethical and emotional before it is cognitive. While dialogic education can involve scaffolding to enable participation in dialogues for beginners it can also require education through challenge in which the teacher withdraws and the learner is left to find their own voice in a new and unfamiliar situation.

Many techniques for dialogic education, that is to say education for dialogue as well as through dialogue, have been developed for particular kinds of teaching in particular contexts. But however 'tried and tested' a technique is, this cannot take away responsibility for judgement from teachers (including the teacher voice in self-directed learners or within learning communities) because contingent responsiveness in the moment is of the essence of a dialogic relationship.

6) Dialogic education is education for learning from and through the Internet

The answer to the question of why we should teach like this, returns us to the context of the Internet Age. Much of what has been said above about a dialogic theory of education could have been said before the Internet Age and probably has been said before by dialogic educational thinkers going back to Socrates, but the advent of the Internet changes everything and makes a dialogic approach to education both more relevant and more possible than ever before.

In the following chapters, I will revisit and develop this loose theoretical framework, adding to it and refining it in the light of the needs of the Internet Age. In Chapter 3, I look at the important role of the Infinite Other as a super-addressee emerging in dialogue and underwriting the notion of a reason that can transcend specific contexts. In Chapter 4, I focus on extending the understanding of dialogic from the context of personalities in dialogue to include the broader and more generic dialogic relationship of an inside with an outside. Augmenting our understanding of dialogic education with the creative dialogic tension of a figure within a horizon (Chapter 3) and with multi-modal dialogue (Chapter 4) sets up an expanded understanding of dialogic education for the Internet Age introduced in Chapter 5 where I look at educational technology.

3

EDUCATING REASON

Recent research in developmental psychology tends to support a dialogic account of how we learn to think. Thinking apparently emerges in the context of taking the perspective of real others such as parents and peers who shape attention with pointing and gaze. More explicit education can continue this trajectory of expanding dialogue by drawing children into taking the perspective of virtual cultural others and indeed into dialogue with the open horizon of otherness itself or what I call the 'Infinite Other'. In this chapter, I give examples that suggest that learning to think implies a shift in self-identification towards, in a sense, 'becoming dialogue'. This theory helps us to understand why some approaches to teaching thinking succeed and others fail and suggests guidelines for improving practice.

Mirroring

Hold up a new-born baby, look into its eyes and stick out your tongue: the chances are that the baby will stick its own tongue out back at you. You can find videos of this amazing phenomenon on YouTube. This is one of a series of experiments that have been used to demonstrate that babies are not born as passive learners but are born primed and ready for interaction with other people.[1]

However, this natural seeming way of putting things, that babies are born primed for interaction, might be misleading. It seems to be natural for us to think in terms of separate physical bodies that engage in relationships. This way of thinking is implied when we say that babies are born with skills that enable them to interact. Dialogic theory, which begins with relationships, can help us see more perspicaciously. When we notice that if one body sticks its tongue out then so does the other and if one smiles, then so does the other it becomes apparent that the invisible relationship between the two bodies causes their coupled behaviour.[2] Shifting our focus of attention from identities that are in relationship to the invisible relationship within which identities form is essential to the shift from monologic theory to dialogic theory.

The recent discovery of mirror neurons offers a neuroscientific way of understanding how it is that a relationship can precede the separation of two parties in an interaction. Mirror neurons in the brain react in exactly the same way to behaviour that a baby observes someone else doing as they react to behaviour that the baby is itself doing. To put it another way, for a mirror neuron, you sticking your tongue out and me sticking my tongue out are one and the same thing. There are even people, grown adults, who cannot see someone else being touched without experiencing their own body being touched.[3] The division between 'me' and 'you' or 'self' and 'other', is not innate but comes only after experiencing sensations in a shared space, a space that precedes the division. This is another way of saying that for the baby at this stage, its mother smiling and the baby smiling are not experienced as separate things but as variants of the same thing.

Questioning and developing Vygotsky's ZPD

Vygotsky's notion of the Zone of Proximal Development (ZPD), the zone in which teacher and learner collaborate in a way that enables the learner to do more than they could unaided,[4] introduced the notion of a type of dialogic space into education and has proved very influential. However, discoveries like that of the mirror neuron and other findings of empirical studies of young children's early learning now make it possible to question Vygotsky's account and to develop it in a more dialogic direction. Whereas Vygotsky proposed a limited version of dialogic space as a tool within the larger project of education, new research evidence suggests that dialogic space is not simply a tool within education but, more radically, it should be understood as the context of education. To put this another way: education is a matter of improving the quality of dialogue from within dialogue, it is not, as Vygotsky seems to suggest, about using dialogues as a means to achieve an end that is outside of dialogue.

Vygotsky writes that babies learn their first sign, pointing, when they grasp towards an object that they want but cannot reach, and their mother, interpreting their reaching action as a desire for the object, gives them the object. Eventually, Vygotsky suggests, infants learn sign-mediated action, that is they learn that they can achieve their desires through others by using signs.[5] Wertsch argues, I think correctly, that Vygotsky's account of how infants first learn to use signs by pointing implicitly contains his theory of the ZPD and his whole theory of education.[6] The ZPD is described by Vygotsky as the place where the emerging fuzzy concepts of the child's spontaneous understanding are grafted onto the more formal and mature concepts already achieved in the culture. This same ZPD process in which children's relatively unconscious meanings are grasped and extended into greater consciousness and clarity by a more knowing adult, is, according to Vygotsky, also at work when babies first learn to use signs.

Vygotsky's story of how children learn to point through trying first to act directly on the external world sounds plausible at first hearing but Vygotsky's later fame should not blind us to the fact that this was just a speculative hypothesis, albeit from a brilliant young man. This hypothesis has since been subjected to more serious experimental evaluation. Baron-Cohen conducted a series of studies on infants first use of signs and he argues, from the evidence, that to understand the genesis of symbolizing we need to distinguish between two kinds of pointing: just pointing to get what you want (proto-imperative) and pointing to draw another's attention to something (proto-declarative).[7] The first kind of pointing does not imply inter-subjective awareness and so is not the beginning of language as Vygotsky mistakenly claimed. Baron-Cohen provides convincing evidence that autistic children have no trouble mastering 'proto-imperative' use of pointing to show that they want something even when they fail to master more communicative 'proto-declarative' use of pointing as a sign intended to direct another's interest.

The significance of this is that in order to use pointing as a sign it is necessary first to have a sense of the other person as someone with their own distinct perspective on the world. Hobson argues from a wealth of evidence that those infants who, for whatever reason, fail to establish a dialogic relationship with their mothers, or other primary care-giver, fail to follow their mother's gaze and so fail to understanding 'pointing' as a sign.[8] So Vygotsky was wrong. Babies do not first learn signs as tools to get what they want. They first learn signs as a way to direct the attention of other people within a relationship. One implication of this is, that while it might make sense to think of bodies as existing outside of relationships and then entering into relationships, this is not the case for selves. Selves, understood as unique first-person perspectives on the world, are always already within relationship.

Introducing consciousness

Vygotsky thought that his account of how children learned to use signs in relationships with others was relevant to his motivating quest, which was understanding the development of consciousness. He wrote rather poetically that

> Consciousness is reflected in the word like the sun is reflected in a droplet of water. The word is a microcosm of consciousness, related to consciousness like a living cell is related to an organism, like an atom is related to the cosmos. The meaningful word is a microcosm of human consciousness.[9]

In this little exergue and elsewhere, Vygotsky seems to follow Marx's suggestion that consciousness can be understood as internalized language. Marx explicitly included language and consciousness as 'tools' that help humans to work on nature and produce a living. Marx had the idea that humans first used signs to coordinate working together, I think he imagined something like a team of hunters having to talk together to bring down a mammoth. Having developed language as 'practical consciousness', the idea was that this social tool turned inwards to become personal consciousness.[10] Vygotsky followed Marx quite closely to argue that first we use words as tools to communicate externally and then we internalize these to use them to regulate our own thinking. We become conscious through this internalization of language and, indeed, through the internationalization of culture.

For Vygotsky consciousness is language experienced on the inside hence the claim, quoted above, that 'the meaningful word is a microcosm of consciousness'. It follows from this bigger picture that Vygotsky's account of how babies learn signs in the cradle and how children learn to use words as concept tools in the ZPD are, for Vygotsky, part of the development of consciousness.

Vygotsky's application of Marx has proved an insightful and fruitful theory for education because it locates individual intellectual development in social and historical context. However, the evidence now suggests that it needs to be revised with the addition of a key distinction that he often failed to make, or, at least, failed to take seriously enough. This is precisely the key dialogic distinction outlined in Chapter 2: the difference between taking an external perspective (Buber's 'I-it') and taking an internal perspective (Buber's 'I-thou'). In his account of learning to point, Vygotsky conflates these two types of relation: the mediated tool use of the baby getting what it wants through pointing, an external I-it relation, with the baby getting its mother to direct her attention which implies an internal I-thou relationship.

This distinction is important because the internal relation presupposes an already achieved intersubjectivity. The need for there to be an intersubjective relationship between the mother and baby for there to be the use of signs, tells us that consciousness and thinking do not start with language but emerge out of intersubjectivity.[11] The augmentation of Vygotsky's theory with the key dialogic distinction between external and internal perspectives on relationships has important implications for how we understand intellectual development. In the next chapter, Chapter 4, I pick up the question of the development of consciousness that Vygotksy raised in order to argue that the dialogic relation is key to understanding what consciousness is, how it arises and how it can be expanded. In this chapter I focus more on issues normally labelled as 'cognition', however, I strongly agree with Vygotsky that cognition and consciousness should not be thought of separately.

Primary intersubjectivity

Search YouTube for illustrations of 'the still face' experiment and you will see just how unhappy very young babies get if their mothers do not respond to them. When mothers keep their faces still, babies seek their attention, becoming more and more desperate until, eventually, they turn away in obvious distress.[12]

An extension of this experiment, called the two videos experiment, was devised to distinguish between the effect of just seeing the mother's face and hearing her voice and the effect of being within a living relationship. In this experiment, after interacting with their babies, mothers went to another room. For half the babies in the experiment their mothers continued to interact with them via a video link while the other half of the babies were shown recordings of their mothers making the same kinds of faces and noises. The babies trying to interact with the recordings showed the same sort of distress symptoms as the babies in the 'still face' experiment.

This experiment is fascinating in showing that real relationship is possible at a distance mediated by electronic sounds and images even for two-month-old babies.[13] It seems that contingent interaction is more important to real relationship than physical presence. This experiment shows the beginnings of the kind of internality that Socrates referred to in his distinction between the living word of dialogue and the dead word that is experienced as external to a relationship. The internality here is not the internality of a self in the face of an objective world. It is the internality of a relationship. The baby is not relating to sounds or faces or smells or any other objective physical phenomena – the baby is relating directly to her mother and she knows this because when she smiles her mother smiles back.

Trevarthen calls this early stage of infancy 'primary intersubjectivity' and this label has been more generally taken up[14]. It is interesting to note that this kind of 'intersubjectivity' seems to come before the development of subjectivity. It seems natural to think, as I wrote just above, that the 'baby' is relating to its 'mother' but the baby does not really exist as a separate self with a separate sense of agency at this point. When the baby smiles the mother smiles and when the mother smiles the baby smiles but the baby does not smile with an intention nor is it aware that it is smiling. Relationship exists first and it is only out of developments within that relationship that a separate self emerges.

This primary intersubjectivity has been described as a preparation for true intersubjectivity[15] but this is misleading, it is not something that babies have but that then disappears as they grow older. There is plenty of evidence that people who live and work closely together attune their behaviours.[16] People in conversation, for example, tend, quite unconsciously, to assume the same accents and rhythms of speech as the people that they are talking to. In other words primary intersubjectivity, or what could be called participatory consciousness, is not an early stage of consciousness that is overcome by education, but is the context of all consciousness at whatever stage.[17] Participation through mirroring is a larger context that both precedes and exceeds the emergence of self-consciousness and also is never overcome or left behind by this emergence so it remains throughout intellectual activity as the ever-present context of self-consciousness and of directed self-conscious thought.

'Thirdness' or the agency of relationships

The relationship between the egg and the surrounding mother moves at conception from being an external or mechanical relationship between physical objective external things to becoming, at least in part, an internal or dialogic relationship. The difference is that while the meaning of an external or mechanical relationship is entirely defined or constituted by the objects in relation, a dialogic relation is constitutive. This idea of a constitutive relationship can be illustrated quite simply by the grammatical truth that an 'I' cannot exist without a 'you' so the relationship between 'I' and 'you' is constitutive of its parts. The relationship between a mother and her baby precedes the separate existence of the baby as a voice or a partner in the relationship and it is only in the context of this preceding and constitutive relationship that the new self emerges.

Understanding that relationships can be causal helps us explain experimental observations. For example, some have sought to explain the behaviour of the babies in the two videos experiment by postulating a 'contingency awareness mechanism' in the baby. This kind of ad hoc explanation in terms of individual brain mechanisms is a product of the assumption that the only real causes of behaviour must lie within organisms. It is in exactly this sort of case that theory becomes useful. Theory helps us to shift ways of seeing. Once we foreground the relationship and see it is primary and causal then understanding what is going on between mother and baby becomes easier. The baby does not cause the mother to smile and the mother does not cause the baby to smile, both are caused to smile by the relationship between them.

Dialogic relationships, in this case the dialogic couple between mother and child, are real, albeit invisible, mechanisms that have causal agency. This is perhaps obvious but is worth stressing only to correct for the tendency of those who hold a physicalist world view to ascribe reality and causal agency only to visible material objects like bodies and to see relationships as always secondary to these physical bodies.[18]

In fact we are all familiar from real life with the experience of relationships that take on a force of their own that compels our behaviour. If you try a dance that requires a partner, like a tango for instance, you may find that sometimes you consciously decide to act and sometimes your partner consciously prompts you to act but if the dance is to be any good then you both have to let go a little and allow the dance itself to take over and prompt both of you to act. The motivation that causes you to act is unconscious and seems to come from outside you but it is not actually just your partner pushing and pulling you – it is the dance itself that moves you both. The same is true in real dialogue or what could be called, dialogic dialogue. The dialogue has its own agency that is independent of the agency of the participants in the dialogue. That is why we often find ourselves prompted to say things that we did not know we were going to say and see things that are new to us. A dialogue can be like a whirlwind in this respect sweeping us up into something that is more than any one of us alone. We see this same phenomenon in the relationship between mother and child where the relationship takes on a life of its own and causes new behaviour to happen.

Bakhtin describes how there is always a 'third party' in any dialogue between two people. He refers to this as the 'superaddressee' or the witness that you are addressing beyond the actual person you seem to be addressing. In a sense this is the voice of the relationship in that it emerges out of the space of the relationship. I am following Bakhtin to suggest that the separate kind of agency that emerges in dialogic relationships can be referred to as the principle of thirdness.[19]

Secondary intersubjectivity

In the visual cliff experiment, infants of about one year old are put on a Perspex table which has half the surface with solid wood underneath and the other half transparent so that the infant can see the floor. A toy is placed on the transparent side at which the mother stands. The child crawls to the toy, but, on reaching the visual cliff, looks scared and invariably looks to the mother. If the mother gives a happy reassuring look then most of the time the baby will cross the apparent cliff to get to the toy. If the mother gives a fearful look then most of the time the baby will stop on the safe side of the table. This illustrates a huge shift in the baby's relation to the world. Before the baby related directly to people and objects in the world without being aware that it was relating to the world. This cunning experiment shows that how the baby feels about crossing the visual cliff is mediated by how the mother feels.[20]

Because the baby looks to the mother first in order to know how to respond to things that the baby encounters, joint attention on the world is established. Through this joint attention the mother can shape the baby's feelings about the world and lead the baby to take on the attitudes and understandings of the mother. But of course this only happens because an emotional bond has been established through give and take, 'peek-a-boo', type games in the earlier stage of primary intersubjectivity. Without this bond babies do not learn how to see and feel the world from the mother's point of view and learning in general is seriously impaired.[21] There is something to learn from this that is general to education. The importance of reciprocal relationships as the basis of education is not simply a phase. Relationships are essential to the motivation that drives education throughout the life-course.

Relationships with real people, mothers, fathers, teachers, role-models, have a huge influence on motivation for education but beyond this the path of educational achievement also requires being drawn into a positive empathetic relationship with the process of educational dialogue itself. To understand how it is possible to relate to something as apparently abstract as a dialogue we need to combine the principle of 'thirdness' outlined in the previous section with the principle of secondary intersubjectivity. To find out how it is possible to get inter-subjective with a relationship rather than just with a person we need to briefly explore recent research findings on the development of symbol use and symbolic thought, which is the next major shift in development illustrated by the way in which children learn how to point.

Becoming a self

In the 'visual cliff' experiment we can see shared emotions such as fear or confidence. This experiment shows the baby forming a relationship with the attitudes of the mother applied to an object in the world rather than just a direct relation with the mother. Emotions here seem to serve as the first intersubjective language. This is joint attention: the baby looks at the cliff and looks at the mother, the mother looks at the cliff and looks at the baby, the way she looks conveys confidence or fear enabling the baby to look again at the cliff in a new way mediated by the mother's emotion.

Signing usually begins with a pointed forefinger meant as a sign for a shared object that the child wants the mother to pay attention to. Real signing like this, proto-declarative signing, means that the child can also follow the gaze of the mother to try to understand what the mother is pointing to. What exactly the mother is pointing to is not always so obvious. Is it the cup or the rattle next to the cup? To find out the child has to, in a sense, hypothesize and error-check, returning to the mother's gaze and her expression. It follows that in order to follow signs like pointing effectively the child must try to take on other's 'point of view'.

The uniquely human capacity to have split attention or to hold two things in mind at once is essential to self-consciousness because self-consciousness implies not only being a self but also observing yourself being a self as if from outside. Hobson describes how this possibility arises in the context of the to and fro of imitation, role-taking and joint attention found in secondary intersubjectivity. If a child is given a strange new toy, shall we say a robot Buzz Lightyear toy that says 'to infinity and beyond', the child might be anxious. The normal response is to check with the mother to find out what the appropriate reaction should be to the new toy, perhaps the face of the mother will show amusement, surprise or even mild feigned anxiety intended to help the child cope with her anxiety, at the same time as reassuring the child about the toy. In this way the child relates to the mother (or other care giver) relating to the world and then looks back at the toy with modified feelings. Through this sort of encounter similar to the emotion sharing and joint attention found in the visual cliff experiment, the child learns to take on another's point of view and so the child learns to take on two points of view about the same subject at the same time. This is the beginning of thinking.

Having two perspectives on the world, one's own and someone else's implies a third perspective, the perspective of the relationship itself from within which the child can see her mother and, in return can see herself. The child does not learn to see herself only by seeing herself reflected in the eyes of her mother, she also learns to see herself from the perspective of her relationship with her mother.

We can see this effect clearly if, when, playing alone, the child says to itself 'I can'. This common phenomenon means that the child sees itself as a separate person, just as the child has learnt to see its mother as a separate person. To be self-conscious is to be able to take the perspective of another person towards oneself, but not just a specific other person but another person in general. This means to see oneself from the perspective of a relationship. First the child has to be drawn out into relationship with other people and from that, even from a relationship with just one other person, the child discovers that there are many perspectives on the world. Once the child knows that there are many different perspectives on the world it is a short step to realizing, by reversing the direction of attention in the relationship, that the child's own perspective is also one of these perspectives on the world and so the child becomes a self in relation to other selves.

Who is thinking?

When children take the third person perspective to say e.g. 'Sammy drives the car', which is very common, if we were to ask 'who sees Sammy drive the car?', the answer is not so obvious. We tend to take the reality of the individual self as the source of self-consciousness so much for granted that it is hard to find the words to make an alternative case. However, the evidence from studies of development does suggest an alternative. This is that it is relationships that carry consciousness rather than any single embodied self. The embodied self is observed on one side of each relational act and children learn to identify with this and say 'me' and 'I' as a matter of learning the rules of the grammar but it is equally possible to identify with people and objects on the other side of the relationship.

Children who refer to themselves in the third person before they have a strong sense of self are not necessarily wrong. Observe 'your own' consciousness moment by moment as your focus of attention shifts and keep asking yourself: 'Who is conscious?'; Who is really seeing this?; Who is thinking this?; and so on. You might find quite a few different self-identities form behind different types and acts of consciousness. Some feelings are really rooted in the body, being burnt by a hot plate for example. Others are quite collective like the real happiness one feels on the streets of England the morning after the English team has won an important football match, and the real collective depression one might feel if the team has lost.

If you maintain this inner attitude of questioning towards the 'self' implied by each of your own acts of consciousness you might experience an infinite regress. Each apparent voice or position can be questioned in a way that makes you, 'the observer', step further back from you, 'the observed'.[22] Each identity position turns out, on examination, to dissolve because it is one of the things thought about and not the thinking itself. So where is the thinking itself to be found? Who is thinking really?

The dialogic theory that I am developing here proposes that we think of the source of consciousness not as a body but as precisely the dialogic gap introduced in Chapter 2. The dialogic gap, which makes relationships possible, is singular because it has no specific content. It is singular not in the way that one is different from zero and from two but in the way that the big bang is posited as a 'singularity' in physics. The big bang event is a singularity because it does not fit in. It cannot be located within space and time because it is the origin of space and of time. In a similar way consciousness emerges from the singularity of the dialogic gap because this is constitutive of the meaning system from within which it must know itself only by reflecting backwards from what it experiences to posit a self who experiences. I hope that makes sense but if not it should become clearer when I look at consciousness and neuroscience in the next chapter. However, I hope that the fact that consciousness is not a product of a physical body or even of an embodied self but is the product of relationship has already emerged clearly from the preceding descriptions of stages on the way of children learning to think.

What is thinking?

So far I have largely focused on outlining the emerging consensus that cognitive development, or how we learn to think, is a dialogic process. But what do we mean by thinking? This word, thinking, originates in human experience and so obviously exploring our experience of what we call 'thinking' from the inside is one important way of trying to explicate what we really mean by it. Another useful way is through taking a more outside stance and observing other people thinking in contexts. I have done some empirical studies of children solving reasoning puzzles, which I think provide excellent data which reflect on the nature of thinking and I will present an extract from this data in the next chapter.[23] A third way is through neuroscience that can now, to some extent, give us a window onto brain activity as people think. Nueroscience evidence suggest, for example, that quite a lot of what we would normally call thinking can be done quite unconsciously by the brain, so thinking is not the same thing as consciousness, or at least not the same as self-consciousness. I will discuss this neuroscience approach to understanding thinking more in the next chapter. Between them these three approaches, phenomenology or the inside experience of thinking, empirical observation of thinking in contexts and the neuroscience of thinking, offer insights that can take us further than the rather abstract models of thinking offered by classical cognitive psychology. In this section I focus on the phenomenology of thinking through the work of two of the most sensitive and insightful, if also somewhat controversial, philosophers trained in the phenomenological tradition of philosophy, Heidegger and Levinas.

'Was heisst Denken?', an essay by Heidegger usually translated as 'What calls thinking?', begins with the claim: 'We come to know what it means to think when we ourselves are thinking. If our attempt is to be successful, we must be ready to learn thinking'.[24] Thinking has to be learnt, Heidegger writes, but the first step in learning thinking, he claims, must be to unlearn all the nonsense that has been taught about thinking. He writes, for example, that 'Science is not thinking'. I think that he means here that algorithmic accounts of thinking (and of science) as facts, linked by logical arguments or as the application of a defined method, are at best accounts of thinking made up after the event that tell us nothing about what thinking is really like. So what is thinking really like? Heidegger does not answer this question directly but he replaces it with another question: 'What calls us to think?'[25] By doing this he is pointing out that while cognitive science has tended to describe thinking as if it was a process that we can control, like applying a set of tools to solve a problem, the actual experience is often much more like being called to think by a voice that originates beyond us. Heidegger writes, rather obviously perhaps, that what most calls us to think is that which we find most thought-provoking. While we can usually never fully grasp hold of that which calls us to think, the very fact that we allow ourselves to be called by it means that our thinking becomes a kind of pointing towards it.

Levinas accepted Heidegger's claim that we are called out to think by something beyond us but this 'something' is not, he claimed, a mysterious abstraction like

'Being', as Heidegger had perhaps implied. Thinking begins, Levinas claims, when we are called to explain ourselves in the face of real other people. From the very beginning, to be a self, for Levinas, is to be a kind of response to others who call us out: they call 'Are you there?' and the self says: 'Here I am'.[26] It is in the context of a relationship of responsibility (a need to respond) binding us to other people that we are first called to think, in order to justify and explain ourselves to others.

The new developmental psychology story of how a self emerges through relationships with others, which I outlined above, suggests how it might be that people can feel called out to respond to others. What is most thought-provoking is often what others provoke us to think about.

Although Levinas writes a lot about concrete real other people, his account of thinking is similar in other ways to Heidegger's original account. He writes that there is something about other people that we can never grasp, their 'Infinite Otherness' from us, and it is this mysterious and ungraspable otherness of the other that is what most calls out to us. Levinas invokes this 'Infinite Other' in an ethical context. It is because other people transcend our capacity to understand them and represent them that we should not use them as means to achieve our own ends but should respect them as ends in themselves. However I think Levinas's notion of the Infinite Other can also be understood as a kind of cognitive causal mechanism if we insert it into a dialogic account of how we learn to think. The description of thinking as a kind of response to the call of Being for Heidegger could be translated as thinking as a response to the call of Infinite Otherness.

Some might say that Levinas's idea of the Infinite other seems just as vague and mystical as Heidegger's concept of Being. But actually I think that it is quite a concrete and straightforward idea. It is simply another way of saying that I am in a relationship with you but that any idea I form of you does not fully grasp you because you are more than my images of you. Cognition in general always occurs within the context of a prior relationship with otherness in general that cognition therefore cannot completely comprehend. In other words there is always an outside to our representations, an excess that we cannot grasp or contain, and it is because of this that Levinas uses the term 'infinite' in the simple sense of 'not finite'. The encounter with the face of the concrete other, Levinas claims, is an encounter with this Infinite Other that outstrips our comprehension and yet calls us to respond.

Heidegger's and Levinas's accounts of thinking can be called dialogic not because they locate all thinking in real dialogues between specific individuals but because their accounts of thinking do not reduce it to 'structures' but assume a context of relationship. This adult phenomenology of thinking makes sense in the light of recent development psychology if we consider how thinking first develops within relationships as described above.

The vertical dimension of thinking

The idea of teaching thinking implies values and criteria for good thinking. I call this the vertical dimension of thinking. It contrasts to me with the horizontal dimension implied by the claim that there are lots of different kinds of thinking and contexts of thinking. Yes of course there are many different kinds and contexts of thinking but if they are all at the same level, i.e. different locations on a horizontal plane, then there is no role for teaching thinking. The enterprise of teaching thinking begins with the claims that some kinds of thinking are at a higher level than others which implies a vertical dimension tangential to this horizontal plane. Piaget, for example, has a clear account of the vertical dimension of the development of thinking from the more concrete and 'operational' towards the more abstract and universal. Vygotsky follows Piaget's vertical account of the development of thinking quite closely but questions the internal mechanism of growth that Piaget proposed in order to give a greater role to culture and to education.[27] Can a more dialogic account of learning to think also offer an account of the vertical dimension of the development of thinking that is required by education?

One possible response to this question from a dialogic or more generally socio-cultural perspective might be that there are many different kinds of thinking for different purposes in different contexts and so it is not possible to talk about teaching 'good thinking' because there is no abstract 'thinking in general'.[28] This is the implication of a situated 'communities of practice' approach to learning.[29] I have responded to this possible criticism of the whole idea of teaching thinking elsewhere.[30] Accounts of different contexts of thinking describe the horizontal dimension of thinking but in addition to this we need an account of the vertical dimension of thinking in order to understand thinking in response to a new event or thinking that cuts across contexts in order to criticize or challenge existing practices.

Bakhtin's notion of the 'witness' position or 'superaddressee' in every dialogue is relevant for re-constructing the vertical dimension of learning to think within a dialogic theoretical framework. In a dialogue we might start just trying to persuade the other person but in doing so we end up listening to our own arguments as if from an outside point of view. For example in analysing the talk of children in primary classrooms I often see children changing their minds in the face of questioning by other children not in fact because they tried to see the issue or problem from the point of view of the specific questioner but simply because they looked at it again as if afresh from the outside and realized that they had got it wrong. In this common move they are stepping back and looking again at their own utterances from the perspective of an outside witness that is not a specific or situated outside person.

As outlined in Chapter 2, the superaddressee, although not a physically embodied perspective, serves as an influential voice or perspective in all dialogues. Bakhtin, distances himself from a 'spiritual' account of thinking which transcends its context, when he writes of the superaddressee:

The aforementioned third party is not any mystical or metaphysical being (although, given a certain understanding of the world, he can be expressed as such) – he is a constitutive aspect of the whole utterance, who, under deeper analysis, can be revealed in it. This follows from the nature of the word, which always wants to be heard, always seeks responsive understanding, and does not stop at immediate understanding but presses further and further (indefinitely).[31]

It follows from Bakhtin's account of the superaddresee that if you try to pin down this position in order to dialogue with it you will find that another superaddressee position is automatically generated. Bakhtin did not bring this out but with the benefit of reading Bakhtin after reading Levinas we can see that the infinite regress implied by the idea of the superaddressee means that it leads on to a cognitive version of the Infinite Other. While within a specific culture the superaddressee might take on a particular form that we dialogue with, shall we say an image of God or of a local god, then there will also be a witness or superaddressee position generated by this dialogue. In other words if one is open in a dialogue and listens closely there is no final position but always a voice from outside the consensus with a new perspective asking to be heard. This takes us in the direction of Levinas's Infinite Other, that part of the otherness of the other that can never be contained or represented within my words but always outstrips my capacity to understand. But it must be emphasized that the cognitive Infinite Other invoked here is not any kind of static thing or image or actual person but simply the name given to an infinite process of questioning.

This analysis of the implicit infinity in dialogues enables us to understand more clearly how children learn to think in the way referred to as reasoning. First they are called to explain themselves in dialogues with specific others. In the act of explaining themselves they become drawn into a dialogue with a third position that every dialogue generates, the position of the super-addressee. This position can become blocked as a particular set of rules or criteria, those instantiated in a particular community of practice for example, or the children can be drawn further into relationship with the Infinite Other.

This account of learning to reason goes beyond the otherwise related account of George Herbert Mead. Mead offered a similar story of how children learn to think by being drawn out to see from the point of view of others and then the 'Generalized Other' who represented the norms of the community.[32] The Generalized Other is certainly a superaddressee figure but if we engage in dialogue with the Generalized Other a new superaddressee position is generated which enables us to question these norms of the community and perhaps revise them. There are always voices outside of the community questioning the rules of good reasoning that the community upholds and listening to those voices with respect takes us in the direction of the Infinite Other.[33]

What is learning?

Lave and Wenger's situated account of learning as joining and becoming more central in a community of practice has been influential.[34] In relation to thinking it is misguided in so far as it implies that thinking is always limited by the criteria of good thinking found within communities.[35] This is an ethically dangerous idea that is disproved every time we are challenged to think by a voice outside of our community. However there is one interesting implication of situated learning theory that I would like to borrow and build upon to understand dialogic education better, this is that learning should be understood as a trajectory of identity within a social context.[36]

It has long been clear that learning anything significant changes who we are and how we make sense of the world around us. This idea is already found, for example, in Piaget's notion of accommodation. However whereas Piaget's and even Vygotsky's ideas of learning as the development of the self are abstract, Lave and Wenger situate this in a cultural context as becoming a self in a society.

1) Identity and identification

Identity sometimes refers to things that do not change much like being British or female or a teacher. However, there is also a more shifting ground of identifications, like the way in which we might identify with being one kind of person at an office party and then shift to identify with being a different kind of person at a family funeral. The way in which Wenger and other educationalists are increasingly using the term 'identity' to understand an important dimension of learning is not so much as a noun but as a verb. The interest here is in the active process of identification and why and how learners identify with different self-images at different times. This is well summed up in a recent article on identity in learning mathematics by Paul Cobb and colleagues:

> We take as our starting point the colloquial meaning of *identifying*, namely, to associate or affiliate oneself closely with a person or group. Our concern is with both how students come to understand what it means to do mathematics as it is realised in their classroom and with whether and to what extent they come to identify with that activity.[37]

2) The vertical in learning

One problem with the learning as identification with social practices model however is that, on its own, it is all horizontal and lacks an adequate account of vertical learning. Learning as a trajectory of identity on Wenger's model can account for how one might learn to be a good citizen in a democratic society but it could equally account for how one might learn to be a good gang member. It is about how we get socialized into different group norms: it does not account for how we might learn to become more aware of our identifications in order to question and transform group norms.

Just as the notion of teaching thinking requires an account of what progress and development in thinking look like so, in a similar way, the idea of learning to think cannot be left as a neutral account of processes of socialization but implies a notion of learning to think well. The dialogic account of learning to think as being drawn into dialogue with the Infinite Other that I have outlined offers the vertical dimension that is required for education and that is missing in Wenger's account and in situated learning theory in general.

3) Identification with orientations in groups

In a similar way to Paul Cobb's account quoted earlier, Neil Mercer and I found that shifting self-identifications seemed crucial to understanding the cognitive implications of the different types of talk we found in small groups in classrooms. Disputational Talk, in which children try to defeat each other and be the winner, depends on an identification with a narrow and defended self-image where what is seen as 'self' is defined against others. This sort of identity can be found in the common phrases 'I win, you lose' or 'winner takes all'. People engaged in Disputational Talk are trying to beat each other, they are not trying to learn from each other. Cumulative Talk, by contrast, depends on all in the group identifying with the group identity more than with their individual identity. They do not want to challenge each other since that might disrupt the harmony of the group. In cumulative thinking there is no incentive to challenge ideas or explore reasoning, instead people seek to agree with each other to maintain the feeling of belonging to the group. We have videos of cumulative groups where different opinions were in fact expressed, almost by accident, but were then just ignored by everyone present in order to maintain the appearance of unity.[38]

As well as Cumulative and Disputational Talk we found a third kind of talk that Neil Mercer followed Douglas Barnes in calling Exploratory Talk. Exploratory Talk involves engaging critically with each others' ideas within a shared relationship. The definitions of this by Barnes and then by Mercer invokes explicit reasoning.[39] However an experimental study led by Sylvia Rojas-Drummond in Mexico shows that teaching Exploratory Talk leads to improvements in collaborative creative or divergent tasks without any explicit reasoning.[40] This finding implies that what is essential to 'Exploratory Talk' is not in fact the explicit reasoning. Just as Disputational Talk and Cummulative Talk can best be defined by the type of identification they imply, so can the intersubjective reality referred to previously by the term Exploratory Talk. I now prefer the term dialogic talk since what seems to be most essential to this type of talk is identification with dialogue itself as opposed to the identifications with particular images which characterize Disputational and Cummulative Talk.[41]

Identification with the 'space of dialogue' was an idea I put forward in 1997 writing with Neil Mercer to explain the trajectory of learning towards learning to think in small group talk.[42] It was meant as an answer to the question: from what standpoint are children able to challenge their own thinking? How is it possible for them to change their minds because of what they hear in a discussion? If they are thinking then they are not simply identifying with their initial position or their self-interest, nor are they simply identifying with the other speaker's position, although they may be listening carefully. If they are able to change their minds it must be because they are identifying in some way with the process of the dialogue itself and the ideal of truth that it generates.

4) Combining identification with verticality

Both Disputational Talk and Cumulative Talk involved identification with limited images, one an image of self and the other an image of the group. Dialogic talk however is characterized by openness and respect for difference. As described in the first section of this paper, dialogic is actually defined by a constitutive dialogic gap or difference. Disputational and Cummulative Talk are at the same horizontal level, they are just different types of talk characterized by different identifications. Identifying with the non-identity of dialogue is at a different ontological level taking us in the direction of the vertical.

This account of how group thinking improves when Exploratory Talk is taught suggests a general direction in the development of more effective thinking away from identification with limited entities or images, and towards identification with the open and non-identical space of dialogue. In a sense this ideal of identification with non-identity is an oxymoron but it is a productive oxymoron pointing us in the direction of a practice of reflection[43] capable of dissolving fixed images and assumptions.

The earlier discussion of the third position in every dialogue and the progression from dialogue with specific others through to dialogue with projected cultural voices and on to dialogue with the Infinite Other makes it understandable why identification with the space of dialogue should lead to better thinking and measurably better problem solving in groups. Identification with Dialogic Space is functionally equivalent to identification with being in dialogue with the Infinite Other – or putting every bounded identity into question – and could also be described more simply as openness.

Illustrations from case studies of teaching thinking in classrooms

The story I have told of learning to think as moving from coming to self-awareness within relationships to engaging increasingly in dialogue with the Infinite Other might sound a bit abstract and philosophical. However it has actually emerged as an attempt to make sense of evidence from studies of teaching thinking. I think that it helps us to understand what is really going on as children learn to think and so it has practical implications for how to teach thinking. To help contextualize this theory a little more I will give brief illustrative accounts from three different studies of young children learning to think in classrooms.

1) Separate moments brought into dialogue

When I first observed a group of 5-year-old children doing a Philosophy for Children session I was struck by how they started with monologues, hardly seeming to listen to each other at all. The activity involved sitting in a circle and discussing a book that they were reading together. Many of the children had things to say but they just give their own stories from incidents that has happened to them without responding to anything that the other children had said.

I continued to observe weekly sessions of Philosophy for Children over a three-month period. The teacher modelled listening carefully and responding to what had been said and making connections. He actively encouraged the children to think about whether they agreed or disagreed with the previous opinion. Before long the terms 'agree' and 'disagree' were taken up by the children.[44] Within a few weeks the group had shifted from all talking in parallel to talking together, responding to and building on what previous speakers had said. As a result more complex ideas were possible involving not only associations with personal stories but also some evaluation of and reflection upon claims.

It was as if previously separate streams of experience were being brought into relationship and as a result some light was being shed. I was impressed at the power of a few simple shared expectations in a dialogue, shared expectations such as listening, responding, agreeing and disagreeing, to transform the quality of the shared thinking. It struck me that this experience in a class of 5-year-olds illustrated the larger dialogic vision of education as bringing isolated voices representing relatively closed off bits of time together into larger and larger dialogues in which each voice was reflected upon and able to reflect on other voices across difference and across time.

2) Physically invoking the absent other

The crucial role that the absent addressee can play in precipitating a shift in understanding can be seen clearly in some data from an American primary classroom.[45] In the data a group of four children had been told to make a graph but had not been told how to make it. They had been growing plants as a class and had measured each plant's height each day. One of the children, Angelina, wanted to write down all the observation data in cells linked to each plant name. She had not really understood how a graph can help display information. Julia and Tom argued with her that they should map the height of the plants on one axis against the days on the other axis. They argued for a long time even turning the graph paper around so that they could literally see it from each other's point of view. At one point in the video it is possible to see that Angelina changes her mind quite dramatically and concedes to the argument of the others. How does this happen? She precedes her change of mind by listening intently to Julia then turning her head away from Julia a little, as if for a moment of private thought, then she lifts her head slowly with a long drawn out 'Ohhh!' her eyes widen as her mouth opens into the 'O' shape which is at the same time a kind of smile.

Is it the argument that Julia has just given that enables her to see things so differently? Before Angelina's conversion, Will had just said: 'That's what you're telling them with the graph – that's why we're making the graph!'

And then Julia had added: 'We're saying: "It's day nineteen – how is it going?"'.

As she said this she turned a little to the side and made an exaggerated welcoming gesture with her hand drawing in an imaginary viewer from outside to look at the graph.

There was something at stake for Angelina in not changing her mind as she had invested time in her arguments and she wanted to be right, yet she found herself led, almost despite herself, to see Julia's point of view. The quality of the relationships in the group is crucial to this achievement of unforced agreement. The ground rules operating in this group meant that challenges were responded to with reasons, not with a breakdown of communication, and that changes of mind were possible (although this was touch and go at times as they got quite angry with each other).

It seems that Angelina's change of mind here did not stem from any abstract logic so much as from a shift in perspective to see the graph from a projected future point of view – the point of view of the future viewer of the graph referred to and brought into the discussion by Julia and Will. This change of mind is preceded by the physically embodied gesture of drawing in the alternative perspective, the future viewer.

It is always the perspective of the other that calls us to think and especially the perspective of the absent other. In thinking about what you are doing it really helps to consider the eventual audience, not just people you know who are close to the task and might understand, but also people you do not know who need you to explain it to them. It is seeing things from the perspective of this potential audience that often helps you to see things more clearly for yourself.

3) From procedure to concept mediated by the witness

My last simple example has a very similar structure but it is more obviously applied to conceptual development in arithmetic. Mathematics education researcher, Carol Murphy and I, with other colleagues at the University of Exeter, put together a project combining Dialogic Talk and mathematics to see if talking together would help young children shift up a level in their understanding of mathematics concepts.

One teacher we are working with, Susan, taught her class of 6- and 7-year olds the ground rules for Exploratory Talk and then asked them to work together in groups of three solving a simple form of magical square. They were given the numbers 3, 2 and 1 on cards and asked to arrange them in a 3 x 3 grid so that every row and column added up to the same.

In one group we video-recorded two of the group, Jack and Amy, who worked industriously arranging numbers and counting them out while a girl called Judy just watched them.

1	2	3
2	3	1
3	1	2

FIGURE 3.1   Magic square

'Two, three and one' Jack counted on his fingers, 'That's six'. 'One, three and two', Amy counted on her fingers, 'Six'.

They were succeeding at the task, finding the way in which the numbers could be used to make all the rows and columns add up to the same total but they did not seem to realize that 3+2+1 was the same as 1+2+3 and the same as 2+1+3, etc. Judy sucked her finger looking on then said: 'They are all adding up to six, look they are all six'. She said it quite loudly and they certainly heard her but they carried on counting them out numbers in rows and columns as if they had not really understood her point.

When Susan the teacher came around to this group she praised them for arranging the numbers correctly to form a magic square and emphasized the point that Judy had seen, that if you use only the three number cards '1', '2' and '3' then the answer is always 6 regardless of the order. She concluded by saying, 'So, there is no need to keep counting on your fingers, you know that they add up to six'.

This group had not been using all the talk ground rules but the collaboration itself seemed to spark an insight in Judy and prepared the ground for teaching the concept of commutitivity: that 1 + 2 is the same as 2 + 1, etc. It is interesting that out of the three children Judy was the one least involved in the procedure of the task but was the one looking on. There is an old saying 'Two is company, three's a crowd'. In groups of three, two children will often happily support each other in doing the task as they see it while one is left out slightly. This knowledge that three is an awkward number often leads teachers to be resistant to the idea of grouping in threes. But the child left feeling a bit spare in the group is often the one who challenges the others to think more about what they are doing.

What I think we might be seeing in this simple episode is the social mechanism for what Karmiloff-Smith referred to as 'representational redescription'.[46] Karmiloff-Smith argued that to understand conceptual development we need to understand how children go beyond succeeding at tasks to understand them by restructuring them. She posited an inner mechanism of 'representational redescription' as necessary to explain how something that is at first procedural, like solving this maths task, become re-described as something more abstract like understanding that the same three numbers always add up to the same answer (cummutativity).

But in this example we see Karmiloff-Smith's internal mechanism occurring externally in the social interaction of three children, one taking the outside position or the witness position in order to re-represent what they others are doing.

A dialogic account of learning to think

This chapter has argued that the central mechanism driving conceptual development is seeing as if from the perspective of others, both real others and virtual others. I have proposed a developmental sequence in learning to think well from responding to the call of real voices, to responding to the call of absent cultural voices, such as the projected future reader of a text or the Generalized Other of Mead, on to a relationship with the Infinite Other which is not a position so much as a process of questioning and a call to go beyond existing images. Since each virtual witness and absent addressee can themselves be questioned, generating a new superaddressee position, this feature of dialogues is a source of an infinite creative potential for seeing things in new ways. Although the Infinite Other cannot be pinned down and described, in practice it is more than an abstract idea but engages like a concrete participant in dialogues. This was made clear in the second case study I described above where one girl stood up and gestured drawing someone towards her in order to invoke the absent and as yet unknown potential future audience for their graph.

It might be argued that the concept of dialogic is not very useful because in fact everything is dialogic. The structure of consciousness itself is perhaps dialogic, if consciousness (self-consciousness at least) can be understood as seeing as if through others' eyes. There is always more than one perspective or more than one voice in play so the idea of monologic is an illusion.

This is all true but if monologic, which is the ideal of there being only one true representation, is an illusion then it is a very influential illusion. In lived reality we experience a continuum between more monologic voices and more dialogic voices. The sign that says 'No Walking On The Grass' is a more monologic kind of voice than a friend who explains to me that the grass needs time to grow and so asks me please not to walk on it today. The first is an outside voice of authority, the second a persuasive voice that enters into my world as if the words were my own words.[47]

Some shout their views and refuse to listen displaying an intersubjective orientation that Mercer called 'disputational'.[48] Others may be more quiet but they agree with 'what everyone says' and ignore any challenges to this groupthink. Such people display the orientation that Mercer called cumulative, again in the context of groups talking together in primary classrooms.[49] These are two ways of not thinking well because blocked by monologic identifications. In each case strong identification with a limited image, a self-image in one case and a group image in the other, prevents the openness to the question which is necessary for good thinking. Teaching thinking therefore means, amongst other things, drawing learners away from over-identification with closed and limited identities (monologics) and to open them up to questioning from other perspectives (dialogic). Doing this is moving them on a scale from monologism towards dialogism: from identifying with a closed image towards identifying with the infinite openness and potential of the process of dialogue itself.

The examples I gave of thinking breakthroughs in primary classrooms illustrated some intersubjective mechanisms for taking thought further. In the first and third examples teaching shared expections that opened a space of reflection enabled children to step back from each other's ideas and leapfrog them into new insights that combined the ideas of others into a new vision. Although each new vision can be partially reified into a concept, a clearly defined mathematical concept such as 'cummutativity' in the third example, in fact each new concept is also a kind of dialogue that brings different perspectives and different experiences together dynamically to talk to each other. Concepts, it turns out, instead of closing things down can open up new perspectives as if starting points for a new dialogues with new potentials for meaning.[50]

Cognitive development, which has often been described in monologic terms, can therefore be re-conceptualized in a more dialogic way as drawing apparently isolated moments of experience up into larger dialogues. This is the development that Bakhtin wrote of when he implicitly talked of moving from the 'narrow time' of the here and now, towards that 'Great Time' in which every voice is in dialogue with every other voice.[51] At the same time this model of teaching and learning thinking has useful implications for classroom practice. It suggests teaching children how to question each other and how to constantly invoke the voice of absent witnesses in order to help make sense of what they are doing and to grow in insight.[52]

The idea of dialogic is not limited to dialogue with this or that image of a specific 'other' person but can lead us beyond the particular other person into dialogue with infinite otherness: that otherness that always outstrips us and that never allows us to say 'now I know the truth so I can stop thinking'. Teaching thinking is drawing learners through relationships into a state of being more at home in openness and multiplicity. Learning to think on this model can therefore be seen as a trajectory of identification from initial identification with closed images of self and group towards an identification with the radical openness of dialogue itself. According to this dialogic theory of learning to think: to learn to think is to become dialogue with others; to learn to think well is to become dialogue with the Infinite Other.

Bruner once claimed that everyone was either following Piaget or Vygotsky or adopting a position between the two.[53] In this he was assuming that the key distinction in theories of cognitive development was that between a focus on individual mechanisms (mostly neo-Piagetian) as opposed to a focus on social mechanisms (mostly neo-Vygotskian). In this paper I have argued by contrast that the key distinction is between monological theories and dialogical theories. Piaget and Vygotsky offered different monological theories of development. Using the stimulus of Bakhtin's notion of the superaddressee I have tried to show that a genuinely dialogic alternative account of cognitive development or 'how children learn to think', is possible. Because this account is not about cognition in the abstract but about thinking as an aspect of relationships in context it fits better than either Piaget or Vygotsky with the new insights that are emerging from research on the brain[54] and the understanding of the essentially dialogic nature of cognitive development outlined earlier on in this chapter.[55]

This rethinking of the nature of thinking as dialogic rather than monologic is an essential preliminary to understanding the role of the Internet in supporting and enhancing thinking. It is possible that schooling has re-enforced a cultural confusion between thinking and literacy. The monologic accounts of thinking and of how we learn to think found in Piaget and Vygotsky are based implicitly on the experience of print. A dialogic understanding of thinking takes us further. From a dialogic point of view we can understand the confusion between print-based literacy and thinking since between Gutenburg and the advent of the Internet, printed books were the main medium for bringing the voices of distant others into the dialogue. Schooling builds upon this tremendous affordance. But from a dialogic theory perspective wisdom does not arise as a result of internal-izing a particular communications technology, such as print-literacy, but from engaging more fully in the dialogue of humanity carried by that communications technology. It is not the writing that is important for thinking but the dialogue.

The quality of thinking in oral cultures is different from that in literate cultures but the reported and recorded voices of oral thinkers show us that this thinking is not noticeably less wise. Before writing, oral thinkers like Socrates could attain wisdom through becoming a space of dialogue between many voices. The shift from print-based literacy to the Internet has provoked fears that we will lose the ability to think deeply. The dialogic understanding of thinking and of how children learn to think deeply that I have outlined in this chapter points to the key role of dialogue between different voices. This prepares the way for understanding how we can best use the Internet not only to support education into thinking but also to widen and to deepen collective thinking.

In the next chapter I turn to evidence and ideas from the recent science of consciousness in order to explore how this dialogic re-working of more traditional ideas of reason can help us to understand how it is possible to identify with the space of dialogue and how this helps us to understand and to promote creative thinking.

4

EDUCATING CREATIVITY

This chapter focuses on the question of where new ideas come from. It begins with an example that helps us to expand Vygotsky's notion of the Zone of Proximal Development to allow for creativity. It follows on with an open exploration of what happens when a new idea pops into play in a dialogue. Insights from empirical neuroscience, evolutionary psychology and the phenomenology of perception are called upon to help track down the path of genesis of this new idea. Dialogic theory is found to be useful in understanding creativity but only when this theory is extended beyond the normal context of verbal dialogues between embodied voices to encompass also the idea of a dialogic relation between the conscious foreground of thinking and the unconscious background. On this theory learning creativity involves a shift from identifying with bounded images of self towards identifying with the inclusive boundary between the apparent field of consciousness and the background context of all that is unconscious.

Hexagon or cube?

Vygotsky's Zone of Proximal Development (ZPD) is the first application of a kind of dialogic space idea to education. The ZPD is proposed as the space within which teachers and children share their perspectives in order to see things from each other's point of view.[1] This sounds quite dialogic and as a result many authors have described Vygotsky as a dialogic educational theorist. But this is a misunderstanding because, as presented by Vygotsky, the ZPD subordinates dialogue to a supporting role in a monological vision of education into the correct way of seeing things. The role of dialogue in the ZPD was, Vygotsky wrote, to lead children from their participatory way of thinking towards the use of pre-existing concepts.[2] The only reason that the teacher has to attune herself to the child in the ZPD is in order to graft their fuzzy ill-formed initial ideas onto the more coherent and consistent system of concepts already in use in the culture. To illustrate why this monological understanding of the role of the ZPD is a recipe for destroying creativity I will give a real example of a type of ZPD that opened up in my educational role as a parent.

One day last year my son Danny came home from his primary school annoyed with a maths problem. A test they had done previously had been given back in class and he could not understand why his answer to one of the questions was marked as wrong. He showed me the paper. The question that was marked as wrong had included a figure, which looked to me like a hexagon made up of six triangles with one angle marked with a question mark.

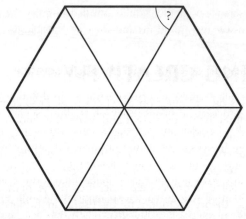

FIGURE 4.1 Hexagon?

He had said that the angle was 90 degrees and he was still sure that he was right. I patiently explained that his answer was wrong because the angle must be 60 degrees being part of an equilateral triangle and we can see it is equilateral because six of them make up this regular hexagon. 'Ohh', he said. He looked a bit embarressed about getting the answer wrong. He was obviously prepared to concede that it must be 60 degrees because I said so, but I could feel his discomfort with this so I remained with him, paying attention and listening in a way that gave him the time and confidence to articulate why he was not convinced. Eventually after a few false starts he was able to explain: 'It is not a hexagon, it is a cube.' I looked at the diagram again. I saw a hexagon. I said so. I could see from his face that he was still genuinely puzzled and even a little upset so I tried again for his sake. I squinted my eyes, I focused in and out, I tried to see it in every way possible and suddenly, yes, I too could see a cube where before I had seen only a hexagon. In case you cannot see the cube immediately here is the same diagram with one face of the cube (two triangles of the hexagon) lightly shaded which might help.

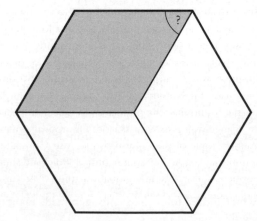

FIGURE 4.2 Cube

I was amused when I realized that Danny had seen the diagram as a cube and so thought the angle must be a 90 degree right angle. This made perfect sense on reflection because reality is experienced by children, by all of us in fact, in 3D, but diagrammatic representations in printed school text books and worksheets usually assume only 2D vision.

This whole episode could be seen as a ZPD in which I, as the more experienced adult, was able to mediate the problem for Danny, and break it down and explain it to him. Now Danny understood what was required and next time he would get the 'right' answer of 60 degrees instead of the 'wrong' answer of 90 degrees. But unlike the ZPD, which is a one-way account of children's learning, this dialogue was two-way because it was also a powerful learning experience for me. I did not see that the picture in Danny's maths test (Figure 4.1) could be seen as a cube until Danny pointed this out to me. At first I dismissed this idea but my strong relationship with Danny motivated me to try to see it as he saw it. This became a learning experience for me because it connected to other experiences and made sense of them. In a similar way Danny did not see that the picture in the test was a hexagon until I pointed this out to him. In order to be able to teach here I had to be able to learn, which means seeing the diagram through his eyes. Similarly, to be able to see the test question in the way that the test-setter had wanted him to see it, he had to first have a relationship with me that enabled him to take on my perspective and see it as if through my eyes. In this sense I was acting in a mediating teacher role, bridging between his reality and the reality that the education system wanted him to inhabit.

We could treat this episode as Danny moving through a ZPD, but only at the expense of ignoring the most interesting aspect of the teaching and learning. As a teacher I was teaching creative thinking by modelling it. I taught creative thinking by listening with respect, remaining patiently with the pauses and breakdowns in the conversation and genuinely responding with interest to the ideas that emerged, encouraging him to give value to his own vision of things whilst at the same time understanding the different way of seeing that others might have.

From ZPD to dialogic space

Concepts, according to Vygotsky's theory of education, are tools and the role of education is to coach the correct use of these tools. Although Vygotsky did not use the term scaffolding, the idea of scaffolding, through which a teacher breaks down a complex problem into simpler forms which students can solve, and then gradually removes the scaffolds until students are able to solve the original problem, is implicit as the model of pedagogy that follows from the notion of the ZPD.

Of course children need to learn how to use concept words appropriately and other cultural tools but there is a problem with this theory of education. It excludes the possibility of education for creativity.[3] Children's participatory thinking is the source of creative new ideas and Vygotsky's concern seems to be with taming this profusion of new ideas in order to educate them to conform with already existing ways of thinking. Harry Daniels has challenged my argument here, responding that because the way in which the pre-existing cultural tools are used is negotiated in the ZPD each child and each generation will use the tools in new ways.[4] Harry Daniels is right to some extent that transmission within the ZPD does not need to be completely uncreative precisely because the dialogic negotiation zone of the ZPD will leads to some changes. However, there remains a more conceptual objection to generalizing the ZPD as a total theory of education. The claim that there is some variation in the transmission process can account for evolutionary and incremental creativity in a culture over time but it does not account for the more revolutionary creativity of coming up with new and surprising ways of looking at things that do not answer any existing problem and are not reducible to using existing tools in a slightly different way.

To understand teaching for creativity all we need to do is to expand and radicalize Vygotsky's original insight that there is a kind of dialogic space in education. In the ZPD Vygotsky applied the opening of dialogic space as a limited tool within a larger asymmetrical educational theory as a way of bringing children from participatory thinking into systematic thinking. Yes, development occurs in the space of possibilities (dialogic space) that opens up in educational relationships, but this space is not a limited zone that learners pass through, it is also the context of education and the end of education. Widening, deepening and fully inhabiting the space of possibilities that opens up in dialogue is becoming a creative thinker. If we take the space of the ZPD more seriously we can see that this space itself, dialogic space, can be taught and personally appropriated by students: not only the cultural tools and concepts that are negotiated and transmitted within this dialogic space.

This implies teaching in a way that always preserves awareness of the larger context of participatory thinking that precedes and exceeds conceptual systems. In teaching a way of thinking, the use of graph paper, for example, or the use of a number system, we need to teach this not as the only right way of thinking but as a perspective which might be useful for some tasks. In other words we need to teach in a way that deconstructs at the same time as it constructs. As I will bring out later with examples, this switch around in education is not necessarily very difficult, it could be as easy as using the language of 'what might be the case' depending on perspective rather than 'what is the case'.[5]

Summary of the argument stimulated and illustrated by the hexagon or cube example

In schools teachers often tell children to read the test questions carefully in order to give the right answers, they tend not to tell children that reading carefully always means taking the perspective of the person setting the test and figuring out how they see the world and therefore how they want you to answer the question. The answers to the questions get labelled 'right' or 'wrong' and this has a strong effect on the children but these answers have to be understood as right or wrong not in the context of eternity but in the context of a relationship between the child and the usually anonymous test setter.

'OK a hexagon could be a cube if you squint your eyes and try hard enough to see the cube but there really are facts in education, for example, two plus two always equals four', you might want to respond. People do say that sort of thing quite often. But any claim about facts always already has a whole history of education behind it and someone without that same history of education, a young child for example, might not always see it the same way. That two plus two equals four is not a fact of experience. If you add, say, two hungry tigers to two tasty lambs, then two plus two will probably equal two. Or what about if you add two female rabbits and two male rabbits and leave them a while, then two plus two could equal eight or twelve or even more.[6]

Numbers, addition, hexagons, and every other concept taught in schools, are part of a special virtual reality created by education. Once you see the world in terms of numbers or other concepts then this comes to seem so obvious that it is hard to see the world in any other way. Of course we need to teach children the ways of seeing that work currently in our society so that they can fit in and share the same world as the rest of us. But we have a choice as to whether we teach how to fit in and see things the same way as everyone else in a manner that closes down the possibility of thinking differently or in a way that preserves creativity by respectfully acknowledging that there are always other voices in the dialogue and always other ways of seeing. The creative dimension of the education that happened in the 'Hexagon of cube' episode is not simply found in the fact that Danny can now see the hexagon and that I can now see the cube. More importantly we are both now more attuned to the fact that everything, however obvious it seems at first, implies a perspective and other perspectives are always possible.

Monologic education is from A to B, replacing the 'incorrect' vision of childhood with the 'correct' vision of adulthood. Dialogic education is from A to A+B, progressing through an augmentation of perspectives and so increasing the range of possibilities. This is one way to understand why dialogic education is intrinsically creative education.

Where do new ideas come from?

I argued previously that a learning dialogue is not simply characterized by empathy for the specific other, it is also characterized by the more fundamental dialogic quality of openness to the Infinite Other. The voice of the 'Infinite Other', which I described in Chapter 3, is the voice (or perhaps the voices) of all that which does not fit in. In the example above it seems that the learning that occurred can be explained by a dialogic attitude of openness to the specific other. Danny listened to me because he loved me and I listened to him because I loved him. However, in many cases, learning occurs not through sharing perspectives but because something new emerges in the dialogue. This requires the openness not simply to specific others but to otherness in general, which I am referring to with the idea of the 'Infinite Other'. The next example, from children talking in a classroom, illustrates how this creative new learning can occur.

In the 'Thinking Together' research programme, a dialogic way of talking was taught in classrooms and the impact of this teaching on collective thinking was assessed, at least in part, through looking at the way children talked in groups of three solving reasoning test problems (Raven's Standard Progressive Matrices). The 'Thinking Together' approach has proven its ability to improve group thinking many times in many contexts since the first research study back in 1994. Just last year a new study in a primary school in China showed a very similar enhancement in group ability to solve reasoning test problems together to that which was found by the original 'Thinking Together' approach in the UK. There have been similar studies in Mexico, Finland, the Netherlands, Australia and South Africa. Each such study gives many examples of improved group cognition. Although there are changes in the cultural context and changes in the way the teaching approach impacts on the children's talk, nonetheless the main effect remains the same. In each of the studies we can see how more dialogic talk helps children to share insights, to direct each other's attention, to challenge each other's ideas, to prompt reasoning and to support focused attention. When the groups talk more dialogically they explore more options, ask for help, change their minds in the face of evidence and reasons and generally think together in a way that leads to more problems being solved.

I began writing about this approach with Neil Mercer and Lyn Dawes, arguing that the success of the 'Thinking Together' programme comes from teaching a way of using language. The way in which children talked together was obviously a very important part of their improved performance in solving more reasoning tests. The guiding dialogic expectations for talk that are taught in the programme lead the groups to talk longer, to consider the explanations of others, to try out more alternatives and to spend longer in states of uncertainty puzzling over the problem. This contributes to better collective thinking and leads to more problems being solved by the more dialogic groups. However, looking again at the videos, I noticed that the actual moment of solving the problem is never fully explained by the way in which they are using language. Raven's reasoning tests have the valuable property of not being solvable through algorithmic reasoning but require an 'Aha!' moment of insight when the key pattern appears. When children are asked to solve the problems in groups it is common to see periods of silent focus on the problem on the paper in front of them followed by one child seeing the pattern and trying to explain it to the others. This observation led me to argue that the way in which children talk together is not directly solving the problem but opening a space for the creative emergence of the solution of the problem. Shared expectations as simple as always asking 'Why?' when someone offers an answer lead to the opening of more spaces of reflection and so to the solution of more problems.

This raises the question, if the talk does not solve the Raven's puzzle then how is it solved? Other researchers have quite rightly challenged my account of creativity as simply saying that a space of reflection is opened up by dialogic talk but without giving any further explanation of why this open space should then lead to a solution emerging. Yes, they say, a space is opened through the talk and then a solution appears to pop into the head of one of the children in the group but what is the actual mechanism underlying this phenomenon of creative emergence?

Revisiting the 'taking the circle out' example

One example that we first used to illustrate shared thinking, the example which became labelled 'taking the circle out', offers a particularly clear illustration not only of the role of talk in creating a shared context through new concept words but also of the role of creative emergence within dialogic space. It has been published several times before. This example was also re-analysed by Christine Howe who argues that the Piagetian operations of contrast and comparison in the motivating context of cognitive conflict can help us to understand the way in which the children generate a solution to the puzzle.[7] I will revisit this example not because I do not have many other similar more recent examples, but because I want to expand and deepen earlier analyses in an attempt to chase down the causal mechanism or mechanisms behind the creative emergence of a new idea.[8]

As we visit them the group of three 9–year-old children, Tara, Perry and Keira, are talking together around a Raven's reasoning test problem (Figure 4.3). This is a problem that they looked at three months earlier and failed to solve. Since then they have had ten lessons, each of an hour, delivered once a week, focusing on how to talk together.[9] In the pre-test episode of talk around this problem, Tara, a girl, and Perry, a boy, disputed the answer without giving reasons for their different choices. Both the alternatives they offered were wrong but they did not consider any other answers. The solution put down on the single answer sheet as the group solution was in fact Perry's answer simply because he grabbed the pencil away from Tara and wrote it on the sheet. In the post-test episode they talk much more responsively and consider several possible answers.

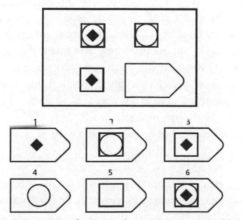

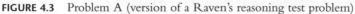

FIGURE 4.3   Problem A (version of a Raven's reasoning test problem)

Transcript extract 1: Post-test, sharing the solution

Perry: I think it's number...

Tara: I think it's number 4 to be honest.

Perry: I don't, I think it's number 6.

Tara: I don't, I think it's number 3 look because that one (pointing) has that in the middle and it's got a half one in the middle.

Perry: Complicated ain't it?

Keira: No, because that one is that, I think it's that one.

Perry: No, because look at that and look at that (pointing) they are the same, you can't have two the same and it's got that one on, look Keira, it's got that one on and it's got that one on so it's out of them three.

Keira: That one, one, 'cause that's a...

Perry: Yes, but it's got to be that.

Tara: That has got to be a diamond, a square with a diamond with a circle in that one, number 6, do you agree?

Perry: No, what do you mean?

Tara: OK, no. it's got to be square.

Keira: I think it's number 6, that's the one.

Perry: No, it ain't.

Keira: I think it's number 6.

Tara: No, 'cause it's got to swing round every time, so there is a circle in it.

Keira: Yes, but it hasn't got a circle in there has it and that one has (indicating).

(Three second pause. Concentrated faces.)

Keira: It's that because look that's got a square so it's just got to be empty.

Perry: With no circle in so it's just got to be an empty square.

Keira: No they are just normal boxes.

Tara: Look, that's got a triangle, that's got a square. Look. That's got a square with a diamond with a circle in, that's got a square with a diamond in and that's got a square with a circle in so that's got to be a square.

Perry: I don't understand this at all.

Tara: Because, look, on that they've taken the circle out. Yes? So on that, you are going to take the circle out because they have taken the circle out of that one.

Perry: On this they have taken the circle out and on this they have taken the diamond out and on this they have put them both in, so it should be a blank square because look it goes circle—square.

Keira: It's got to be a blank square. Yeah, it is.

Perry: Do you agree on number 5, do you agree on 5?

(Perry writes '5', which is the correct answer.)

The 'Thinking Together' programme explicitly taught the importance of asking questions, giving reasons and seeking agreement. This programme transformed the quality of the talk. When Tara thinks she has a solution she asks 'do you agree?'

and Perry does not agree so she thinks again. The talk is full of signs of shared thinking and openness to the views of the others. After a long pause Tara seems to see the answer. She tries to explain her vision, Perry then admits that he does not understand her in a way that invites her help. Tara then tries again using the phrase 'taking the circle out'. Perry suddenly seems to see it now. His eyes light up and he shows signs of excitement. He then repeats Tara's words 'taking the circle out' with energy and animation to express his new understanding.

The phrase 'taking the circle out' acts like a proto-concept. The action of 'taking the circle out' is not in the picture at first but can be seen now by Perry when he looks at the picture mediated by this use of language. However the words alone are not enough here for understanding – both the words and the new way of seeing are needed together. Language clearly helped in sharing the correct answer. Language also helped in keeping the group focused on the problem and allowing them to try out different alternatives without giving up. But how is it that Tara managed to see this movement of 'taking the circle out' in the picture? Here language was not obviously involved.

The two-sided nature of creativity

Research on the neural activity occurring around 'Aha' moments of insight like that which Tara experienced in the extract above, suggests the importance of unconscious thinking processes. Research has shown that problems requiring creative solutions which cannot be solved straight away can often be solved the next day even when subjects report not thinking about them at all in between times.[10] This finding fits well with Christine Howe's discovery that dialogic talk about science problems in class often does not help children solve the problems at the time of the talk or immediately afterwards but it does have a significantly positive effect on their understanding when they are tested two weeks later.[11] It is even sometimes possible to tell from EEG brain patterns whether or not people are going to solve a problem up to 8 seconds before they actually solve it. The clue comes from an increase in the 'alpha' brain rhythms normally associated with deep relaxation.[12]

In Tara's case the 'Aha' moment came after an incubation period in which, presumably, implicit bodily operations like 'taking out' and 'turning around' were applied to all the bits of the diagram at a speed faster than that possible for conscious verbal thought. The metaphor that solved the problem was one of a bodily action, 'taking the circle out'. So here, as with all creative thought, we have two sides; one side, the setting up of goals and the monitoring of goals, reflectively self-conscious and controlled and amenable to verbal description; the other side, the generation of connections and alternative perceptions, seems to operate below the threshold of self-conscious thought. When one of the alternatives generated fits the goal the process stops and Tara experiences an 'Aha' moment. The fact that she could not at first explain her new perception in words to Perry suggests that the process of thought leading to the moment of insight was not verbal.

The two-sided nature of consciousness

In the still emerging new science of consciousness there are few certainties but one area of growing consensus is that consciousness comes in two main types: top-down analytic consciousness and bottom-up generative consciousness. This two-sided nature of consciousness mirrors the two-sided nature of creativity. The top-down ability to direct our attention and so to be conscious that we are conscious is one type of consciousness. But this top-down type of consciousness operates within the larger field of an older type of consciousness which, to avoid confusion, I will call 'sentience'.

There is good evidence that most animals are aware of the world around them and of their position in the world without their necessarily being aware that they are aware of the world and of their body within it. Humans also are sentient of many things that they are not consciously paying attention to. The creative problem-solving thinking required to solve Raven's reasoning tests requires both of these types of consciousness. Top-down consciousness, or the ability to actively direct attention, is required at the beginning of the process to set up the problem and it is also required at the end of the process to recognize the solution, to characterize it and to share it with others. However it is sentience or bottom-up generative consciousness that actually works on the problem in the period of incubation and then deliverers the solution up to the level of consciousness in the 'Aha' moment.

Universal metaphoricity

Deacon calls most animal consciousness or sentience 'iconic', because sensations represent things through shared features. Some patterns on moths' wings are clearly iconic in this sense. The colours and lines on the wing might appear to represent tree bark, for example. Deacon points out that this animal iconicity starts with the act or non-act of not making a distinction. Moth wings that look like bark are iconic for the bird because of a distinction that the bird does not make. The bird looks at the bark and it looks at the moth wings and it does not see the distinction between them so it does not swoop in on the moth.[13]

The implication of this simple example of iconicity through not making a distinction is that sentience works with differentiation down from wholes rather than with building up complex structures from units. The moth wing is the bark until another sign, perhaps a movement of the moth's wings, indicates that it is different from the bark. More generally, everything starts off by meaning everything unless and until a distinction is made that reduces its referentiality. Deacon's account of the kind of meaning appropriate to sentience can be perhaps be understood more clearly if we relate it to accounts of the holistic nature of meaning given by many creative artists. The Swiss abstract painter, Paul Klee, for example, described, in his notebooks, how each dot drawn on the canvas radiates outwards to cover the whole canvas in lines of force that can then be manipulated by further dots and lines. The French symbolist poet Stéphane Mallarmé similarly claimed that the white page before he began to write a poem was pregnant with all possible meaning. The meaning was to be brought out and, in a sense, carved down from the whole of the white sheet by the distinctions that he made with black marks of ink on the page. As he pointed out, the meaning of the words was not contained within the words themselves but remained in the white spaces between the words. The point that these artists are making is a rediscovery of the holistic way in which meaning works in sentience. Every little bit of the world can, under the right circumstances, be taken as a metaphor to represent other bits of the world because every little bit of the world already contains, potentially, the field of all possible meaning.[14]

Paying attention

Education begins with the act of pointing things out to others. Some primates show signs of educating each other into new techniques. In one famous example Japanese Macaques given sand-covered yams over a long period learnt to wash them to make them easier to eat and then trained their young to wash them. But this example is famous because on the whole education of this kind, and the ability to intentionally pay attention to things and point them out, is much more characteristic of humans than of other animals. Paying attention is not simply an individual achievement. As I described in Chapter 3, children first learn to pay attention to things by having their attention directed by others. Children only become self-aware or aware that they have a perspective on the world, when they learn to see themselves from the perspective of their relationships with others.

In a recent book, Tomasello sums up the evidence supporting the view that our capacity for reflective self-consciousness is intrinsically a social achievement.[15] This can be seen not only in the ontogenesis of self-consciousness in children but also in the phylogenesis of self-consciousness in the species. According to evolutionary psychologist, Merlin Donald, brain expansion was driven forward, not by the cognitive demands of tool-making, as some had speculated, but by the growth in the size of the social groups of early humans, imposing greater demands on learning.[16]

Dehaene and Naccache summarize the results of careful experimentation on the neuroscience of consciousness (his focus is self-consciousness rather than sentience) in a number of conclusions that have considerable implications for education:

1   Paying attention is a necessary condition for being consciously aware of something. Many events stimulate neural activity but unless we pay attention to them they do not become conscious. Experiments show that even quite big events can be shown to people and processed in the brain while the people deny being aware of them if they are not paying attention to them because they are focusing on something else.

2   Cognition is possible without consciousness. Evidence from patients with brain lesions and from brain scanning experiments indicates that many generative perceptual, motor, semantic and emotional processes can occur unconsciously. For example, in the phenomenon of 'blind sight' patients who, due to a brain lesion, are unable to see anything on their right side can, nonetheless, point accurately to objects in their blind field. So in a way they can see them (sentience) but without consciousness of being able to see them.

3   Some mental operations, however, require consciousness. If the brain can function so well on so many tasks without consciousness some have questioned the usefulness of consciousness arguing that it is an illusion and epiphenomenon of no great value.[17] Dehaene and Naccache, however, refer to experimental evidence that makes the useful function of consciousness clear. Operations that require consciousness include all forms of intentional activity, preserving information over time and also solving problems that cannot be solved automatically because their solutions requires new combinations of processes.[18]

The findings as to the unique role of consciousness, summarized by Dehaene and Naccache, suggest that consciousness has an essentially educational role. When automatic functions work well consciousness is not needed but when there is a new problem and we do not know how to proceed, consciousness is needed. As Donald puts it, consciousness brings extra resources to bear on a problem. Consciousness has an executive function, it is needed for selecting what to focus on, and also what information is important and needs to be kept available and what can be discarded.

The Global Workspace Theory of consciousness

Paying attention (top-down consciousness) is more than just an inner experience. Electrical activity levels in the brain increase enormously as we pay attention to things. If a sound is played in the background there will be some electrical activity in the brain showing that the brain is aware of it in the sense of sentient awareness but if someone is asked to pay attention to that sound the electrical activity associated with the sound will increase by up to 500 per cent.[19]

There is a growing convergence in the neuroscience of consciousness on a functional model for explaining what happens when passive bottom-up awareness, or sentience, shifts into active top-down consciousness, or paying attention. This is called Global Workspace Theory and is presented by its originator, Baars, using a theatre analogy for the mind.[20] The idea is that neural processes are rather like a multitude of voices murmuring away in the dark of a large theatre, none loud enough to be heard clearly. Once a neural process makes enough connections, or is heard by enough neighbours, then it crosses a threshold and climbs onto the stage of the theatre where it finds itself bathed in light and its voice picked up by microphones and broadcast to the entire audience.

This model of consciousness as a kind of global broadcasting of key events is supported by experiments that have shown that there is an 'attentional blink' in which, for a short time span, an event which becomes conscious will prevent other events from becoming conscious even if they have equal or greater activation.[21]

Creative thought as a combination of top-down and bottom-up consciousness

Let us turn back to consider what happened when Tara managed to see the key to solving the puzzle, which she described as the movement of 'taking the circle out'. Before, in the pre-test, she had moved too quickly to thinking that she had the correct answer, along with the others in her group, and they had ticked the wrong answer without fully considering the alternatives. This time, after lessons focusing on how to talk in an exploratory way, the group paid more attention to the problem, which meant exploring it from multiple possible perspectives.

According to Global Workspace Theory paying attention to a problem means globally broadcasting it to a large number of neural processes all of which are then primed to work to find associations and possible solutions below the threshold of self-aware consciousness. These billions of processes are working with neural resources developed over the lifetime of the individual and also over the millions of years of the evolution of the species.

The basic metaphoric nature of the animal mind supports a search for any kind of connecting similarity to the focus of attention. Varela calls this aspect of paying attention 'searching the inner web' because it has similarities to the kind of open pattern-matching search conducted by a search engine on the Internet such as Google.[22]

On the other hand, the mind searches patterns stored in any modality, mixing image, sound, touch, smell and movement and twisting them together in the way that it generates solutions or throws up new questions.[23] In this case, the 'Aha' moment of Tara that solved the reasoning test puzzle, the search seems to have focused on virtual bodily movements and operations within the world: putting something in, spinning it around, taking it out and so on. The Global Workspace theatre image suggests that there are billions of voices murmuring away talking about an issue in the darkened theatre but once one voice generates sufficient attention or neural links it is moved from the background audience to the foreground stage.

The attentional blink effect is implicated also in the 'Aha' experience blink where people are often observed to close their eyes or to turn their head away just before the insight hits them. A burst of alpha wave activity is associated with this effect that appears to indicate the turning of the focus away from the strong stimuli of the outer world to pick up the often weaker messages coming from the neuronal assemblies that have worked out a solution to the problem in the background.[24]

The stage is an image of self-consciousness and here a solution mysteriously popped into Tara's mind. The solution she came up with, and which she later labelled 'taking the circle out', is implicitly an imaginary action performed on objects. This was clearly represented initially only in terms of a bodily movement because she could not describe it in words adequately. Under pressure to communicate she then re-described it in verbal terms and found the phrase that worked for her team mates: 'taking the circle out'.[25] In the context of understanding a pattern in a line drawing this is a metaphor based on a potential movement of the body.

The multi-layered nature of the mind

Vygtotsky proposed that we understand cognition not only through micro-genetic studies, studies of the kind presented above of how a single new idea emerged that helped solve a reasoning test problem, but also in terms of ontogenetic and phylo-genetic analysis, or how cognitive abilities develop in the life of the individual and in the life of the species. Tara was not thinking alone. She was thinking within her small group which framed and motivated her individual search for a solution, but also with an embodied mind that had developed as a result of interactions throughout her life-time and through millions of years of human history and that was operating within a complex social system.

Another consensus emerging from neurophysiology related to consciousness studies is that the brain has regions that have developed in different stages. Self-consciousness of the kind that is able to intentionally pay attention to things is a recent development in evolutionary terms and is associated with activity in the frontal cortex. This is the only area of the brain that has expanded significantly in recent evolutionary history. Every conscious act of attention also shows signs of activation in other older parts of the brain. Top-down intentional acts of paying attention to things necessarily operate within the larger context of the animal mind that is also conscious of things but in a different generative and metaphoric kind of way, which, following Deacon, I am calling sentience.

Donald suggests several stages in the development of human consciousness each of which has left a trace in the development of the brain. The brain architecture of humans has developed gradually through augmentation from an animal brain without the development of any new separate modules. The conclusion we can draw from this is that self-conscious and symbolically mediated thinking operates within the context of layers of evolutionarily earlier types of thinking which still remain with us and are essential to creative thinking.

Understanding something, as Tara understood the solution to the problem, involves links between these levels. Understanding is not a purely verbal or symbolic act but implies connecting verbal explanations to metaphors drawn from experience as well as to gestures or movements of the body.[26]

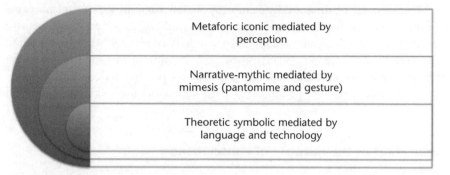

FIGURE 4.4   Layers of mind

The relationship of individual mind and cultural mind

It is interesting that the most recent layer of mind, according to Donald's schema, is mediated by technology beginning with cave paintings and continuing through written language to the Internet. Writing symbols on a page or a blackboard does not necessarily imply that there is a need to express outwards something thought earlier 'in the brain' but the act of writing can in fact be the very thinking itself. In this way technologically supported shared spaces of thinking extend the working memory. When Tara was searching for a solution with multiple mental operations below the threshold of self-consciousness, the space that she searched seamlessly combined experiences stored in her individual brain with the diagram on the paper in front of her. The apparently external visual field is a shared space that is also a mental or semiotic space. The apparently external world is always already internal to the larger mind.

Distinctively human self-reflective consciousness begins with the division of the working memory to be able to hold two perspectives in mind at the same time.[27] In the previous chapter we explored how this occurs in ontogenesis as the baby learns to see things as if through its mother's eyes as well as through its own. In phylogenesis the evidence similarly points to the advantage of intersubjectivity, or being able to feel what others feel, being the driving force behind the evolutionary step to reflective consciousness. Pantomiming or gesturing to attract the attention of another and to shape their perception makes use of this division in the working memory. To pantomime one must, at one and the same time, be inside one's own body shaping it from within and also outside, aware of how it must look to others. In acts of self-awareness the first thing we are aware of is our own location as a body in relation to others and to the otherness of the world around us. However, such acts already presuppose the unity of the preceding field of sentient consciousness, which includes the others and the world around us with our 'inner' or bodily mediated sensations in a seamless way.

Thinking can be mediated by culture, by shared diagrams for example, because of this double nature of human consciousness. Although it often seems to us to be individual, thinking always implies a pre-individual phase where it is outside us perceptually embodied in a shared world. It is because of this collective moment of consciousness that creative thinking can be augmented and expanded by the use of the Internet to become more global: a theme that I will explore in the next chapter.

Education as the purpose of consciousness

Reflective consciousness is educational, it is a kind of creative collective learning machine. Automatic routines evolve slowly over time to deal with problems. Bees for instance have learnt to dance collectively in order to show the direction of flowers. However their lack of reflective consciousness means that they cannot learn new dances to deal with new situations. It is plausible that humans developed reflective consciousness to deal with the increased complexity and change of social life. The research on reflective consciousness summarized by Dehaene and by Donald suggests that this kind of consciousness has an executive function, bringing attention to bear on problems in order to mobilize greater resources to try to find creative solutions to those problems.

While we are aware of ourselves only through being behind the paying attention moment of consciousness, this moment necessarily also implies the field of sentient consciousness within which we are paying attention. Although we experience ourselves as unconscious of the processes that we rely on to creatively solve or resolve problems this does not mean that these processes have nothing to do with us. Much has been made of the fact that brain scans sometimes reveal that 'the brain' knows what decisions we are going to make before we make them.[28] A brain scan could similarly have revealed that Tara was about to solve the problem several seconds before she herself was aware of this.[29] This does not mean that it was not Tara solving the problem. She had, after all, initiated the process by paying attention to the problem. Or rather the group had decided to pay attention to the problem after being asked by their class teacher as part of a research project that later published books and articles about this experiment linking it back to earlier work. My point here is that to understand agency and identity it is not enough to focus on the tiny moment of the process when we come to self-consciousness and experience ourselves thinking on one side of the process, located somewhere about 1.5 inches behind our eyes, as if in isolation from others and from the world. These moments of self-consciousness are always part of larger flows of meaning best understood as a dialogue within which we participate but over which we have limited control.

The realization that creativity is not a property of self-consciousness alone but a kind of dialogue implies that we need to learn to be on both sides of the dialogue at once, perhaps at times consciously asking the questions but then waiting patiently and listening carefully to what both inner and outer voices have to say in response. Consciousness of how things work is functional because it leads to self-education and to collective education. Realizing how important de-focusing, relaxing and then listening to quiet inner voices is to creativity can lead to changes in behaviour.

Guy Claxton, for example, has developed an approach called 'Thinking at the Edge' (TATE), to help children become more aware of voices at the edge of consciousness. TATE offers a clear example of how learning dispositions may be cultivated in classrooms. Examples of the sort of activities that can help develop TATE are:

• Encouraging children to have one book with the left-hand page for drafting and doodling, and the right hand for the 'the best draft so far'. Allowing time and space for students to share their preliminary thoughts and experiments with each other, and to talk about what was at the back of their mind when they were sketching, and perhaps why they decided to go with one idea instead of another.
• Asking children to keep a book of snippets from life that are interesting but you don't really know why, like overheard conversations, images, quotes, fleeting thoughts etc.
• Putting displays on the walls that show successive drafts of a painting, a poem, or a design, so that the creative process of drafting and re-drafting is made visible, and thereby given legitimacy, value and status.[30]

The location of dialogic space

The neuro-physiologist and general polymath, Raymond Tallis has recently argued vehemently against what he terms neuro-mania which seeks to apply neuroscience to illuminate every issue. What he is objecting to is that invoking neuroscience appears to give some sort of causal argument for phenomena when it is really just redescribing them in different and often quite misleading terms. His concern is that neuroscience can be invoked as if finding a brain mechanism linked to an experience somehow explains that experience. He argues that our experiences, which take the form of feelings and appearances, are just too different from neural mechanisms to allow for any kind of causal explanation of this kind.

The problem that Tallis is perhaps pointing to is that our models of the brain are always already models within the field of our consciousness and so cannot be used to explain that field of consciousness. As Max Velmans puts it, when I stick a pin in my little finger I feel the pain in my little finger. If I were to localize the part of the brain where the pain is signalled this is not a better answer to the question 'where is the pain'. What we are really studying in neuroscience is not just the empirical observable brain processes but also the underlying causal processes that lead to there being a world and a little finger and a pain in the little finger.

The argument that consciousness must be presupposed by any kind of scientific enquiry is hard to refute. We must be conscious of the world before we interrogate it and build models of it. However, scientists and those who appeal to science often seem to forget this simple fact. As Tallis writes, science is often written as if it assumes a view from nowhere, whereas in reality we only ever have a view from somewhere. Time, space, the hardness of matter and so on make no sense unless an implicit and embodied observer is smuggled into the picture.

Kant defined the term 'transcendental' in a precise way that makes it useful to understanding the issue of the location of consciousness. Kant's definition of transcendental was a precondition of experience as opposed to an object of experience.[31] So for example he argued that space and time are transcendental preconditions of experience since to experience something implies to locate it in space and time. Space and time are properties of our human experience, he argued, but not properties of things in themselves. Contemporary physics supports Kant in this argument.[32] The following transcendental argument explains why we cannot reduce appearances to neural processes:

a) It can be assumed that the world as we experience it including space, time, objects etc. is a construction of the brain on the basis of stimuli from outside the brain.[33]

b) BUT the brain as we experience it is also a construction of the brain within the field of our conscious experience. To observe a neural process in the brain presupposes not only scanning equipment but also an observer and a construction of the meaning of the perception which locates the process in space and time.

c) It is obviously nonsensical to argue that an element of the constructed world caused the phenomenon of the construction of that world in the first place.

d) We therefore need to distinguish between two meanings of the word brain: brain 1 – the transcendental constitutive brain (think of it as a holographic data projector) and brain 2, the observed brain in the empirical world that is, like the rest of the world, a projection from brain 1.

This argument is simply an unpacking of the common paradox that brain is in the world but the world is in the brain. The processes that we observe in the brain cannot be exactly the same processes that led us to be able to see a brain in the first place. The logically prior process of constitution of a world with a brain in it, is invisible to us because it is transcendental. However, the fact that it is transcendental does not mean that it is not accessible to reflection and to science.

When people take psycho–active drugs such as LSD their brain activity changes and their experience of reality changes in ways that we assume are correlated. Both the changed experience and the altered images on brain scanners are indirect effects of an underlying causal mechanism that is not directly visible but that can be modelled and tested. Neuro–educational research, as in other sciences, is not observing the causes directly but using the creative process of thinking that Pierce called abduction to build models that fit both observed events and personal experiences in order to conjecture an underlying and invisible causal mechanism described in terms of neural activity. In this context neither the phenomenology of experience nor the external and objective view of brain processes mediated by FMRI scans should take precedence. Both perspectives are needed if we are to approach more closely to understanding aspects of thinking such as creativity.

The argument that in studying some neural activity we are not only studying events in the world but also the creation of the world for us is a compelling one. Clearly neural activity is involved in constructing our experience of a world in space and time and in so far as we study that activity we are studying the preconditions of our experience of reality. This argument suggests that creative thought is not simply to be found 'in the world' or 'in our brains' in ways that can be fully observed and measured. Creative thought also participates in the invisible prior movement that is the creation of a world for us. The dialogic space that opens up between people in dialogue is a version of the space of possibilities that opens up beneath the gap between sentient and sensed (or observer and observed, toucher and touched etc) in embodied experience out of which a world issues.

In so far as we can argue that dialogic space is what could be called a 'causal mechanism' underlying and to some extent explaining creativity, and I have been making that argument in this chapter, then it is both real and transcendental. It is 'real' because it has real causal effects: when we open dialogic space, children are measurably more creative. It is 'transcendental', because it is not simply located in the observed world but is also a precondition for any self-conscious act of 'location' through which we experience ourselves as being within a world. In other words dialogic space is one aspect of the underlying space of possibilities, the underlying unbounded design space one might say, within which and out of which we construct the many different actual worlds of experience.

The unit of consciousness

From the inside point of view studied by phenomenology the unit of consciousness is a figure on a ground.[34] This fits rather well with the claim from Dehaene's summary of the neuroscience evidence that there is no consciousness (he means self-consciousness) without the act of paying attention. When we pay attention we pay attention to something and that something must stand out against a background that we are not paying attention to. As we found through discussion of the nature of animal consciousness or sentience, the meaning of any figure on a ground is not intrinsically limited. Any figure could potentially mean anything and everything. The universal metaphoricity implied by this potential epiphany of each and every moment is the simple corollary of the Global Workspace Theory that becoming conscious means a single focus point of attention being 'globally broadcast'.

Through phenomenological study of perception Merleau-Ponty argues that there is a chiasmic relationship between figure and ground. In rhetoric the term chiasm refers to the reversal of subject and object in a sentence. Reversing the sentence 'I see the world' into the sentence 'The world sees me' leads to an example of a chiasm: 'I see the world, the world sees me'.

Chiasm is the idea that you can either see the figure or you can see the ground but you cannot properly see both at once. However, both sides, figure and ground, depend upon each other and can reverse around each other. Merleau Ponty's understanding that perception is chiasmic, can help us to track down the source of creativity.

The figure and ground structure of all perception that comes from the act of paying attention also characterizes our sense of being a self in a world. It is not only true that I touch the world, the world also touches me. According to Merleau-Ponty my physical image of myself and my physical image of the world are both constructed out of this intertwined 'sensing and being sensed' process. When I say that our perceptual world is constructed in this way I mean the world of space and time that we inhabit. Merleau-Ponty's chiasm idea is the claim that the gap between me and the world or between the sentient and the sensed as he puts it, is not really a physical gap, but a kind of hinge around which the perspectives of outside and inside turn around each other. This hinge or gap ('ecart') between the inside perspective and the outside perspective, is an opening onto the unknowable transcendental outside of all possible experience. Although it means nothing in itself this opening in a context becomes a source of possible new meanings.

What Merleau-Ponty is saying with this gap idea is that while we construct images of the world on the outside and of the body on this inside, really we are neither in the body nor in the world but always in between. In creative thinking we inhabit this gap between opposites which is always there before the solidification of forms. To teach for creativity is therefore to encourage a shift in identification back from fixed forms towards the original opening or gap out of which all forms have to be born. To put this another way, Merleau-Ponty's hinge or gap opens up into a space of possibilities in which the creative artist can re-imagine the world differently.

As we have already seen, this idea that the most fundamental unit of meaning is a figure and ground separated by a gap or hinge, can potentially be investigated by empirical neuroscience. Dehaene conducted experiments which demonstrated what became known as an 'attentional blink', something that I have already referred to. If a sequence of visual images are shown in rapid succession at the same spatial location on a screen participants fail to detect a second relevant image occurring in succession if it is presented between 200–500 milliseconds after the first one. This implies that there is a threshold or bottleneck preventing all neural processes reaching consciousness but only allowing one through at a time.

Although the language of Dehaene's empirical neuroscience and the more elliptical language of Merleau-Ponty's phenomenology are very different it is possible that they are describing one and the same thing seen from different perspectives. The mysterious flash of alpha wave activity observed just before 'Aha' experiences is an aspect of the transition of a background voice to becoming foregrounded and so conscious.

In exploring moments of consciousness, neuroscience is therefore exploring the basic building blocks used in the construction of reality. The most basic unit turns out, as gestalt psychology and the phenomenology of perception had already argued, to be a figure on a ground. The figure is separated from the ground by a boundary that is also a kind of gap or a hinge around which the inside figure and outside ground exchange perspectives in a dialogic dance. Further light is shed on this gap or hinge phenomenon by research on the attentional blink effect.

Creative thought is not to be found within the illuminated stage of foreground conscious awareness alone and nor is it reducible to the billions of sentient brain processes murmuring away in the darkness of the background mind but it is precisely to be found in the dynamic relationship that unites these two moments of thought as two sides of a dialogue. It is out of this relationship over time of a central focus of attention and a background unconscious process that the 'new idea' that solves the puzzle suddenly popped into Tara's mind.

The question we have to ask as educators is why do some minds seem to block salient ideas from the background context entering into the foreground consciousness whereas other minds always seem to have the knack of coming up with new ideas when they are needed? The problem of uncreativity may be that people become trapped in constructed ideas that lead to the premature rejection of new faint voices that do not fit in with the constructions that they have become comfortable with. To address this problem we need to teach in a way that is deconstructive. This requires moving into the gap between foreground and background, between self and other, through stepping back from or de-identifying with the images that we construct.

Why creativity is the default setting

Trying to understand the talk of children in classrooms, for example, the talk of the group illustrated around the reasoning test in example 2, I argued that language does not work directly to promote creativity, new ideas are not simply constructed together with words, but that language works indirectly, opening a space out of which creativity can emerge. This 'opening a space' argument implies that creativity is already the default setting so that the problem is not teaching creativity so much as not teaching uncreativity in the first place.

My assumption that creativity is the default position that therefore does not need to be explained has been influenced by the thinking of Jacques Derrida. Derrida made a simple and clear argument for revaluing the thinking of difference as opposed to the thinking of identity. To understand why it is plausible to think of creativity as the default setting and therefore not as something that needs to be explained it is useful to revisit this argument.

Normally, this argument goes, we think in terms of identity and assume an already constructed world in which differences are negatively defined as the difference between existing things. The rethinking of the significance of difference that I rely on in my argument about creativity is sometimes associated with post-modernism. It was begun by Heidegger[35] and taken up in different ways by Merleau-Ponty[36] by Deleuze[37] and also by Derrida.[38] This rethinking offers a more positive account of difference as being a creative force at the origin of every type of identity.

Step 1: Think of a thing, anything

Ordinarily we think we inhabit a world of things with clear identities demarcated by boundaries. This is the way that thinking works. Think of a thing, anything at all, and you will be able to draw some sort of boundary around it in your mind. Even if your 'thing' is something vague like 'happiness' it is still separated by a boundary from other feelings like 'sadness' or 'fear'. The way in which we draw a boundary around 'now' to separate it from 'then' and a boundary around 'here' to separate it from 'there' and a boundary around 'self' to separate it from 'other' all follow this same general pattern. This is illustrated by Figure 4.5: Identity.

Identity, presupposes that someone somehow has already drawn a line separating the figure (A) from the background (B). This act of drawing a line around a thing is 'constitutive' because it brings the thing into existence in the first place see Figure 4.6.

A boundary around a space illustrates this basic building block of thinking: a thing with an identity. Classical logic begins with the idea of identity that 'a thing is what it is and not another thing', a claim written formally as $A = A$ and $A \neq B$.[39] But identity is also used to refer to people, contrasting me as 'self' to you as 'other'. This seems like common sense. It should do because, as discussed, it is the basic structure of consciousness. Experiencing a figure on a ground is simply what it means to be conscious. However, there is more to reality that our conscious experience.

Step 2: But what must have happened already to make this picture possible?

Since we need the figure-ground structure to be self-conscious in the first place we cannot be conscious of the prior movement constituting a figure-ground relationship by making a difference, but we can work backwards from experience

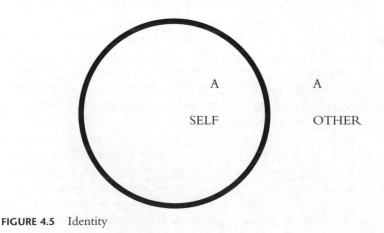

FIGURE 4.5 Identity

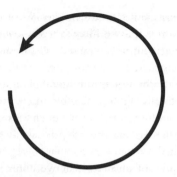

FIGURE 4.6 Drawing a boundary line

to figure out that this must have happened in order for us to be conscious. To put this another way, since I only come into existence as me after I have separated a 'me' from a 'you' (and a 'now' from a 'then' etc.) I could not possibly be conscious of this prior movement of the creation of my world.

And of course, drawing a boundary to create an identity (Figure 4.5) presupposes a field that one draws the boundary within. In this case the underlying sheet of paper upon which one draws.

A figure always appears against a ground but in looking at the figure we often ignore the ground. Figure 4.7, a sheet of paper, is just symbolic of the kind of background space, which must be assumed if we are to make a constitutive difference by drawing a boundary around a figure.

Every figure is a figure standing out against a particular background. The poet Mallarmé, for example, spoke of how the white page in front of him before he wrote upon it was already pregnant with all possible meanings.[40] By drawing a letter or a word on the page he brought out some of those meanings but always at the expense of other possible meanings. These are metaphors and analogies but they point to a pre-existing space of infinite possible meanings that is then carved up into particular figure–ground configurations.

FIGURE 4.7 The background sheet of paper

So, to recap, my argument is that we normally live in a world of stable and bounded things. This world, the world of our experience (not to be confused with the real underlying structures and transcendental causal mechanisms explored by science[41]) must be constructed by a movement of drawing a boundary around things. The space where this movement of drawing a boundary happens is not the physical space and time that we experience, because this is the world that we can only experience after a lot of boundaries have been drawn. This implies that there is another kind of space underlying the boundaries, a space of possibility before boundaries become fixed.

Dialogic space, the space of meaning that we enter into when we engage in dialogue together, is not a physical space, so where is it then? Dialogue, whereby the outside enters the inside and the inside enters the outside, is a way of unpicking some of the boundaries that locate us within identities. The space that dialogues open up is the space of the boundary, that is to say, the space of infinite possibility that was there before the boundary was drawn.

Understanding 'flow'

Mihalyi Csíkszentmihalyi is well known for introducing the concept of 'flow' into research on creativity; people enter a 'flow state' when they are fully absorbed in activity during which they lose their sense of time and have feelings of great satisfaction. Csíkszentmihalyi describes 'flow' as:

> being completely involved in an activity for its own sake. The ego falls away. Time flies. Every action, movement, and thought follows inevitably from the previous one, like playing jazz. Your whole being is involved, and you're using your skills to the utmost.[42]

The concept of 'flow' came out of a major research study.[43] Csíkszentmihalyi and his team interviewed ninety-one people who could be called creative because they had transformed their field in a publicly acknowledged way, scientists who had won the Nobel Prize, artists who were leaders of new movements and so on. He found that when they really engaged with their field and with producing new ideas or products, all reported a sense of joy and of inner reward. Some reported that the quality of time itself changed from being the external context of actions to becoming an internal flow in which awareness of the passage of time disappeared. So many creative people described being carried along by a current that Csíkszentmihalyi decided upon the word 'flow' to describe this state. *Flow* is the mental state of operation in which the person is fully immersed in what he or she is doing, characterized by a feeling of energized focus, full involvement and success in the process of the activity. A key component is the loss of a division between self and world.

Csíkszentmihalyi identifies the following features as often but not always accompanying an experience of 'flow':

1   *Clear goals* (expectations and rules are discernible and goals are attainable and align appropriately with one's skill set and abilities).
2   *Concentrating and focusing* (a high degree of concentration on a limited field of attention – a person engaged in the activity will have the opportunity to focus and to delve deeply into it).
3   *A loss of the feeling of self-consciousness* (the merging of action and awareness).

Freeman Dyson, who made a major contribution to quantum theory, was interviewed by Csíkszentmihalyi. Like many creative people he echoed the point that creative work seems to have two sides to it. He describes how, after he immersed himself intensively in reading the relevant literature about a cutting-edge problem in physics, he took a break and went touring across California. The solution to the problem suddenly came to him and he felt impelled to write it down. He writes of his experience of creativity:

> I always find that when I am writing, it is really the fingers that are doing it and not the brain. Somehow the writing takes charge. And the same thing happens of course with equations ...The trick is to start from both ends and to meet in the middle, which is essentially like building a bridge.[44]

Summing up the findings of his interviews with creative people Csíkszentmihalyi adds:

> Creative thoughts evolve in this gap filled with tension – holding on to what is known and accepted while tending towards a still ill-defined truth that is barely glimpsed on the other side of the chasm. Even when thoughts incubate below the threshold of consciousness, this tension is present.[45]

This corresponds well to Merleau-Ponty's findings within the field of aesthetics. Merleau-Ponty reminds us that Cézanne claimed that 'nature is on the inside' and that Klee heard the forest speaking to him. One point of his chiasm idea, or the mutual envelopment of the sentient and sensed (the body and the world, the seer and the seen or the toucher and the touched etc.) was to help understand creative art as a kind of turning inside-out and outside in through which the artists becomes the world and express what it wants to say.

While 'flow' is a very valuable description of what creativity feels like from within, it is not really a theory of creativity. By adding the dialogic analysis developed so far we can create a theory of what creativity is, where creativity comes from and how to promote it through education.

The altered experience of time and identity discovered by Csíkszentmihalyi and described in his concept of flow corresponds to a shift in identity away from being on one side of the dialogic gap to dwelling within the gap itself.

Dialogic theory applied to creativity in physics or in fine art is a long way from its origins in face-to-face talk. My argument is that the underlying chiasm structure of an inside and outside reversing about each other around an invisible gap or hinge is the same in all cases. Keith Sawyer, who was one of Csikszentmihalyi's research students at Chicago University, underlines this point when he writes: 'Csikszentmihalyi *found that the most common place people experienced flow was in conversation with others*'.[46]

Why dialogic education is education for creative thinking

The example I explored in depth in this chapter was not typical of what most educators think of as creativity. Tara's 'Aha' insight helped her to solve a reasoning test problem. The task was a convergent task with a right answer. Creativity is more commonly thought of in the context of painting a picture or writing a story; divergent tasks which do not have correct answers. Creativity is about framing problems not only about answering problems, like reasoning tests, that have been framed by others. But the value of dialogic talk has been assessed in many contexts including the context of more divergent tasks such as collaborative writing.[47] Dialogic ways of talking help children to be more creative and more successful in the context of divergent tasks as well as in the context of convergent tasks. The results of this research confirms the view of Guy Claxton that creativity can be summed up as simply the skill of coming up with a new idea when you need one.

Tracing creativity back to the chiasm structure of consciousness can help us to understand why the opening of dialogic space in a relationship between children talking together in a classroom should promote creativity. The essential structure of the chiasm is that of an inside and an outside revolving around a gap or a hinge. In any dialogue the other or addressee appears outside of me. This other is at the centre of their own world with me within it. In other words my perspective envelops and includes them just as their perspective envelops and includes me.

When their perspective appears on the inside of my speech informing it from within and when my perspective informs their speech from within we have a situation of mutual envelopment in the context of the tension of separation around an unbridgeable gap of difference. To appropriate the perspective of the other implies the transformation of turning inside out through the dialogic gap that both connects and divides us. This gap between inside and outside is not simply a social gap. It is not contained or defined by language alone. It opens onto the same space as the gap between sentient and sensed in perception. Dialogic space is the space before space, a space pregnant with potential voices not yet thematized by which I mean not yet clothed in categories.

In the last chapter we described how learning to think well involved a shift in identity from identifying with an image of the self or of the group, or indeed, any fixed image whatsoever, to identifying with, and feeling comfortable with, the dialogic space of uncertainty and multiplicity that opens out of the dialogic gap. We can now see why this good thinking that helps groups solve more reasoning test problems is also creative thinking that helps groups and individuals come up with new ideas and new perspectives that not only solve problems but also ask new questions and see things in new ways.

Towards education for creative thinking

Much of the discussion of creativity in this chapter has been at a highly gener-alized and abstracted theoretical level. However, the provisional dialogic theory of creativity that I have sketched has practical implications for pedagogy. Some of these are highlighted by the research of Ellen Langer. Langer conducted a number of experimental studies that point to the importance of whether we learn things in a 'mindless' or a 'mindful' manner. By 'mindful' she means seeing all the possibilities. In one study,[48] Langer compared what happened when students were educated mindlessly or mindfully. The context was how to use a new kind of racket in a ball game called, 'Whak-it-ball'. One set were taught how to play the game using the words 'is' and 'can only be' the other were taught the same content using language like 'could be', 'perhaps', 'from one perspective'. Both conditions fared equally well when using a normal size ball. Then a much smaller ball was introduced. With this new ball the ways of playing the game had to change. A significant number of the students who had been taught in the mindless condition did not adapt their behaviour and so played badly. The students who had been taught in the more mindful way were able to adapt their behaviour more easily and so fared much better. In other studies Langer and colleagues extended this work to more academic educational contexts such as understanding texts in History and similar benefits were found to follow.[49] Langer concludes:

> Almost all of the facts most of us learned in school were taught to us in a perspective-free way that encourages mindless use of the information because it does not occur to us to question it again. In contrast, information presented in the mindful, perspective-taking condition was learned better by high school students, even though they had to deal with more information. Clearly, mindful teaching practices can have a pronounced effect on student learning.[50]

Langer is convincing that teaching in a way that encourages students to see from multiple perspectives at once is a good idea. Her 'mindfulness' education is a version of the dialogic education that I have been advocating. To see everything from multiple perspectives at once only happens if we move from only identifying with being just one position in the dialogue to identifying with the multi-perspec-tival space of the dialogue as a whole.

Possibility thinking

That creativity can be taught or at least that teaching can be done in a way that supports and encourages creativity, has been demonstrated by a series of studies by Anna Craft and colleagues. Building on insights from Csíkszentmihalyi, Langer and others, Anna Craft and colleagues have been working for schools for some years to develop and to assess an approach to teaching for creativity which they call 'possibility thinking'.[51] According to Anna Craft this can be summed up as posing the question 'what if?' in different ways and contexts, combined with perspective taking, or 'as if' thinking. Teaching possibility thinking therefore involves a shift from the question 'what is this and what does it do?' to 'what can I or we do with this?'. Working with teachers the research team have developed ways of promoting possibility thinking in classrooms. The focus has been on enabling children to pose their own questions in the context of play in immersive environments where there are opportunities for risk-taking and for showing agency as well as opportunities for innovation and imagination.

The series of research studies on teaching possibility thinking adds to our understanding of what teachers and adults can do to encourage and sustain creativity in ways that are quite practical. In a recent study with nursery-age children for example, the teacher behaviours that generated more creativity were found to be provoking or stimulated the children with open-ended challenges, allowing time and space for children's responses and 'being in the moment' with the children while they were engaged with their activities.[52]

Summary and conclusions

In Chapter 3, I argued for a dialogic understanding of good thinking, meaning the kind of thinking that we should be teaching in schools. A key part of this dialogic understanding of good thinking is a broadening of the traditional conception of reason to give a central place to creativity. In this chapter I have followed the question, 'where do new ideas come from?' This exploration has led to a theory of creativity that can be used as a basis for education into creative thinking. When I call this a theory of creativity I obviously do not mean to imply that it is a theory of the pinned-downable kind that enables the prediction of results from actions. This is theory in the looser sense of a way of seeing things that can serve as a provisional guide to action and as a way of choosing the focus of further research. Through a combination of classroom research on children's talk, neuroscience research and reflection on experience (phenomenology) I hope that I have demonstrated that research can gain insight into the nature of creativity and how best to promote it. Creative thinking implies finding new ideas popping up when you need them. These ideas are creative firstly because they are surprising, meaning that they do not follow in any algorithmic way from the past, and secondly because they are useful to the task at hand. Creative thinking is normal thinking for humans because it follows from the essential structure of thought as a chiasmic relation between figure and ground where chiasmic combines the idea of mutual envelopment with the idea of reversibility of perspective. Because of the nature of consciousness as paying attention we only ever experience one side of this chiasmic relationship and tend to over-identify with the figures in the foreground and under-identify with the background. Education for creativity works by shifting identification into the space between figure and ground. This is another way of saying identifying with the dialogue between figure and ground. It combines framing questions with listening for answers, even when those answers take an as yet unheard of form.

The lesson for educational theory can be understood as a radicalization of Vygotsky's original introduction of the space of dialogue in education, the Zone of Proximal Development or ZPD. The ZPD notion implies scaffolding children into the use of pre-existing cultural tools and cultural voices. Teaching for creativity does not focus only on persuading children to master the correct use of cultural tools but also on allowing them to appropriate the dialogic space that is characterized by uncertainty and multiplicity. To appropriate dialogic space means to learn how to step back, to de-focus and to listen to the almost inaudible voices of the multiple possible perspectives that underlie everything. As always with dialogic theory this theory of education for creativity is not a replacement of the past but an augmentation. As well as teaching mastery of tools we must teach dialogic space, as well as teaching construction we must teach deconstruction. The figure-ground structure of consciousness means that creativity is in a sense the default setting. We do not so much need to teach children to be creative as to stop teaching them how to be uncreative.

This chapter has hardly mentioned the Internet but actually it has been essential in setting up two new ideas which make it possible to understand how and why the Internet Age could see a leap-frogging advance in consciousness. Firstly, while dialogic has normally been assumed to be verbal in this chapter I have argued that it is also perceptual and therefore multi-modal. Secondly, the real dialogue has been shown to be between a focus foreground and an unbounded background. Dialogic education on the Internet occurs much more through this kind of dialogic creativity than through explicit verbal dialogue between two or more clearly defined individuals. By expanding the notion of dialogic in this way we take it beyond its origins in oracy and into the Internet Age.

The chiasmic structure highlighted by the Global Workspace Theory of consciousness explains why we always find ourselves only on one side of acts of consciousness, standing as if alone at the centre of an island of visibility surrounded by darkness. But in fact this is just one moment, the individual and self-conscious moment, in a movement that unites us with everything else and with all other voices. Just as in a dialogue we find the voices of others on the inside of our thoughts so in creative thinking we find the world outside can turn inside out and reappears on the inside of our thinking. The chiasmic nature of creative thought as both individual and collective, both internal and external, explains why thinking can be supported and extended by communications technology and why the Internet can support the emergence of collective creative intelligence. In Chapter 7, I apply this understanding to explore how the Internet can support collective creativity and what education can do to help to improve the quality of collective thinking with the Internet. The next chapter, Chapter 5, focuses on understanding the role of technology in education.

5

EDUCATING TECHNOLOGY

The title of this chapter, educating technology, is meant to bring out the double role that technology has in education: it is not only a neutral tool that we can use for our educational ends, it also shapes our understanding of education and what education is for. Currently the way that we think about education seems to be very much influenced by the technology of writing, especially print. As the Internet becomes the dominant communications technology how we think about education will inevitably change. If we are to rethink educational technology in ways appropriate to the new Internet Age we need to look at educational technology in a historical context going back to its origins before print and even before writing. This chapter therefore begins with a short and highly selective history of educational technology before moving on to a theory of the role of educational technology in the Internet Age. It ends with an illustration of how we can apply this theory to educational design for the future.

The new cave?

Like many parents today I am worried about the apparently addictive nature of online games. Every day my son comes home from school, sits on the sofa with his laptop and disappears into another world. He looks distracted, like someone in a trance, as his hands twitch rapidly on the keyboard and his eyes flick to and fro following movements on the screen. I talk to him and he does not respond. Sometimes, just to annoy him, I pass my hand in front of his eyes, he continues playing, hardly noticing the interruption. The Internet game that is so absorbing for him, Team Force 2, is very similar to the cops and robbers or cowboys and Indians games that I used to play as a child. The difference is that I used to play these games in my physical body running around in a muddy field. On the other side of my son's laptop screen is a world where children and people of any age take on new bodies and run around shooting each other. They communicate via chat, boasting, complaining and sharing news about their game. They also trade, swapping guns and costumes, especially prized hats that can make them look more 'cool' or fierce or funny. One of the children often on this site is his cousin who lives hundreds of miles away. They always chat a lot when they are playing at the same time. Most of the other players he does not know but he thinks of some of them as his friends. He has no idea who they are in real life or where they are from. He tells me that lots of them seem to be Russian from the script of their chat messages.

The gateway into my son's game is the small screen of his laptop filled with flickering pixels. Yet it is obvious from his demeanor that he is inhabiting another world which he finds more vivid and more engaging than the physical world around him. The experience of space for him is not the same in his other world, nor is the experience of time. For example, he was helped by another player to find a way to jump very high above the buildings in the shared game space, shooting down at the other players below, which is not something one can do easily in real life. Sometimes, when I point out how long he has been playing, he seems surprised and says it only seemed like a few minutes when it was actually an hour or more.

The contrast with his school is quite interesting. The school exists in physical space and each subject has a physical base, a classroom, which he and his physically embodied companions have to walk between carrying heavy bags full of books. Because his companions are physically embodied there are only about twenty of them at a time and they remain always the same, not popping in and out from Russia or Japan. The writing is almost always physically embodied in space either in a book or on a static whiteboard or, less commonly, on loose sheets of paper that he has to stick into his book and carry around with him in his backpack.

The virtual shared meaning space that the school exists to induct him into, the shared meaning space of culture and science, is mostly mediated by books and by written exercises firmly located in a physical environment. Compared to his online game experiences this seems like a very indirect and labourious way to participate in shared meaning.

The first cave

The first educational technology that we know about is that of cave paintings that date back some 30,000 years. The oldest cave paintings are found in France and Spain but those in Southern Africa are almost as old dating back 25,000 years. Other ancient cave paintings are found in Asia, Australia, and North America. According to David Lewis-Williams all exhibit similar themes. These include large animals, hands, geometrical patterns, wavy lines called 'finger flutings' and occasional stick men sometimes with animal masks. Some of these paintings are stunningly beautiful and evocative and have inspired contemporary art. I would encourage you to Google for images of eland painted by the San of the Western Cape. The use of crushed hematite red rock, yellow ochre and black charcoal make for elegant and powerful images similar to those found in Lascaux and Altamira.

At first all of these paintings were widely thought of as a kind of magic intended to increase the number of animals and improve the hunt This theory was developed by Henri Dicuil at approximately the same time as Vygotsky developed his theory of tool-mediated action. The two theories fit together well. Put into Vygotskian language, the idea is that the first communications technology functioned as a cultural tool to help with stone-age hunting. This theory held sway until it was challenged quite recently by David Lewis-Williams of Witwatersrand University in South Africa. Lewis-Williams offered three kinds of evidence in support of some compelling arguments. First, the bones of the animals eaten by the people who did the paintings are not the same as those animals they painted. For example, at Lascaux the bones that have been found from that period were mainly reindeer whereas the animals painted were mainly horses. The second and more convincing evidence Lewis-Williams produced is ethnographic. He gained access to thousands of unpublished pages of transcribed notes of interviews with San hunter-gatherers from the 1870s which was a time when the San still created cave paintings and still used painted caves for special gatherings. The third kind of evidence he applies comes from neuroscience research into brain generated imagery during altered states of consciousness.[1]

Lewis-Williams concluded from this evidence that the cave paintings were essentially an educational technology for the group. The shamans, or those able to voluntarily enter into trance states and see visions (amongst the nineteenth-century San group interviewed this was said to be about half the men and a third of the women), used the paintings to record visions and evoke them later. The paintings were particularly important in initiation ceremonies for new adults. The paintings themselves evoked the altered states they recorded, bringing with them the emotions and feelings of energy or awe or joy associated with the animal forms.

The link between the paintings, often found in remote caves not used for other activities, and altered states of consciousness, was confirmed for Lewis-Williams, by the fact that many of the apparently abstract line drawings found in caves around the world are those produced by all human brains in altered states of consciousness associated with trance and visions. The eland was often painted in San caves not because this helped them hunt eland but because the eland had a special cultural significance as a personification of a potent spirit which was invoked in San initiation ceremonies. The most effective way of evoking the spirit represented was by touching it with the palm of the hand hence, Lewis-Williams claims, the many hand paintings found in caves.

The idea of stone-age hunter-gatherers using painted images to evoke spiritual energies after engaging in rhythmic trance-dancing and hyper-ventilation to induce an altered state of consciousness probably sounds rather remote from contemporary education. It is interesting however, because the use of the paintings was clearly educational and this kind of use implies a rather different implicit theory of education than that commonly found in print dominated cultures.

Ethnography reports initiation ceremonies in every small-scale society. Most initiation ceremonies apply what could be called a pedagogy of extreme challenge involving inducing disorientation through various means including vigils, isolation, hunger, sensory deprivation, drugs, rhythmic dancing and rhythmic chanting. The art or artifact (sometimes a mask) is then used to provoke an encounter with voices that are not everyday but belong to the shared cultural life of the tribe. Often these are described as ancestors, even when they take animal forms, and they inhabit not normal space and time but the 'dreamtime' or the spirit world.[2]

To enter this cultural world via the bridge of the painting or other artifact students have to de-identify with their everyday world and their everyday self. Lewis–Williams writes that the painted walls of caves became like a thin membrane between the everyday world and spirit world beyond, a membrane that the shaman could cross at will serving as a guide for others. On the other-side was a world of shared visions, which the new members of the community could be initiated into.

This new world was not chaotic but had landmarks that the guide could point out to newcomers to help them orient themselves. These landmarks might be, for example, powerful spirits that everyone could see, like the eland for the San. Initiation is often described as when a person becomes truly human by entering the cultural life of the tribe and so acquiring a spiritual body in the shared spiritual space of the tribe as well as having the original physical body in their shared physical space. In extreme states of trance shamans did sometimes become totally possessed by animal spirits, a process described alarmingly by the San as 'when the hair starts to grow'. More commonly icons like the eland paintings, do not possess the viewer completely but they come alive and communicate. So on this early theory of education; education serves to make young people fully human by teaching them how to talk with and how to walk with the spirit voices often referred to as the ancestors of the tribe.

Vygotsky described signs as tools to get things done. Signs could be used to get things done externally or, taken inward as cognitive tools, they could be used to get things done internally helping us to think more logically for example. The very first signs, however, paintings on the wall of stone-age caves, had a different function. They were epiphantic signs[3] serving to lead people into the presence of the cultural voices of the tribe. Oral peoples do not think of themselves as using these signs to achieve their own intentions, it is the other way around, the signs come alive and possess them and give them a new voice, new visions and new intentions.[4]

How communications technology educates minds

I am interested in looking at education into the shared cultural space of the San hunter-gatherers and other oral societies for how this might inform a larger under-standing of education and of educational technology. If we contrast the experience of cave painting mediated education to the experience of print mediated education, the cave painting model seems to be more engaging. I doubt if young members of the group need to be bribed to participate in communal trance dances nor threatened with punishments if they refuse. Adventures in the communal spirit world are quite literally awesome. It is clear from the ethnographic evidence that this heightened experience of shared virtual reality, mediated by the technology of shared artefacts such as cave paintings, is not seen as functioning to support other ends but as very much an end in itself and even as the most important end for each individual and for each community as a whole.

The experience of my son, along with the billions of other children and young people who play Internet-mediated video games, suggests that communications technology has the potential to reproduce something of the intrinsic motivation of the first virtual reality. However, these games are often currently being used for distraction rather than for the kind of profound adventures in worlds of shared meaning once experienced by the San hunter-gatherers.

For those students who can reach into it, the virtual reality world of meaning accessed via education, the dialogic space that Oakeshott referred to as the conversation of mankind, has the potential to inspire and engage just as much as the virtual reality of the San. Unfortunately, in contemporary schooling, it is only experienced as intrinsically motivating by very few students and often even then for very limited moments in time.[5] This means that voices behind the pages of school textbooks do not often leap out and possess students to give them new visions of how things could be. My question is, can we use educational technology to bridge these now distant seeming worlds and restore the intrinsic motivation that was once felt by young people learning to participate in their shared virtual reality?

But before trying to answer that question I will turn back to a question raised already throughout this book, this is the question of how education into the use of a particular communication technology, writing and reading, shapes our brains and our ways of thinking. One reason for doing this is to try to explore the complexity of arguments about changing education systems. The problem is that each system, to some extent, constructs its own reality with its own criteria for the evaluation of what counts as good education.

In so far as we inhabit the reality constructed by print-based education it might be hard for us to see how any other reality could be possible. As Lewis-Williams found, neuroscience can give us, to a limited extent at least, a way of getting an outside perspective on these social constructions of reality in order to see how reality is constructed in general. In this sense neuroscience offers us a perspective from which we can question the way in which reality is shaped by print in order to develop a theory of education in general, a theory which can apply equally to the San hunter-gatherers and to children born into the emerging Internet Age.

Lewis-Williams emphasizes that all human brains have the same capacity for a range of states of consciousness including dreams and the altered states associated with trance dancing. He claims simply that different societies at different times have valued these states differently. This is partly true but there is more to it than that.

Human brains are designed for education into culture and the process of becoming educated involves the shaping of attention and so the shaping of consciousness and the shaping of brains. Dehaene's research referred to in Chapter 1, shows that literate brains are distinctly different from non-literate brains. Language requires a huge amount of processing power and yet human brains do not have a specialized module for language. This means that the original ape brain has been taken over and modified for new functions. Oracy has colonized and made use of the auditory cortex used for the processing of sounds. In literate societies education into literacy leads to the colonization of the visual cortex. This has consequences for how minds work. Literates are distinctly worse at face recognition than non-literates, for example, presumably because so many of the neurons in their visual cortex have become specialized for the recognition of letters and words. Dehaene's research also suggests that literates show less capacity for holistic perception, that is, seeing the context as well as the foreground focus, and more capacity for analytic perception, which focuses on the foreground only as if it were independent of its context.[6]

However it is also true, as Lewis–Williams points out, that all brains have access to all of the states that he mentions and indeed similar experiences to those, which I attributed to the San are common in every culture. Research suggests that even in highly literate cultures many people still have the experience of hearing external voices for example.[7] The difference that education makes is not only in directly shaping the brain but in shaping the way in which we value or fail to value different types of experience.[8] So in the next section I briefly discuss how technologies used in education have indirectly shaped experience through shaping default understandings or thought and of reality.

Socrates notes in the *Phaedrus* that the living word of face-to-face dialogues has the potential for stimulating understanding in others. He contrasts this living word of dialogue to the dead words of writing that are just like shadows or ghosts because, he claims, they are not inhabited and cannot answer back. Many have noted that face-to-face dialogue assumes a certain 'mutual attunement' between participants.[9] Utterances in dialogues do not stand alone but they respond to previous utterances and they are designed to influence the person addressed. In a dialogue, in other words, the other (the addressee), is not simply outside me but appears on the inside of me shaping my utterances from within even as they form. Even to engage in dialogue I need to be able to see myself to some extent from the other's point of view and see the sense of each of my utterances in the context of the dialogue as a whole.

Socrates' account of the power of the living word remains valid today and provides an important intellectual source for this book. However, Socrates shows a certain naïvety as to the impact and limitations of the spoken word as a medium of dialogue. He sees only the negative potential of the new technology and only the positive aspects of the old technology that was in the process of being displaced. The limitations of oracy as a medium of thought have been brought out by others looking back from the vantage point of established literate cultures.

In oral cultures words are only found in the ephemeral context of face-to-face speech. By the time I have grasped the import of my interlocutor's words they have vanished and I cannot turn back to re-examine them. This means that words, and the ideas they carry, are inevitably closely bound up with specific times and local places. Drawing out the inner logic of this feature of orality, some have argued that without literacy there can be no universal abstract concepts including universal moral codes.[10] Writing, it is argued, enabled ways of thinking that were not possible with face-to-face dialogue alone. One example is the way in which the 'religions of the book' could disembed themselves from a physical context to cross seas and mountains and claim adherents in different cultures. They could separate their truth from sacred places and located rituals, for example particular caves and the dances and chants that occurred in them, because truth was now contained in writing and so became transportable.[11]

As we noted above, Socrates, an oral thinker, is reported as criticizing writing precisely for taking the idea of truth away from the living context of words in face-to-face dialogues and claiming truth for what he referred to as the dead words of writing.[12] In the Christian New Testament there is an interesting passage that appears to state that the writing is now closed and anyone adding a word to it will be cursed.[13] This is indicative of a new idea of truth that arrives with writing. Truth here is being presented as a closed finished thing of universal relevance separate from any specific context of utterance.

Of course literacy did not suddenly take over nor did it ever completely replace oracy, but at a certain point, according to Toulmin, it seems to have shaped not only how people thought but also how they understood their own thinking. Toulmin investigates the origin of 'modernity' and finds it in a shift from respecting dialogic modes of thought to respecting only written modes of thought. Before 1600, he writes, both rhetoric and logic were seen as legitimate modes of philosophy.[14] He contrasts Montaigne's highly contextualized and dialogic brand of philosophy to the abstract universal certainty sought after by Descartes only a little later. After Descartes there was a shift from seeing truth in terms of utterances in dialogues in situations to seeing truth in terms of propositions and proofs that were unsituated and universal.[15] In other words modernity can be characterized by 'monologicality', the assumption that there is only one true perspective or voice. This assumption is not possible in a dialogue but is made possible by the use of the written words, symbols and representations. The dominance of monological ways of thinking in the education system reflects the dominance of written modes of reasoning over oral modes.

If orality and literacy impacted on ways of understanding thinking then what impact will the Internet have? It is too early to say. Whilst oracy and literacy have had millennia to shape collective cognition, the widespread use of the Internet is still just beginning. One possible impact noted by Gabi Salomon some years back[16] as the 'butterfly effect' and recently made into a bestseller by Nicholas Carr, *The Shallows: What the Internet is doing to our brains*,[17] is to make us all more superficial and distracted. Whereas reading books takes commitment and can lead to depth understanding, use of the Internet encourages browsing nuggets of pre-processed information condemning us to superficiality, or so the argument goes. This analysis fits reasonably well with those who argue that the rise of the Internet marks the end of the modern self, said to be individual and autonomous. Mark Poster, for example, argues that:

> Electronic culture promotes the individual as an unstable identity, as a continuous process of multiple identity formation and raises the question of a social form beyond the modern, the possibility of a post-modern society.[18]

If we accept Toulmin's account that a focus on print has had a monologic effect, turning 'utterances' in dialogues into 'propositions' in proofs; it seems possible then that the Internet can restore us to a more participatory and dialogic way of understanding thinking. However, while the Internet supports dialogue this is different from the oracy that preceded literacy, for one thing this is no longer a dialogue limited to a physically located community but a dialogue without any necessary spatial limits. Ong has argued that practices around writing and reading books led to the formation of a sense of an individual inner autonomous space that contrasted to the more collective identity of selves in oral societies and enabled critical thinking leading to political change. It seems plausible that some forms of blogging promotes similar kinds of 'inner space' capable of standing back from and criticizing tradition, but in a collective form without the same strong sense of individual autonomy.[19]

One clear lesson that can be learnt from the literature about the impact of modes of communication on thinking and society is that mentality is not just a causal effect of the technology. Ong brings out how one way of writing and reading can cement communal solidarity, the reading aloud of a manuscript such as the bible which was common in the middle ages,[20] whilst another way of writing and reading, silent and solitary writing and reading of books, can support the formation of a separate autonomous inner self able to stand back from the culture around it.[21]

The message we can take from this is that the apparent fragmentation and superficiality induced by Internet use according to Carr and others is not an inevitable effect of the Internet but a possible consequence of one way of using this new technology. Just as the previously dominant media of communication, oracy, and then print literacy, can be a part of cultural practices that have quite different effects on thinking, so can the Internet. This analysis suggests a possible role for educational research as determining what are the new pedagogical affordances of the Internet and thus how it can best be integrated into the practice of education.

Print-based education

There is good reason to think that the use of writing, especially print, has had a huge impact on ways of thinking and learning.[22] Schools, as we know them today, were created around the technology of writing. Collins and Halverson do a reasonably sympathetic analysis of the history and nature of mass schooling and conclude that print-based schooling is a system that is coherent and which works well in its own way, which is what makes it so resilient to change. Reading, Writing, and Arithmetic remain the core curriculum everywhere followed by the transmission of specific subject knowledge embodied in text-books or work-sheets. Teachers are knowledge experts who transmit their expertise through various methods including lecture, recitation, drill, practice and, very occasionally, dialogue.[23] Wherever there are schools there are children divided into year groups, bells ringing to mark lessons, teachers at the front of the class with a blackboard, a whiteboard or now sometimes an interactive whiteboard, a curriculum organized in separate discipline areas and written tests of individual knowledge. Of course this is a simplification of a complex reality but it reflects an instantly recognizable 'ideal type' which has remained essentially the same for the last one hundred years at least and is now found all over the world.

Cathy Davidson echoes Castells and many other authors in claiming that schools reflect the logic and the needs of the Industrial Age, writing that:

> The chief purpose of [schools] was to make the divisions of labor central to industrialization seem natural to twentieth century workers. We had to be trained to inhabit the twentieth century comfortably and productively. Everything about school and work in the twentieth century was designed to create and reinforce separate subjects, separate culture, separate grades, separate functions, separate spaces for personal life, and all the other divisions.[24]

There are good reasons for thinking that mass schooling was originally designed to meet the needs of the then emerging industrial economies for more literate and disciplined workers. It is clear that the structure of schooling, with separate subjects, stages and quality checks, mirrors the design of production processes in factories. However, I refer to the Print Age rather than the Industrial Age to draw attention to the fact that the design of factories and industrial production depended on ways of thinking associated with the dominance of print. The subject-divisions of school reflect the eighteenth-century taxonomical way of thinking of Enlightenment encyclopaedists trying to map all human knowledge. The idea that knowledge takes the form of representations that can be put in books and transmitted across generations is not so much an industrial idea as a graphocentric idea. The analytic focus on representations of truth found in science text-books, as if these were separate from any perspective or dialogue, is symptomatic of the monologic way of thinking which came to dominate theory in eighteenth-century Europe.

My suggestion is that the monologic vision of reality and truth, sometimes referred to as Enlightenment rationalism,[25] underpinning the structure of modern schooling is not an inevitable product of print but it is an affordance of print technology. This particular affordance may well have had adaptive value in the eighteenth century when the great Enlightenment reform movement was devised and in the nineteenth century when mass schooling rolled out across Europe and the world. It is not so obvious that it meets the needs of the emerging Internet Age. However, the print-supported monologic vision of reality and truth has become self-reinforcing because it is sustained by print-based educational institutions that reflect it. Many attempts to change schools through the use of new communications technology have proved ineffective. Whatever their affordances for new kinds of pedagogy new technologies do not get adopted in a major way unless they can be used within the current school system.[26]

Using a term borrowed by business studies, what has happened to print-based education can be understood as a form of 'producer capture'. Producer capture is said to be what happens when an institution supposedly offering a service to customers ends up generating its own needs which dominate over the needs of the consumers. Ask any student in secondary school why they are reading what they are reading or writing what they are writing in school and they are most likely to tell you that they need to do this in order to pass the next test or exam. When I taught first year undergraduates, fresh from school, about Freire's dialogic approach to education starting with the words and concerns of the learners, the most common reaction from my highly educated UK audience was, 'That is all very well but then how would they pass their exams?'

Internet-based education

If the business studies term 'producer capture' serves to sum up print-based formal education, then another term from business studies, 'disruptive technology' can help us understand the impact of the Internet on education. A disruptive technology is one that improves a service in a way that is unexpected and so goes on to create its own new way of doing things and its own different 'value system' eventually displacing an existing technology. An example of unexpected disruption might be the way in which peer-to-peer music file-sharing software running via the Internet has already undermined the market in physical CDs. Nobody expected this use of the Internet and the big business interests did not want it but it turned out to provide users with music in a way that many preferred to the existing technology of CDs.

In the Introduction to this book I mentioned how I learnt to get help with computer problems simply through Googling the problem and especially any obscure error codes I was receiving. This invariably led me to forums in which others had raised similar problems and more expert participants had offered solutions. This experience, which I am sure that many readers share, is paradigmatic of the main affordance that the Internet has for a new kind of education. One could call it peer-to-peer education. It combines a focus of interest – lets us call this the question – with resources generated by others that can help answer that question. Of course here the Internet is not being viewed as an external network but internally from the point of view of participation. This kind of education is through participation even in the simple case where I have a problem, Google that problem, and find a bit of a previous exchange on an Internet forum that provides a solution to my problem. But where the question is less closely defined such searches easily lead not only to vicarious participation in other people's past exchanges but to becoming drawn into participation in a living shared enquiry or a shared construction on the Internet.

The programming language and learning environment called 'Scratch' provides an example of how this simple 'question within a dialogue' structure can lead on to kinds of education that rival the education provided by schools. Scratch is a simple programming language that is supported by a community of users. Anyone can join. There are currently over one million registered members of the Scratch online programming community and 306,000 project creators.

Thomas and Seely Brown give the example of Sam, aged 9, who became engaged in making simple games using Scratch.[27] When he uploads his programs others can comment and borrow the code in order to remix it but with a tag that shows their new version was based on Sam's original. When Sam likes programs he finds he also downloads the code and gets into conversations with the maker about remixing it. This approach offers an engaging way to learn programming but more than that Sam has learnt from this how to learn from others. Thomas and Seely Brown report that Sam told them that the single most important thing he learnt was 'not to be mean' and also to make sure that you commented on something good when you came across it. What he looked for in a programme was 'something really cool you could never know yourself'.[28]

Sam did take some classes to help him improve his programming and Scratch is used within many schools. Despite this there is a big different in the two approaches to education represented by the ideal type of print-based schooling on the one hand and this example of Internet mediated education on the other. Sam started with participation and then learnt the skills and knowledge he needed to improve his participation. The print-based curriculum tends to start with a list of skills and knowledge that it is assumed that children will need in order to be able to participate later on. This principle of starting with the dialogue and then remediating skills or knowledge as they are needed for participation in the dialogue is a core principle of dialogic education. There are other things that can be said about Internet-mediated education such as that it is 'personalized', in that everyone's experience is unique and tailored to their needs, that the learners are in control of the topics and pace of the learning, that it is multi-modal and not only mediated by writing, and that it is shared enquiry or shared construction with a real audience. But all these characteristics follow from the basic idea of learning that follows from engagement in Internet mediated dialogue.

Education and digital role-playing games

The way that Sam was learning programming as part of the Scratch community is similar to the way that players learn together in online games. My son plays an online game with about 26,000 other players and when he sees others doing things that are new to him he asks in the chat how they did that and normally they help out. Even though the theme of the game seems to involve everyone killing each other they have learnt to be collaborative when teaching and learning new and even more fun ways to play.

The facility with which children learn things in Internet mediated games compared with the difficulty many experience at school has led James Paul Gee to outline a number of principles of games based learning. These include things like working at the edge of competence so that everything is challenging but not impossibly difficult and being able to experiment and take risks without facing serious consequences. Gee, who plays World of Warcraft with his family, refers to how learning in games occurs through 'cycles of new learning, automatization, undoing automatization, and new re-organized automatization' which are closely related to cycles of enquiry, 'probing the world (doing something); reflecting in and on this action and, on this basis, forming a hypothesis; reprobing the world to test this hypothesis; and then accepting or rethinking the hypothesis'.[29] All of this learning is situated in what he refers to as 'embodied experience', even if, in World of Warcraft, your Avatar can be tall and purple with wings, this still counts as embodied experience.

Shaffer has taken this analysis of game-based learning further using a design-based research approach through the development of several games for learning which he calls 'epistemic games'.[30] His idea is that the rules and the roles that we learn through games provide us with ways of thinking and knowing. In online games players assume control of an avatar body and are faced with challenges in a simulated world. Rather than fighting trolls or finding treasure, Shaffer and others have built games that enable players to learn how to think from the point of view of professionals. In Pandora Project players become high-powered negotiators, making decisions about transplanting organs from animals into humans. Through this engagement, they learn about biology, international relations and mediation. In Journalism.net players become reporters for an online newspaper. Working with experienced journalists and interviewing community leaders, these novice reporters learn about how journalists think about the news and how the news relates to local communities.

MOOCs and the emerging new model of education

MOOCs are Massive Open Online Courses. The concept is inspired by the success of MMOGs, or Massive Multiplayer Online Games, like World of Warcraft. The term MOOC was coined in 2008 in response to the experience of a university course in Canada which was opened up to participation on the Internet. Course materials and discussion forums were shared. While the fee-paying students numbered 25, there were over 2000 open course students. These extra online participants enhanced the course with additional conversations and readings.[31] This innovation in online education took off with a course opening in Stanford in 2011 with over 160,000 students, and similar models being tried by MIT and Harvard. In an online TED talk entitled 'What we're learning from online education', Daphne Kohler emphasizes the extent to which the MOOCs she has run from Stanford reached ordinary people across the world who would not normally have access to a world class university[32]. One of the interesting innovations she describes is replacing some tutor marking of assignments, which would be too expensive in a MOOC, not only with machine assessment but also with peer assessment.

MOOCs are part of an exciting new model of education that has the potential to bypass much traditional schooling. At the moment this model seems particularly relevant in countries where there is a shortage of access to high quality place-based education. There is now a vast amount of open courseware and educational material at every level available for free on the Internet. The Tecnológico de Monterrey, probably the most innovative university in Latin America, has a research programme to catalogue these resources and produce guides for educators on how to use these catalogues to create courses in almost any subject at almost any level.[33]

In addition the Tecnológico de Monterrey is running over 2000 small local study centres called Centros Comunitario de Aprendizaje (CCA).[34] Each centre has a number of computers connected to a virtual learning environment and is staffed not by a teacher but by a learning guide, usually a member of the local community who offers advice and keeps a record of progress. Although currently these centres mostly support courses in basic skills of literacy, arithmetic, computing, and accounting, the potential of joining such local study centres to the almost infinite resources for learning now available on the Internet is obvious.

From these and other experiments a new model of education is emerging. On this model initial compulsory primary education in basic skills including learning how to learn together with others online, could be combined with guided individual educational trajectories through the almost infinite array of high quality educational resources already available on the Internet. Study centres as well as partnerships with industry and with community groups could support the embodied social side of learning. There is no need for paper qualifications if all learning experiences are available to view on the Internet, all that would be needed for access to work would be interviews supported by Facebook-like portfolios providing evidence of projects already accomplished.

Prompts and preludes to a new kind of education

There is a convergence between the educational affordances of the Internet and related technologies and the dialogic theory of education which I have been developing in earlier chapters of this book. If education is understood as induction into the dialogue of humanity and the dialogue of humanity is carried by the Internet then education should become education into learning how to learn together with others using the Internet.

Cave paintings, the first educational technology in oral societies, used signs as mediating means for the induction of new members into the dialogic space of the tribe. But these signs did not act as tools but as cultural voices. The eland painted on the wall of the cave spoke to the San and the San shamans learnt to speak with the voice of the eland. The essence of education has not changed with the changing of technology. It is still about induction of new members into a virtual dialogic space as it always has been. Writing technology and print-based education introduced a monologic misunderstanding of this central role of education. According to this print-based ideology education is the transmission of knowledge. On some versions this knowledge is universal on others it is grounded in the nation where the nation is an imagined community created and supported by print-capitalism.[35] But in both versions, the universal and the national, the space that education inducted learners into was not characterized by participation but by the authority of true knowledge. With the advent of the Internet it is possible to return to the participatory nature of education in small-scale oral societies on the other side of the globalization made possible by print. The dialogic space is not limited by physical spaces or ethnic identities, it has no boundaries. But for this new global role of education to develop the virtual near monopoly of print-based education needs to be augmented by Internet-based education. So what exactly what does Internet based education look like?

Web 2.0 social networking technology such as Facebook, Twitter and YouTube support social interaction, essential to forming a more global sense of identity, but they also offer a tantalizing glimpse of how easily people could organize themselves to learn together online in communities. This potential is now being explored by new experiments in teaching and learning online such as the MOOCs described earlier. Bakhtin defined dialogues as social interaction where answers give rise to new questions. This contrasts them to conversations which are more about establishing and maintaining social identities through mutual grooming activities and displays. The later kinds of interactions practiced by higher apes and early humans for millions of years before even oracy appeared on the scene are an essential context for true dialogue, but do not have the same educational potential for new learning. Is there a way to convert the global social interaction potential of Web 2.0 to become a global education potential?

The success of immersive 3D gaming environments with young people shows how learning complex new domains can be fun and engaging, occurring almost naturally as a by-product of acting in a simulated environment. As with the first educational signs, cave paintings, the signs in games are frequently not tools but voices. Avatars in Shaffer's epistemic games enable learners to take on embodied perspectives from which to experience the world differently. Frequently the learning of skills in games is enhanced not only by the immersive representational media itself but also by individuals joining together in collaborative groups mutually engaged in achieving the ends set within the game through developing communication, strategic thinking and problem solving skills. These kinds of skills are precisely the ones that, in a different context, could greatly help young people to understand scientific and mathematical ideas.

In the 3D online game, World of Warcraft, players can learn how to collaborate together effectively in order to bring down a monster. In the real world we face many potential 'monsters' of different kinds that require collaboration for their defeat: global warming, pandemics, dwindling supplies of fresh water etc. Why could not education be education into learning how to learn together online in order to collaboratively defeat the many monsters that challenge us?

When, in April 2010 an explosion in the Gulf of Mexico caused a flow of oil, BP responded by assembling a team of experts to find a solution. This team was not co-located and so they had to work together sharing ideas and co-constructing plans of action supported by web-mediated communication tools. Distributed teams of experts working together to solve problems and inquire into issues are an increasingly common way of working in the Internet Age. Computer supported collaborative teamwork of this kind is not only a response to time-sensitive crises but it is also the main means by which new knowledge is constructed in the sciences. However, current education systems do little to equip children and young people with the complex competence of problem solving and learning together with others online. In the case of the 2010 oil spill the team of experts failed to come up with a successful solution until the oil had flowed for three months doing great damage to the environment. It is possible that a lack of knowledge about and experience of learning together effectively may have contributed to this delay. Perhaps if all the varied experts around the globe involved in this incident had trained beforehand by collaborating together on World of Warcraft as a team bringing down monsters the outcome might have been different.

Learning to Learn Together online

There has been some research on ways to teach for learning how to learn, which is often referred to as the most important knowledge age skill as it equips people to adapt flexibly in a time of rapid change. However there has been little research on how to teach for the skills involved in learning how to learn together, which is possibly even more important for surviving and thriving in the knowledge age since most knowledge work is conducted by teams and not by individuals. Increasingly those teams are mediated by online environments. The new essential competence that emerges as a requirement of the Internet Age is therefore Learning to Learn Together (L2L2) online.

The online element of L2L2 online is not just about the mediation of dialogues within the team, as if this was simply face-to-face but via online tools such as Skype, but the online element points to the dialogic relation between the foregrounded project goals and questions and the background of almost infinite multi-media resources and voices made available by the Internet.

An illustration of L2L2 online

The new Web 2.0 tools available on the Internet making teaching L2L2 online much easier than one might think. A few years back, here at Exeter University, I was given the responsibility of devising a new core module in ICT for around 70 undergraduates doing a degree in Education Studies. Most of the students on this course planned to specialize later as primary teachers. The team were all enthusiasts for the possibilities of new technology but the students were not. They were used to face-to-face lectures, suspicious of new technology in education and not sure why they had to do this compulsory core module on ICT. As a team we therefore designed a course which would illustrate, through experience, the potential of Web 2.0 for learning how to learn together and yet manage to fulfill the expectations of the students and of the university system.

The course model was simple. Learning by collaborative blogging. We used an open source educational environment very similar to Facebook.[36] The course was set up as a group in this environment rather like a group of friends on Facebook. Each student was asked to keep a learning blog and to write something each week in response to the stimulus of the lecture. They were encouraged to share links, videos and other resources relevant to the course on the blog and on shared spaces such as the group blog. In addition, and this was a key requirement, they had to comment on at least two other blogs of students on the course. The main assessment was to be their personal blogs but to ensure that they interacted with others online we also assessed their comments on other blogs and in online discussion spaces. There were other activities, developing group online presentations on topics of their choice etc., but collaborative blogging was the backbone of the course.

Tutors on the course were all also participants supporting with their own learning blogs in the same way as the students and commenting on the student blogs just as the students had to. The tutors' blogs modelled how to use the multimedia resources of the Internet, integrating videos of big names talking about the issues, music, photos and web-links into their blogs. They also modelled being supportive and facilitative in their style of commenting on student blogs.

As predicted, some students hated the topic and hated being forced to use new technology in this way but most students really took to the approach. I was heartened by the number of very reflective blogs on the issues of the course. Many of the blogs used links to appropriate videos and Internet resources and also shared personal experiences. A case study of the kind of learning on this course by PhD student, Amal Al'Ibrahim,[37] combining discourse analysis and interviews, led to the following meta-coding of the types of communication on the course.

Reflecting	*Reflecting on their work, reflecting on the lectures, reflecting on their reading.*
Sharing	*Personal comments, sharing articles, sharing their thought, sharing websites, writing their assignments.*
Stimulating	*Stimulation from articles, stimulation from reading posted blogs, feeling stimulated to do research.*
Enriching course materials	*Enriching course materials, formal debates, learning new skills, linking with their experiences, new issues.*
Managing	*Asking technical questions, asking questions, organizing group members, arranging group work, answering questions.*

Amal's interviews and studies of online comments found several students who had initially been skeptical of the course changing their minds and acknowledging that the online collaboration really helped them. The use of links to Internet resources including news stories and you tube video led to a widening of the discussion and gave it contemporary energy. The students interviewed emphasized how much they learnt from each other. Having other students read books and papers and offer summaries online was felt as a great time-saver. Comments on blogs often expressed the value of the stimulation they received from us, such as: 'Thank you ..., you just made me think!'

They also appreciated the possibility to express their views and feel listened to. One relatively shy participant who had trouble participating in face-to-face seminars commented:

> ... The Hive makes it [debate] easier ... wait your turn to speak, in modules that do not use The Hive you raise your hand and wait. Sometimes you don't... . But in The Hive any time whenever ...

Another comment which I have heard before and which I find interesting is that for some the pace of the online communication was much better for thinking than in face-to-face discussions. Face-to-face dialogues can put you under pressure to come up with answers when really incubation time is needed. Online discussions and collaborative blogging can help reflection because the stimulus of reading a blog can be allowed to incubate for a while and lead to creative results before coming back later, whenever one wants, perhaps at two in the morning after a social evening, and giving a response.

The evaluation of this course revealed that what students were really learning on the course, independently of the official learning objectives, was how to learn together with others online. They were motivated to do better by the fact that their blogs were read and commented on by their peers. They learnt that if all contribute resources and ideas the end result is more enjoyable and more enriching for everyone. And because it was online and it was easy to link in to the rest of the Internet the blogs were multi-modal, enriched with voices and stories, and connected to issues of recent media concern.

From designing tools to designing voices

A key part of educational design for the Internet Age is to participate in educational dialogues on the World Wide Web. One weakness with the 'ICT Futures' course described above was that it was a little cut off from the rest of the Internet. If and when almost all students are on Facebook it might make more sense just to use Facebook or other widely used social networking sites for educational courses rather than a separate university-controlled environment with a separate login and a different interface. In the MOOCs mentioned earlier the learning communities that form around courses use any and every available media including Twitter, YouTube, and public forums on websites.

Many innovative educators are now experimenting with using Facebook for running educational courses. An issue that arises is that the Facebook environment and plugins are designed to support social exchanges rather than educational exchanges. One EC funded project, Metafora, is trying to remedy this by experimenting with the development of the kinds of tools which could support deeper learning with social networking sites.

Learning together online is a complex competence. It implies that all in the group are able to coordinate, regulate, and plan the learning task, balancing issues of individual ability, motivation and expectations through constant dialogue. When starting to work on a collective task, the group need to be able to show distributed leadership, motivate one another, ensure engagement (or find ways to respond when this does not occur), reflect on the quality of the work delivered, deal with (constructive) criticism, reflect on the overall direction of their work (and consult outside experts if needed), and make sure all group members are doing what is expected. Towards the end of the task they need to be able to wrap things up, judge if the learning goals are reached, peer review their work and submit it in time.[38]

A web-based Metafora learning environment is being developed that includes a planning and reflection tool that implements an understanding of the key features of learning together in a visual language (a language made up of manipulable visual icons) intended to facilitate greater awareness of the process of learning together.

The Metafora system is currently being developed with the help of secondary school science, mathematics, and environmental education teachers in the UK, Spain, Greece and Israel to support collaborative enquiry-based learning in science and mathematics and environmental education stimulated by complex real-world questions. Beyond this use in schools, one motivation of the project is to design and test the sort of tools that would help extend Facebook and other Web 2.0 sites to be a good support for groups who wanted to learn things together.

We developed a set of visual icons for the stages, processes, roles and attitudes in collaborative enquiry learning, out of an extensive literature review. Design workshops were used to test and refine the resulting list of characteristics of learning together. The exact format of the workshop varied across the partners but all involved giving a group of between four and six teachers and/or students a complex challenge to solve and asking them to plan together how they would approach solving this challenge. For example in Lleida in Spain, five students aged 17 were introduced to the real-world problem that the local river Segre has pollution levels beyond those that are acceptable. Using a set of laminated cards implementing our initial iteration of the visual language they then planned together how to set about first understanding and then solving this problem. This project is reported on in greater detail in Chapter 6, which focusses on dialogic science education. Other inquiries were conducted with similar small groups in schools in the UK, Greece and Israel.

The final visual language had main activity stages, activity processes, attitudes, roles and connectors. The stages, implemented with big blue square icons, were things like: explore; define questions; build model; test model; refine model; draw conclusions; prepare presentation. The processes, implemented with smaller green icons, occur within each stage, things like: experiment; hypothesize; make notes; propose an alternative; report; reach agreement; evaluate; gather information, and so on.

In a way these sorts of things are familiar from schemas for teaching scientific method and also Bereiter's progressive enquiry.[39] Attitudes were a little different. These were implemented as icons with different colours representing the attitudes:

open, positive, critical, creative, ethical, rational, intuitive, and, of course, a blank (for students to define if required).

The visual appearance of these icons is illustrated in Figure 2: The Metafora Planning and Reflection Tool Interface.

The use of the cards made them consider the need to build models, test models, take notes, observe, reflect on observations etc. Secondary science teachers in Lleida, Spain and in Bodmin, UK fed back in interviews that they valued the visual language because it gave the children the vocabulary that they need to understand the process of enquiry. In this way many of the icons served as concept tools in a way that fits well with a Vygotskian approach.

However in addition we had some icons, attitude icons, which were designed to be 'voices' rather than tools. These icons were inspired by Edward de Bono's six thinking hats. Rather than tools to operate on the world they are ways of looking at the world. Students reported that trying out the different attitudes helped them to think through problems by seeing them in different ways. We included them to emphasize that learning how to learn together is not only learning about project management but also about working in a team and intersubjective attitudes are a key part of that.

The design of education for the Internet Age

Chapter 4, established that thinking is collective rather than individual. Each individual is in a dialogic relationship – a chiasm – with their whole context. Communications technology does not simply mediate relationships between individuals but also this more collective relationship between each individual and their context. Learning on the Internet works by bringing a central foregrounded question into dynamic relationship with a vast background of resources and voices such that they resonate with the question and produce potential answers that often lead to further enquiries and engagement in collaborative learning online.

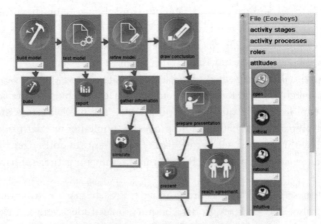

FIGURE 5.2 The Metafora Planning and Reflection Tool Interface

The first communications technology that we are aware of because it has endured, is that of cave paintings. Signs painted on the walls of caves were physical forms of cultural voices. They had an educational function helping to induct new members into the dialogic space of the group. In the oral societies that used cave paintings in rituals the signs were not used as tools for thinking in the way that concept words are seen by Vygotsky as tools. These signs were 'epiphantic' signs evoking voices.

The Internet, because it is participative and also multi-modal, returns us to some of the affordances of oracy but on the other side of the globalization of communication afforded by print and the cumulative development of areas of shared knowledge enabled by print. Education once again means participating in a shared dialogic space in which signs are not merely tools to be mastered but cultural voices that possess us as much as we possess them. The Internet is full of signs and multi-media that evoke voices. Shaffer's video game designs and the Metafora project give examples of signs that were designed specifically to evoke voices in order to help students explore issues from different perspectives.[40]

Education for the Internet Age means induction into the global dialogue of humanity. This implies that print-based education systems need to be augmented with Internet-based education. Key pedagogical moves in this education can be characterized as opening spaces, widening spaces, deepening spaces, resourcing spaces with conceptual tools and resourcing spaces with epistemic rules or 'ways of seeing'. The key skill or competence that is needed for the Internet Age is learning to learn together (L2L2). This competence implies dispositions such as openness to otherness and resilience in the face of uncertainty as well as the ability to communicate and to use new technology to manage complexity.

An aspect of the story of the move from oracy to print-based education is, at least in part, a story about the loss of embodied meaning. The move from print-based education to the dominance of Internet-based education has the potential to restore the meaning that is given to knowledge through its inherence in living relationships. The shift from understanding signs as nodes in a system representing reality to understanding them as voices, i.e. not as representations but as presentations, is one example of this shift.

Assessment shifting from bits of paper representing past achievements to presentations of actual achievement might be another not yet realized educational potential of the Internet. Every employer knows that people cannot be summarized by their qualifications, the 'bits of paper' that they hold, but they want evidence of what people can do. In the example I gave of education through collaborative blogging the multi modal blog that was kept during the course, responding to stimuli and to other students, was the main assignment that was assessed. This is not a representation of knowledge but a presentation of engaged participation. It is easy to see how presentations of actual achievement of this kind could address the needs of assessment in the future.

The assessment of work that will always count for the most in the end is the judgement of the relevant community. But the Internet is open in a way that makes it hard to draw a boundary delimiting a specific community of readers and responders. This means that when creative works are put out for review on the Internet, the ultimate addressee of that work is not just someone in particular, nor is it really everyone in general, but rather it is everyone in particular. In other words the Internet gives a certain kind of concrete embodiment to the otherwise abstract seeming idea of the Infinite Other.

All over the world we can see examples that suggest that a new model of education is emerging. Online learning communities, often working in combination with face-to-face study groups, are emerging in parallel to print-based schooling and in some cases as an alternative that is leap-frogging the old model. In this chapter and in this book I have not attempted to collate all the examples of innovative pedagogy that contribute towards the emerging model of education for the Internet Age. What I have tried to do is provide some pointers towards the new theory of education that is also emerging with these new practices as a way to understand them and to support future design. I have done this by locating the shift from print-based education to Internet-based education in a larger historical context including earlier changes in our understanding of education that came in with changes in technology.

Looking at the evolution of educational technology in a larger historical context suggests the importance of thinking of educational technology not only in terms of representations and tools but also in terms of relationships and voices. Education for the Internet Age occurs within a responsive relationship not only with specific others but also with online communities and ultimately with the unbounded horizon of the Internet itself personified in the form of the Infinite Other. This theory suggests that the agency that drives education in the Internet Age will be less the will of 'society' in the form of prescribed curricula written by nation states, or the will of the student as an individual consumer making choices but the agency that emerges in dialogues with horizons of otherness and ultimately with the unbounded horizon of otherness which is the Infinite Other and is embodied in the Internet itself. On this theory the role of directed teaching needs to focus on opening, widening, deepening and resourcing dialogues. Once students are engaged in dialogues they need the knowledge and skills required to participate more fully and more effectively. The complex skill or competence of learning to learn together with others online emerges as a new essential for education to be taught as early as possible with the same importance now given to reading, writing and arithmetic.

6

EDUCATING SCIENCE[1]

This chapter argues that a dialogic understanding of the nature of science should lead to a dialogic approach to science education, which is more open to engagement with diverse voices. It combines this argument with a description of an approach to science education developed in the context a large European Commission funded international project called 'Science Education for Diversity'. The project surveyed school students aged 10 to 14 and their teachers in Malaysia, India, Lebanon, Turkey, the Netherlands and the UK and developed a framework for the design of education in the context of diversity in science education. This approach to science education is 'dialogic' both because it is about responding to the diverse voices of students without prejudging the nature of that diversity and because it is about teaching for dialogue, where the quality of dialogue is understood as being central to science.

Introduction

In Europe there has been a decline in young people who are interested in pursuing science topics for further education. This has led to concern from the European Commission (EC) expressed in several reports such as 'Europe needs more scientists'.[2] The concern expressed by the EC is mainly that there will not be enough scientists to make the discoveries leading to new products on which it is assumed the knowledge economy will depend. But there is also a concern that citizens with insufficient knowledge of science will not be able to participate fully in democratic decision-making about the increasing number of controversial issues that are hard to understand without some scientific literacy, issues such as nuclear power, global warming and genetically modified crops.

The evidence suggests that young people in the 'Facebook generation' choose school topics to support their developing sense of personal identity and in this context most find science education unappealing or not as appealing as other subjects.[3] This challenging situation has led to considerable investment in research on how to teach science in a more engaging way. One such project, the one million Euro 'Science Education for Diversity' (SED) is what the EC calls an International Project including partners outside of Europe because it takes the innovative approach of seeking to learn from the experience of countries where science education remains a highly popular choice amongst young people.

The SED project focuses on issues of diversity, including cultural diversity and gender diversity, and seeks to explore how Science Education interacts with diverse populations and how it could be re-designed to respond better to the challenges that diversity raises. The partners include Science Education researchers in Malaysia, India, Lebanon, Turkey, the Netherlands and the UK·

In each country we conducted a literature review of the science curriculum and initiatives that addressed issues of diversity in science education. We then worked with ten schools in each country, five primary (focusing on ages 10 to12), and five secondary (focusing on ages 12 to15) thus addressing the point raised by previous research that the key window for engagement or disengagement with science appears to be from age 10 to14.[4] Within each primary school 50 to 100 students aged 10 to 12 completed questionnaires and within each secondary school around 200 students aged between 12 and 15 completed questionnaires. Thus, the project team in each country selected schools that represent the mix of locations including urban, rural and suburban communities and representing, where relevant, the main religions of the country; we focused on state schools accessible to students of all backgrounds; and looked for mixed gender schools or a balance of boy-only schools with girl-only schools; and where possible we sought out schools that have cultural diversity and students from a diversity of socio-economic backgrounds.

Based on the analysis of the questionnaires we selected four schools in each partner country for further study and within each school a sample of students were selected, including cases that hold positive and negative attitudes towards science education. These students participated in focus groups and individual interviews. Within each of these four schools the full complement of science teachers was also interviewed (where possible) alongside other key staff involved in deciding on the science curriculum such as the head teacher.

The data from the literature review of curricula and initiatives in each country, as well as the questionnaires and the interviews, were analysed and synthesized in discussion between all the partners to produce a framework for the design of science education that could address the issue of diversity. In this chapter I do not present in detail the findings of our survey as some of the analysis is continuing and this will form the basis of other publications. The second half of this chapter describes and reports on the development of the framework for design. The development of this framework has formed the basis for the next stage of the project, which focuses on designing, implementing and evaluating interventions based on the framework. However, before I reach that part of the chapter I want to discuss a question that we had to face in developing a new approach to teaching: what is science?

What is science?

Despite the relative uniformity of science education traditions in all the six countries of our study, questionnaires and interviews revealed that the understanding of what science is held by students differed greatly between each country. We explored this by asking what sort of activity should be called science. Answers to these questions revealed that in India, Malaysia, Lebanon and Turkey practical aspects of science (including farming and building a bridge) were more likely to be included in a definition of science than in the Netherlands and the UK.[5] This finding is consistent with differences in understanding of science reported in both Japan and Korea.[6] In the Netherlands social science was mostly included within the concept of science but this was not the case for most students in the UK. This difference may be due to the different normal usage of the Dutch term *Wetanschap* which is used as a translation for the English term science.

Interviews with individual children in the UK revealed some quite narrow images of science, which were, as one might expect, closely connected to their attitude towards science and their attitudes towards careers in science. One image conjured in several interviews in the UK was of a man in a white coat in a laboratory mixing chemicals or inventing things. There was often some reference to large machines and/or electronics when the young people interviewed were asked why some subjects were science and others not. These provisional findings suggest that if we are to address the issue of how to improve science education so that it better responds to diverse audiences it is necessary to raise once again the controversial issue of what is understood by the word 'science'.

Alters surveyed the members of the US Philosophy of Science Association and found eleven distinct positions on the nature of science.[7] He concluded that there is no shared ground to serve as a basis for teaching the nature of science in science education. However, this claim was immediately disputed.[8] Another survey using the Delphi method and including not only philosophers, but also leading scientists, science educators and communicators about science found considerably more consensus.[9] Taking consensus in a rather arbitrary way to be 66 per cent agreement, Osborne *et al.* found consensus on nine themes to be taught as part of the nature of science. All but one of these themes were already covered by science education curricula according to a review of a number of existing standards in science education for the Nature of Science within the USA, Canada, England and Wales and Australia.[10] Using the more normative formulation of McComas and Olson, the eight areas of overlap between the two reviews were:

1   Scientific knowledge is tentative
2   Science relies on empirical evidence
3   Scientists require replicability and truthful reporting
4   Science is an attempt to explain phenomena
5   Scientists are creative
6   Science is part of social tradition
7   Science has played an important role in technology
8   Scientific ideas have been affected by their social and historical milieu.

However the one area where Osborne *et al.* found a discrepancy between existing standards and their Delphi review of the experts is a crucial one. This is the theme they labelled 'Diversity of Scientific Thinking' which refers to the growing consensus within philosophy of science that there is no single 'scientific method' but many methods appropriate for different areas and different problems.

Osborne *et al.* illustrate the importance of this theme by pointing out two areas where the UK science curriculum fails to include reference to important methods within the different sciences. First, the distinction between historical reconstruction and empirical testing: as Rudolph points out, historical reconstructions such as the phylogenetic history of various species or records of climate change might use models to help them at times but they are not really about testing models but more essentially about establishing correct chronologies.[11] To give a well-known example that illustrates Rudolph's point: finding out exactly when *Tyrannosaurus rex* became extinct is of scientific interest even if this extinction cannot be predicted by a model because it was due to contingent factors. Secondly, Osborne *et al.* claim that the correlational methods common to many media reports of science and basic to medical science are absent from the curriculum, perhaps, they speculate, because school science in the UK focuses only on the three large natural sciences, biology, chemistry and physics.

This issue of the unity or diversity of scientific methods is obviously relevant to science education but it has been even more central to debates in the philosophy of science. To help explicate this issue the Exeter research team organized a seminar with Professor John Dupré, a leading philosopher of science working at the University of Exeter where he heads up the Centre for Genomics in Society (Egenis). The argument that follows is influenced by John Dupré's work.[12] There is now near consensus in the Philosophy of Science community (certainly considerably more than the 66 per cent agreement that Osborne thought enough to use the term consensus!) that there is no single scientific method but a variety of methods and practices used for different purposes in different contexts. While there is no easy or simple way to demarcate science from non-science, established sciences often share a number of epistemological criteria which some claim can be used to distinguish them from non-sciences. Examples of these epistemological criteria are:

- the use of empirical evidence
- consistency with known facts and theories
- elegance and simplicity
- the power to generate useful implications
- testability, i.e. that they could be proved wrong by the right observation.

However, it is possible to a) find established and respected areas of science that violate each of these criteria and b) find areas of knowledge not normally called science that meet each of them. For example, taxonomies in biology and elsewhere are based to some extent on empirical evidence and can be very useful but they are not testable and no single taxonomy is likely to be consistent with all relevant known facts and theories.[13] Much work in theoretical physics has little relation to empirical observations, for example the Penrose-Hawking singularity theorems relating to black holes have already been celebrated as a breakthrough in physics yet have no supporting empirical evidence to my knowledge.

Many more such examples of accepted and effective methods of knowledge generation that do not fit any unified account of 'scientific method' could be found if we were to consider the full range of practices found in all the established natural sciences from astronomy through to zoology.

Empirical evidence from the sociology of science, i.e. looking at what scientists actually do rather that what they say that they do, undermines the claim that there is a single 'scientific method'. Despite this many still hold to the view that science can be distinguished from non-science through epistemological criteria. A Google search on 'scientific method' finds over seven million hits and the first 100 hits thrown up consist mainly of un-self-critical accounts of exactly what the scientific method is and how to teach it, often accompanied by a flow-chart diagram.

Of course some methods are better than others for answering particular types of questions in particular areas. The experimental method, which involves building a model and testing its predicted consequences against observations of a key variable or variables whilst controlling for the others, has proved particularly effective in many contexts within the physical sciences. However, as we have noted looking at taxonomies and historical reconstructions, even this quite vague account of scientific method is not universally applicable. What counts as a model, a variable and a valid observation are very much subject to debate in different areas of enquiry. If, in reality, there is no foolproof method that we can apply to find the truth, then in every case we need to resort to dialogue to justify ourselves, which means that we need to be creative and flexible and open to alternative perspectives.

The implication of arguments from Rorty and Habermas is that communicative virtues such as honesty, trust, relying on persuasion rather than force and respect for the opinions of others led to more effective knowledge construction in some areas of enquiry and so become institutionalized in cultural practices such as the transparent publication of all methods, meetings where all have the right to challenge views and a blind peer review procedure to avoid the influence of status on the criticism of ideas. In this way the social ground rules or expectations and norms of scientific institutions and scientific communities have been to some extent designed to encourage criticisms and the considerations of alternative views. These social rules and procedures as well as expectations of moral virtues, seek to prevent the imposition of views through manipulative or coercive means.[14] If this reconstruction of the logic at work in the history of the development of science is true then it seems that the success of some sciences in generating consensus behind their claims to knowledge may be more to do with the quality of their dialogues than with the power of any specific methods that they used.

The arguments against there being any unique scientific method do not undermine the importance and value of science but they do suggest that science is not unique but remains part of the larger human dialogue within which we collectively try to make sense of our situation. Claims to a fixed scientific method as the only way to truth are attempts to remove science from the global dialogue of humanity spoken of by Oakeshott and accepted as a key component of dialogic education in Chapter 2. In fact though, while some methods seem to work to solve some problems for some periods of time, all methods are ultimately open to question and that questioning returns them to dialogue.

The decision about whether or not a new method is scientific cannot itself, by definition, be made according to any pre-existing rigorous scientific method but requires the reaching of consensus within a community. The boundaries of that community are permeable and ultimately include all of us. The success of argumentation in achieving consensus implies the need for communicative virtues such as intellectual integrity and respect for the views of others, within the decision making community, as well as institutional procedures for reaching and maintaining consensus.

Attempts to limit the community of those who can engage in debate as to the validity of scientific methods to those who share the same technical language and assumptions shaped by a shared educational background are self-defeating for two reasons. First, scientific activity depends on support and funding from the whole society and if only the insiders can understand the grounds on which science claims validity then that support and funding will eventually cease. Secondly, there is empirical evidence that where research groups share the same language and background too closely breakthroughs to new understandings do not occur. Creativity in science, as elsewhere, requires a diversity of voices. The effort of explaining things to outsiders is often precisely what is needed to see them in new ways.[15]

Monologic, dialogic and diversity

The issue of how we treat the variety of methods in science points to a larger issue. For Ayer and other logical positivists the essential distinction was between what he called 'sense', meaning claims that could in theory be grounded on empirical observations and/or logic, and what he called 'non-sense', which was everything else. For Popper the distinction was between science, which produced claims that could be falsified, and pseudoscience, which could never be tested. These attempts to draw a boundary around science have failed to convince.[16] The more fundamental distinction that they reveal impacts on how science education deals with diversity. This is the distinction between monologic and dialogic.

Science and scientists have a long tradition of aspiring to monologic. This, as the name suggests, is the ideal of the single voice, the one true perspective outside of any dialogue. The dialogic alternative that Bakhtin articulated is that truth is not found in a single utterance but always in a dialogue. Different positions held together in a dialogue do not take away from the truth they enable truth: not truth as a proposition but what Bakhtin refers to as 'polyphonic truth', truth in action which is found through and across a number of different voices.[17] Bakhtin was not referring to the truism that there can be many different but compatible perspectives on the same object but to the more radical idea that meaning takes place as an event only in the gap opened up by different perspectives in dialogue. Facts are, he pointed out, answers to questions and those questions only emerge within dialogues.[18] Bakhtin defined dialogue as shared enquiry in which answers give rise to further questions.[19] Since our dialogues develop and change over time, our questions also change and so the facts we find in response to those questions change or even dissolve as the dialogue moves on.

In practice science is dialogic but its monologic image remains hard to shift and is often reinforced by science education. This is significant for addressing the issue of diversity within science education. Where there is a diversity of views a dialogic approach to education suggests the need for engagement and the need for a greater focus on the quality of dialogue. A diversity of perspectives gives meaning and is an opportunity to teach science as shared enquiry and to explore not only the alternative voices but also how, if at all, consensus can be built in answer to some specific questions. As I mentioned in Chapter 2, Bakhtin relates monologic and dialogic to the difference between an authoritative voice and a persuasive voice. The authoritative voice remains outside of me and orders me to do something in a way that forces me to accept or reject it without engaging with it whereas the words of the persuasive voice enter into the realm of my own words and change them from within.[20] This distinction gets to the heart of the approach needed to engage young people in science in the context of cultural diversity.[21]

How do we conceptualize diversity?

The evidence we gathered from questionnaires and interviews in the SED project confirms the findings of the earlier Relevance of Science Education (ROSE) project that young people in more developed countries have less interest in pursuing science as a career than those in developing countries.[22] The key problem is expressed well by Osborne and Dillon:

> [O]ne of the issues behind the decrease in those opting to study (science) is the diversity of life-styles, religions and youth cultures, not all of which are appealed to by the somewhat limited approach to science education that dominates throughout Europe.[23]

Provisional analysis of the interview data further supports the claim made by Sjøberg and Schreiner[24] that identity formation is an important factor behind this relative lack of interest in a career in science. In more economically developed 'Western' countries, Sjoberg and Schreiner claim, young people are expected to construct their own identities rather than having these ascribed to them by their parents and the culture around them. This analysis fits with some sociological accounts of the continuum between more traditional and post-traditional or 'modern' societies.[25] In this context the image young people have of science and of being a scientist does not always fit with their own identity project. Our data shows that young people in the UK and in the Netherlands were less interested in science as a school subject than children in Malaysia, India, Lebanon and Turkey. The data also suggests that this relative lack of interest might be linked to a narrow image of science and of the life of a scientist, images which did not always fit with their image of themselves and of what they wanted to be in the future.[26] The marked decrease we found in interest in science between primary and secondary school could have many causes but preliminary analysis of the interview data suggests that one cause is the increased need young people have, as they get older, to establish their identities through their interest in school subjects at an age when they come under pressure to define themselves in other areas of their lives such as their clothes, music and Facebook profiles.

This issue of the 'image' of science in relation to the identity formation of young people questions the relevance of some approaches to diversity in education. In many guides for practitioners diversity is defined in terms of gender, ethnicity and ability. While all three factors are significant their impact is mediated by the identity formation projects of young people and these identity projects lead to other potential groupings. For example the group of those who do not identify with science because of what they see as the negative ecological impact of science and technology is not defined by gender, ethnicity and ability alone, although these factors have relevance, but is a more direct reflection of issues of adolescent identity-formation project linked to a particular life-style and a particular youth–culture.

The literature review of science curricula and innovations in the partner countries of the project indicates that most science education initiatives designed to respond to the issue of cultural diversity in the last ten years have been based on external categories such as membership of a particular ethnic group.[27] I would not reject this approach and would want to judge the impact of each intervention on the evidence, however there is an obvious potential danger of imposing an identity on students that they themselves might not find empowering. Nanda, for example, claims that the greatest advocates of indigenization all have secure trans-national cultural identities and children in Western schools.[28] Carter sums up some recent criticisms of traditional approaches to educational diversity based on cultural comparison thus:

> Comparison is seen to compartmentalize difference within continually reasserting borders, paradoxically putting a break on those processes of inter-cultural understanding multiculturalism seeks to promote. Further, it does not take account of the newly emergent mixed, hybrid, and diverse identities consequent to intensified globalization and diaspora.[29]

The Bakhtinian notion of 'voice' is more useful than more objective and externally visible categorizations previously used in the classification of cultures. The use of 'voice' here to indicate a lived perspective on the world that is both cultural and individual is articulated by Hermans in his article 'The dialogical self: towards a theory of personal and cultural positioning'.[30] Drawing on both Bakhtin and William James, Hermans argues that selves and cultures are made up of 'a multi-plicity of positions among which dialogical relations can be established'. In other words individuals form their sense of themselves by taking up positions that they first find outside themselves in the culture: cultures are in turn formed by the way in which individuals take up, mix, and transform, positions.

The value of this theoretical perspective is that it breaks down fixed views of cultures and cultural differences of the kind criticized by Carter and others in favour of an understanding of cultural differences as fluid. 'Voices', in this sense, are cultural rather than purely individual and are in dialogue with each other. So, for example, the voice of techno-skepticism tends to be articulated in relationship to the voice of techno-enthusiasm and while this 'voice' only exists in the utterances of individuals who identify with it while they are speaking, it has a cultural rather than a purely personal existence.

Because voices are internal to cultural dialogues and define themselves in relation to each other, the number of possible voices is not limited or determined by any external or objective features. However, in practice, a relatively small number of clear cultural voices emerged in our study and emerge in every similar study. For example a team-member on the project, Helen Haste, conducted a survey of the values and beliefs that 704 individuals aged between eleven and twenty-one held about science and technology and found four distinct groups defined by their identifications, which we would now call cultural voices, 'Greens' interested in environmental issues but with a specific agenda, 'Techno-investors' enthusiastic about the potential of science, the 'Science-oriented' keen on science as a way of thinking and the 'Alienated from science'.[31] Similar groupings were found in analysis of the ROSE data.[32] These included a mainly male group fascinated by technology, and a mainly female group who just wanted to work with others and develop themselves as people. So far the analysis of our interview data suggest that similar identity-based concerns and cultural voices mediate the interest in pursuing science at school.

Understanding diversity in terms of a range of cultural voices has significance for pedagogy. Sjøberg and Schreiner write:

> When young people make their educational choice, they have a range of options. Young people wish to develop their abilities and their identities, and they want a future that they find important and meaningful. Only by being aware of the values and priorities of the young generation can we have a hope to show them that S & T [science and technology] studies may open up meaningful jobs in their lives.[33]

The implication is that what is required to engage young people in science is a more dialogic approach that is responsive to their interests and concerns. This is a challenging proposal for science education. Our questionnaire responses from teachers indicated that a majority in all countries claimed that they responded to cultural diversity by treating all students the same way. This implies that there may be a gulf in attitude to overcome if we are to adopt a dialogic approach because a dialogic pedagogy takes the opposite approach to diversity. Meanings in dialogues with different voices are never 'all the same' because they are always co-constructed between voices. A dialogic pedagogy in science education implies to engage with the diverse voices of students in such a way that these different voices are respected and enter into the joint construction of scientific knowledge.

In summary, diversity does not only refer to obvious and easily counted differences such as gender, ethnicity, or religious tradition: it also refers to the many differences that there are between students due to their different attitudes and identifications. We refer to these as cultural voices. As I mentioned before, while sometimes these 'voices' coincide with obvious religious, ethnic and gender divisions, sometimes they do not. In the project our aim is to address all the forms of diversity that might impact on how young people respond to science education. This is why the guidelines we developed for the design of educational activities and outline below stress the need to be responsive to the different concerns, interests and experiences of all students.

This approach to science education can be called 'dialogic' in part because it is about engaging students in a dialogue in such a way that each person feels able to express themself, secure in the knowledge that their voice will be listened to with respect. This pedagogical orientation follows from the dialogic view of the nature of science outlined earlier. The theory that all particular science discourses are part of the general dialogue of humanity puts the emphasis less on the content of what has been found out in the past and more on the process of shared enquiry and dialogic argumentation that leads to shared knowledge. This emphasis fits with the definition of dialogic education offered in Chapter 2, which is that dialogic education is education *for* dialogue as well as through dialogue. In this case dialogic science education is education for participation in the dialogues that carry science and in the democratic decision-making dialogues that are informed by science.

How do we make science education more relevant?

As already mentioned, we found evidence of a considerable disengagement from science education occurring in the transistion from primary school to secondary school, especially in the Netherlands and the UK and especially amongst girls. Our interview data suggest that one reason for this might be a sense that science often seems disconnected from the concerns of students and from other real-world concerns and motivating interests. From a dialogic theory of education perspective motivation comes from participation. The agentive power of dialogues was a theme raised in Chapter 3. It follows that the more disconnected a dialogue is from a) the internal dialogue of the student, b) the local social face to face dialogues the student participates in and c), the larger world-historical dialogues carried by communications media and the Internet, then the more likely it is to be experienced as boring and irrelevant.

To re-establish a relationship between school science and the interests of students we should emphasize science content that is socially relevant (including science for development), science topics that are high-profile cutting-edge science, and science topics that impinge on students' everyday lives. Topics most likely to engage students' interest and commitment to in-depth study are topics where they feel they have the opportunity to shape their own learning about science topics that make a social impact and that they see as relevant to them as 'global citizens' or that empower them to make a difference in some way in their own local environment.

Inquiry Based Science Education (IBSE)

In Europe there is a tendency to see IBSE as the solution to the current crisis in science education. The recent Rocard *et al.* report *Science Education Now* (2007) argues that IBSE:

> has proved its efficacy at both primary and secondary levels in increasing children's and students' interest and attainment levels while at the same time stimulating teacher motivation. IBSE is effective with all kinds of students from the weakest to the most able and is fully compatible with the ambition of excellence. Moreover IBSE is beneficial to promoting girls' interest and participation in science activities. Finally, IBSE and traditional deductive approaches are not mutually exclusive and they should be combined in any science classroom to accommodate different mindsets and age-group preferences.[34]

However, the notion of IBSE encompasses a wide range of definitions and interpretations. A key idea is that students can 'inquire' by exploring existing information in science in ways that may be led by a teacher or by the students themselves, and by building on or contesting that knowledge, again through investigations led by a teacher or by the student.[35] Since IBSE focuses on problem finding, data finding, argumentation and solution finding it can be used for the teaching of socially relevant science in a way that draws young people into science as an open-ended process of shared enquiry.

A recent review of research on IBSE confirms to some extent Rocard's claims but points out that the evidence in favour of IBSE is not quite as overwhelming as this report implies:

> The evidence of effects of inquiry-based instruction from this synthesis is not overwhelmingly positive, but there is a clear and consistent trend indicating that instruction within the investigation cycle (i.e. generating questions, designing experiments, collecting data, drawing conclusion, and communicating findings), which has some emphasis on student active thinking or responsibility for learning, has been associated with improved student content learning, especially learning scientific concepts. This overall finding indicates that having students actively think about and participate in the investigation process increases their science conceptual learning.[36]

The conclusion of this survey is that 'some emphasis on student active thinking and responsibility for learning' has a positive effect on understanding scientific concepts. In particular this survey did not find any advantage in what they call 'saturation' by enquiry learning. This would suggest a) that IBSE should be seen as one amongst a range of pedagogical approaches but not necessarily the only one to be used and b) that what is sometimes referred to as guided enquiry may well often be appropriate given the need to understand key concepts in order to discuss relevant topics.

The evidence with regard to what is effective in IBSE is compatible with the broadly dialogic view expressed in the introduction that teachers need to listen to and respond to the voices of students taking up ideas from students and building on them thereby allowing students to participate in a shared construction of knowledge.

A dialogic approach to pedagogy rejects the opposition between teacher led and student led enquiry learning. On the one hand teacher explanations only make sense to students once they have struggled for themselves with the problem for which the explanation offered by the teacher provides an answer and so it follows that effective teacher transmission of conceptual understanding in science needs to be combined with active student engagement. On the other hand student enquiry is often naïve and requires the guidance of an expert learner if it is to result in conceptual learning rather than frustration.[37] Polman and Pea try to isolate the key moves in what they refer to as the transformative dialogue between students and teachers that is required for IBSE to be effective:

> The dialogue sequence we identified for achieving transformative communication is as follows:
>
> 1 Students make a move in the research process with certain intentions, guided, as well as limited by, their current knowledge.
> 2 The teacher does not expect the students' move, given a sense of their competencies, but understands how the move, if pursued, can have additional implications in the research process that the students may not have intended.
> 3 The teacher reinterprets the student move, and together students and teacher reach mutual insights about the students' research project through questions, suggestions and/or reference to artefacts.
> 4 The meaning of the original action is transformed, and learning takes place in the students' zone of proximal development, as the teachers' interpretation and reappraisal (i.e. appropriation) of the students' move is taken up by the student.
>
> The reason this dialogue sequence is transformative is that it allows initial student actions and ideas to be incorporated into later teacher-influenced actions which push students' development and learning, while maintaining intersubjectivity between teacher and students.[38]

The literature suggests that IBSE has the potential to engage young people in a way that allows them to express their own voices and find themselves recognized and valued within the construction of scientific knowledge. However this is not a simple or easy solution, since, as Polman and Pea bring out, to be effective it requires contingently responsive and creative teaching.

Explicitly dialogic pedagogy

Although the overall approach to science education that we are proposing is dialogic there is a useful distinction to make between this theoretical framework for understanding science education and dialogic teaching and learning as a specific pedagogical technique. Mortimer and Scott suggest two dimensions in classroom talk in science education: authoritative *vs* dialogic on one axis and interactive *vs* non-interactive on the other. The four styles of talk identified by these dimensions are all valuable at times in science education.

Dialogic pedagogy teaches students how to engage in dialogue for learning together as well as teaching content matter through dialogue and implies that all members of the class have a voice, and that they expect to respect, listen to, discuss, and develop a range of views including partly formed, tentative points of view. Such a pedagogy provides one means of respecting the range of cultural explanations, and the whole set of students' alternative frameworks including misconceptions, held by members of the group. Through dialogue the conceptual foundations of the topic can be strengthened, its social significance explored and the opportunities for action considered.

There are various specific techniques that can help teach for dialogue. Philosophy for Children offers a tried and tested programme for coaching effective dialogue for conceptual understanding and this has been applied to science education.[39] Similarly the 'Thinking Together' approach which relied on coaching the use of 'Exploratory Talk' has proved effective in improving the quality of dialogue in science classrooms.[40] These and other explicit approaches to promoting and supporting dialogue in classrooms promote ground rules of debate that make it possible to tackle controversial issues of interest to students.

Connecting to real science

Both in the discussion of socially relevant science and in the exploration of high-profile science, it may be useful to make links with practicing scientists and people who use science in their careers: the industrial research scientist, the university lecturer, the High Street optician or the local health worker. Either through face-to-face meetings, or visits to the workplace, or through electronic communication, such scientists could be expert witnesses whose role is to provide insight into the science involved or they could be fully involved as contributors to or observers of the students' debates. A dialogic approach to science education means not teaching science in the abstract but drawing young people into the real dialogues and practices of science in action. Evidence from practice suggests that contact with real science could address the very narrow image that many young people have of science.

Mastery learning combined with dialogic science pedagogy

Enquiry approaches are good for developing the process skills of science as shared enquiry but are not always the best way to provide the deep understanding of concepts from the tradition of science that is required to participate fully in the ongoing dialogue. As Oakeshott has argued, induction into the tradition of a dialogue should not be understood as a limitation to freedom of action but an essential empowerment giving the freedom to act as a participant in dialogue.[41] In this context a modified version of mastery learning is suggested.

Mastery learning focuses on concepts and is teacher led. The teacher determines the core objectives to be learnt and plans whole-class teaching to cover those core objectives taking account of the prior learning of the class. This whole class phase can make use of all the teaching tactics mentioned above: for example, approaches relevant to dialogic teaching and learning, to teaching controversial issues, to enquiry-based science education. There is then a formative assessment of the students' understanding. This might be based on observation of the students, on inspection of their written work, on a test – or on any other method of assessment. The remaining time available for the topic (about half the total time) is then spent in different ways by different students. In this enrichment/remedial phase, those who have attained the core objectives work on enrichment and extension tasks (which may go just beyond the core or may, for the most able, be very challenging). Those who have not attained the core objectives revisit those parts of the topic that they have not yet mastered. They engage with the work in more individualized ways in order to address their remaining problems. The topic ends with a summative assessment.

One way to integrate the strengths of mastery learning into the kind of dialogic education required to address issues of diversity is to emphasize engagement with the voices of students. An example of this might be to work with students and the curriculum to identify a topic that is of interest to the students and to start with dialogue about this topic in order to find out more about the goals relevant to the class and about what the students need to find out. At the end of the topic further dialogue could relate the concepts taught to the lives and concerns of the students.

Teaching the nature of science

We propose two responses to the problem of a limited image of science. One is to include more contact with real working scientists. Young people in our survey who had such contact and knowledge often had a much more positive image of science and scientists than those who did not. The other is to explicitly reflect on and teach the 'nature of science' in a way that can lead young people to focus more on the process of science as flexible open-minded enquiry creatively and collectively seeking to answer real questions and solve real problems.

Teaching thinking in science and through science

Engaging with the beliefs and concerns of students in different contexts implies a focus more on the processes of science than on teaching specific facts or concepts. This coincides with a broader interest that science education should place value and emphasis on the processes of shared enquiry and argumentation that enable students to understand science as a way of knowing.[42]

Several researchers have argued that science education needs to focus more on how evidence is used to construct explanations through examining the data and warrants that form the basis of belief in scientific ideas and theories, as well as exploring the criteria used to evaluate evidence.[43] Knowing how to read and understand such arguments is an important part of scientific literacy. However research shows that reasoning and argumentation is not found in classrooms unless it is explicitly taught.[44] Instead of being presented as a body of contestable findings that are part of an ongoing process of enquiry, science is often taught as a body of facts.[45] Research in this area suggests that argumentative discourse is important for engaging students in science education and that it can be taught.[46]

The role of ICT

In some of our partner countries it is common to have separate schools for boys and for girls. In every partner country different faith groups and ethnic groups are often educated in different schools. Education for diversity that only operates within classrooms is therefore not sufficient alone to address diversity issues. Collaborative enquiry projects that bring together students from different backgrounds and different countries are one way to go beyond these school-based boundaries. For the dialogic science education for diversity proposed it is important not only to relate to local dialogues but also to engage as a participant, in however modest a capacity, in science understood as a long-term global dialogue bringing together many voices from different backgrounds. The Internet offers a medium that facilitates this vision of science as a dialogue of diverse voices.

One study that inspired us was conducted in Exeter from 1997 onwards. Schools in Norway, Sweden, Denmark, the Netherlands, UK, France, Germany and Spain collaborated using the Internet to monitor the population of selected species of butterflies as indicators of climate change over a one-year period.[47] European environmental experts worked with the teachers. One of these, for example, was Constanti Stefanescu who had co-authored an important study in Nature entitled 'Poleward shifts in geographical ranges of butterfly species associated with regional warming'.[48] In this way the collaboration engaged school students in real science that was cutting edge and in the news.

Evidence gathered and analysed by students, indicated a northerly shift in butterfly flight. Data collected in the collaboration was made available through a website, for partner schools to use and interpret, which allowed them to consider the implications of the appearance of butterfly species for climate change. Feedback from the teachers suggested that being able to see the work of other students, seeing their own work on the web and knowing that they were involved in real science was motivating for the students. Although this project was not designed to address diversity issues it followed many of the principles that we suggest should be followed in education to address diversity. Through conducting a real science enquiry collaboratively mediated by the web this project motivated and engaged students from schools with very different cultures from the arctic circle in the north to the Mediterranean coast in the south.

In Exeter we are currently working with science teachers in two local schools, one secondary and one primary, to implement an intervention based on the framework for the design of science education for diversity outlined above. These two schools plan to collaborate via the Internet, teaming up the group of mostly female 16–18-year-olds doing non-compulsory advanced level (A level) science courses in the secondary school with the 10- and 11-year-old primary school students. The idea is to use video links and text messages to allow the primary pupils to ask the advanced level students questions and get advice on their projects. This use of ICT for communication across schools will address an issue we noted in our initial survey: a marked fall-off in interest in science from primary to secondary that particularly impacts on girls.

Dialogic science education for the Internet Age

This chapter began by pointing out a connection between theories as to the nature of science and how science education responds to diversity. A monologic theory of science focusing on finding correct and unique knowledge through a correct and unique method, seems to lie behind and inform an approach to science education which does not respond to or engage with the many different world views of students. I argued that claims that there is a single scientific method have been exaggerated and that in fact there are many sciences with many methods all of which have to be justified ultimately by the same dialogic processes of argumentation as are found in other areas of human life. This led to a dialogic vision of science and a dialogic vision of science education as being about drawing students into those ongoing scientific dialogues through which shared knowledge is constructed and human understanding is increased.

The metaphor of dialogue applied to understanding science puts the emphasis on those virtues, skills, and procedures which enable communities to reach consensus. These include intellectual integrity, listening with respect to alternative views, being open about procedures, the use of empirical evidence in combination with arguments in order to justify claims, and so on. A dialogic approach to science education which emphasizes and promotes the virtues, skills, and procedures required for the construction of understanding in the context of multiple voices would be the best way to engage with the increasing diversity of cultural voices.

The initial research findings in the SED research project, combined with literature review, led to a number of principles for the design of science education that addresses the challenge of increasing cultural diversity.

1   The overall pedagogical approach is *dialogic*: this means teaching 'for dialogue' as well as through dialogue and implies:
    a)   Being responsive to and engaging with multiple voices and perspectives;
    b)   Teaching dialogic argumentation in science including the use of evidence and effective ways of 'talking science'.
2   Science education needs to be *relevant to students* in some or all of the following ways:
    a)   Using science content that is related to events in the media
    b)   Using science content from the everyday world of students
    c)   Addressing controversial issues of interest to students
    d)   Involving real life work in science and technology.
3   To engage with diversity the pedagogy should incorporate *reflection on knowledge and different ways of knowing*, including:
    a)   Reflection on one's own thinking and assumptions
    b)   Reflection and discussion on the nature of science.
4   The research team recommended the use of two approaches to pedagogy: *guided collaborative enquiry based science education and dialogic mastery learning*. Guided collaborative enquiry based learning implies student led enquiry combined with guidance towards scientific concepts. Dialogic mastery learning implies planning teaching of key concepts in a way that is responsive to student's interests and understandings.
5   The Internet and related technologies should be used to bridge diverse cultural contexts and to draw students into live collaborative science inquiries.

The dialogic focus of this framework reflects a vision of science education as drawing learners into participation into science understood as a form of shared enquiry. It suggests that education into science should participate in real science inquiring into response to the many challenges that confront the world. This means engaging students with inherited concepts and traditions of sciences in order to empower them to act in the future. Although this dialogic approach to science education is a response to the challenge of engaging and motivating the full range of cultural voices found in science classrooms, it also reflects a vision of science as a living dialogue, open to and engaged with the larger dialogue of humanity. Increasingly this living dialogue of science is carried by the Internet which is why drawing children to participate in scientific dialogues on the Internet has an important potential role to play.

An Illustration

In Lleida, Spain a research team led by Manoli Pifarre, conducted a pilot study of using the visual language of Metafora, described in Chapter 5, in a way that illustrates many of the principles of dialogic science education in the Internet Age offered above. The context was a small class of 17-year-old school students taking general science lessons and needing to learn about 'scientific method'.

Step one, was a real-world challenge from their local environment. The river Segre, was too polluted in the Lleida area to meet the Water and Environmental European committee requirement that all European rivers have to be in good ecological condition by 2015. Why was this? And what could be done about it?

In small groups they used a draft version of the visual language software on a single laptop per group to focus a discussion of how they would set about investigating this challenge. They had some preparation for group work based on the 'Thinking Together' approach to establishing shared 'ground rules' or expectations. This preparation in combination with the concept mapping space on the screen helped to open and sustain a shared dialogic space. The pedagogical value of the idea of dialogic space here is that they were not simply mastering and appropriating tools but also a space of reflection. This space of reflection combined the infinite potential of dialogic space with a focus on the issues and positions that arise in a dialogue planning and reflecting on a shared enquiry. In other words they were learning creative reflection at the same time as learning how to use cultural tools for thinking. Discussion of alternatives in the group opened up this space of reflection, which each individual could, it was hoped, appropriate for themselves and take away with them to apply to other problems.

Focusing on the specific icons helped to deepen this shared space. For example bringing up the stage of exploration and holding it as a shared focus over time enabled them to unpack it into component activities such as 'brainstorm', 'literature review' and 'observation'. The dialogic space was widened by bringing in other embodied voices when each separate map was uploaded in turn to the Interactive Whiteboard on the wall of the classroom and discussed by the whole class. The students were all local and knew the river and some were related to the farmers and others whose practices might be the cause of the pollution. This topic therefore engaged their experience from outside of the classroom and empowered them to speak about what they knew. In the research phase this space was widened further using the Internet to find information and to engage in critical dialogue with other perspectives by asking local farmers and officials for their views.

With the initial plans as their guide, the groups each then went away to enact the stages and activities suggested. They searched for information, collected data, conducted interviews, built models, tested them with experiments etc. and then came back to the Metafora environment to revise their plans. The aim of the software is not so much to help groups conduct inquiries together as to support learning to learn together. This means raising their awareness of the aspects of a complex enquiry, including the attitudes and social relationships as much as the task management, so that if and when they are called upon to work in a team with others to solve a complex they will know how to proceed.

This was a real enquiry into a real problem for the local community. The end result was to write a letter to the mayor of Lleida detailing all the steps that could be taken to help address the problem of the pollution in the river Segre so that it might meet the minimum standards by the deadline of 2015. I am not sure yet if they really found the best way to solve the problem or how the authorities responded to their advice, but I am sure that they learnt a lot about collaborating as a team and bringing diverse voices to bear in responding to a real-world challenge.

Conclusion

School science has come to focus on physics, chemistry and biology and has the tendency to teach these subjects as if they were matters of fact and 'laws of nature' that need to be learnt. This way of teaching science has reinforced the dominant monological view of reality: the idea that there is a single true representation somewhere that we can get access to and that explains all the apparent variety. The increasing diversity of identities that accompanies the global interconnectedness of the Internet Age has challenged this monological approach to science education.

This chapter began with a philosophical investigation into the nature of science. The conclusion reached through this was that no specific content or method could be used to define science but that it was better understood as a dialogic process of open-ended shared enquiry and very much a part of the larger dialogue of humanity. This has implications for pedagogy. If science is a dialogic process characterized by specific dialogic virtues such as open-mindedness, fairness and respect for alternative views, then these virtues should be made explicit and taught.

The term 'science' is often used to demarcate an area of the school curriculum but the broader meaning of science is simply knowledge. The Internet Age issues of diversity and globalization that challenge established approaches to science education also challenge other knowledge focused areas of the curriculum. The dialogic way of teaching science that has been developed in response to these challenges is an illustration of a more general pedagogy appropriate for education in the Internet Age.

Although these principles were, of necessity, developed to apply to teaching science as part of the existing curriculum within existing schools they could all also inform pedagogy in the emerging alternative model of education for the Internet Age outlined in Chapter 5. Dialogic mastery learning in particular is a contribution to the challenge of how to teach useful conceptual knowledge in a way that arises out of the contexts and interests of students and returns to connect these concepts in order to illuminate those contexts. This approach to pedagogy is as relevant in the context of a MOOC (Massive Open Online Course, see Chapter 5) as it is within the four walls of a traditional science classroom.

The illustration of dialogic science education addressing the real issue of pollution in a local river suggests the value of structuring the content of education, the core conceptual knowledge and key skills that we should teach, through the current and future challenges that are faced both locally and globally. The role of dialogic education is not simply to transmit knowledge from the past but, more centrally, it is to bridge knowledge and voices from the past in order to engage these in ongoing dialogue with real issues that students face today so as to empower them to become more effective and complete participants in their own lives.

7
EDUCATING THE PLANET[1]

This chapter begins with the argument that different communications media tend to 'afford' different kinds of selves with different kinds of ethics and different kinds of 'citizenship'. This leads on to the claim that the Internet has the potential to support a new kind of identity, which implies a new ethics and a new kind of citizenship: this is a dialogic identity characterized by its infinite openness and responsibility to the other. The dialogic self is not an isolated individual but a self with others acting as part of a global creative intelligence. This new kind of citizenship, participation without boundaries, is not something that will just happen on its own. It is a future possibility that crucially depends upon the action of all involved in education for its realization.

Communications technology and identity

There is an interesting strand of literature on the affordances of communications media for different kinds of identity. In the following brief review of this literature I will look at the impact of oral dialogue, written media and the Internet on conceptions of the self and on conceptions of citizenship. But before I do that I want to establish the link between communication and ethics.

Dialogue and values

It was clear from the analysis of dialogic relations in Chapters 2 and 3 that dialogue has implicit ethical ideals. There is often a misunderstanding about this. The linguist Per Linell, for example, criticizes Habermas and other writers, perhaps myself, for working with a normative model of dialogue instead of studying real dialogues with all their messy tensions and peculiarities.[2] But normative ideals are not always simply added to reality by researchers they are sometimes constitutive of social phenomena. Face-to-face dialogue is not a neutral thing occurring in the world that can be studied empirically 'from the outside' as Linell seems to imply. Dialogue is always an achievement that assumes a certain effort at 'mutual attunement' between participants implicating shared expectations that have the force of moral ideals.[3] To engage in dialogue I need to be able to see myself to some extent as if from the other's point of view. Seeing things as if from the other's point of view is an ethical ideal but it is also a necessary ideal for successful communication and mutual understanding.

It is true that we are often aware of unsuccessful communication but this awareness in itself implies that communication must be successful to some extent at least some of the time. The analysis of cognitive development in Chapter 3 argues that the kind of separate self which is able to strategically manipulate dialogues emerges from and is derivative upon an initial open relationship with the other Successful communication implies that mutual attunement or seeing as if through others' eyes sometimes succeeds which in turn implies that certain ideals and values are part of the fabric of social life. If values are implicit and emergent from communication then the communication practices supported by different communication media might well have an impact on values and this indeed seems to be the case.

1) Orality: local ethics and universal warfare

It is widely held that while physical facts are universal, values are relative, changing with each culture. There is one value that seems to run counter to this. This is called the 'golden rule' often phrased as 'do as you would be done by'. When asked what is the most important concept to guide ethical conduct, Confucius replied 'reciprocity'. He emphasized this point many times, repeating in various forms the central message 'Do not do to others, anything you would not want done to you'.[4] The form 'do as you would be done by' is derived from the words of Christ in the New Testament[5] but with similar claims found in the Old Testament and in Judaism. In the Hadith, or sayings of Muhammad we read:

> A Bedouin came to the prophet, grabbed the stirrup of his camel and said: O the messenger of God! Teach me something to go to heaven with it. The Prophet said: 'As you would have people do to you, do to them; and what you dislike to be done to you, don't do to them. Now let the stirrup go! [This maxim is enough for you; go and act in accordance with it!]'.[6]

According to those who have studied such things essentially the same ideal of reciprocity can be found in every cultural tradition.[7]

From what was said earlier about the need to take the perspective of the other in a dialogue it seems likely that the ubiquity of the golden rule is a consequence of the ubiquity of face-to-face dialogue. The sources of most ethical traditions lie in predominately oral societies with the spoken words of prophets and sages often written down later and every small-scale oral society has a similar ethical code. Unfortunately though, if recognizing the rights of the other in a dialogue is the universal basis of ethics then ethics does not need to extend much beyond the community of those who are frequently in face-to-face dialogue. 'Do unto others as you would be done by' sounds to us like a universal moral law but in the context of oral societies it would not be interpreted as such.

The whole idea of universal moral codes only makes sense from the perspective of writing and especially print. Luria's account of his research in Uzbekistan makes this clear. He found a marked difference between the way of thinking of literates and non-literates. Oral people connected things on the basis of concrete experience in contexts and often refused to generalize to things that they did not know or had not experienced unless perhaps they had heard it from a trusted source. Here is an example of oral thinking reported by Luria from his notes of the interviews researchers held with local people:

Q: All bears are white where there is always snow; in Zovaya Zemlya there is always snow; what colour are the bears there?

A: I have seen only black bears and I do not talk of what I have not seen.

Q: What do my words imply?

A: If a person has not been there he cannot say anything on the basis of words. If a man was 60 or 80 and had seen a white bear there and told me about it, he could be believed.[8]

Questions of identity and ethics follow a similar rule. Ethical responsibility is situated in the groups of face-to-face people and cannot be easily unsituated. When I studied Social Anthropology I was struck by the fact that the name of each tribe or group studied turned out, when translated into the language of that tribe or group, to mean 'people'. There are many thousands of separate languages in the world in each of which the word 'people' means the members of the group. This use of language implies that those who do not speak the same language, those with whom we are not in dialogue, can never fully be 'people' in the same way that we, the shared language speakers, are people.

The hypothesis that a sense of reciprocal responsibility in small scale oral communities depends on face-to-face dialogues appears to fit the facts reasonably well. There is some similarity in ethical codes everywhere based on the golden rule.[9] Yet small-scale oral cultures mostly live in a state of constant warfare with their neighbours and have always done so.[10]

The reason for the apparently situated and concrete form of thinking that Luria observed is presumably that in oral cultures words are only found in the ephemeral context of face-to-face speech.[11] Some have argued that without literacy there are no universal abstract concepts.[12] It would seem to follow that an ethics based on a universal sense of obligation to all other human beings (a Kantian type ethics) is unlikely to make sense in a purely oral culture. On the other hand, an ethics based on a sense of recip- rocal obligation between people who know each other because they are in dialogue together is a simple side effect of the participatory nature of dialogue. Where face- to-face dialogue is the only medium of communication it is perhaps understandable therefore that the rights and obligations of 'citizenship', understood in a broad sense, should not be seen as extending much beyond the group of those who talk together.

However, to describe oral thinking as situated and concrete is to apply a deficit model describing it only by contrast with a more abstract and universal image of conceptual thinking which depends upon literacy and education. The thinking of oral societies is also metaphoric and mythopoetic in a way that allows every part of the world to become a perspective on the whole.[13] This richly evocative perceptual and embodied thinking remains the context of all human thinking.

The problem remains, from an ethical point of view, that the signs that carry this thinking, the animals and plants in the environment, the warm breath of face-to-face speech and the sculptures or cave paintings, remain culturally and environmentally situated. Orality as the only or main medium of communication, augmented by the technology of painting or sculpture, constrains education to being only induction into the shared dialogues of the tribe. Ethical tribalism is the inevitable result. In order to sustain Oakeshott's concept of the dialogue of humanity, a more disembedded means of communication technology is required.

2) Writing: the authority of the centre

Writing enabled ways of thinking and being that are not possible with face-to-face dialogue alone. One example mentioned in Chapter 5 is the way in which the 'religions of the book' could disembed themselves from a physical context to cross seas and mountains and claim adherents in different cultures. Writing does not only, to some extent, disembed meanings from their origin in places and in face-to-face dialogues but it also disembeds them from their origins in time. Socrates' dialogues were written down so that they can inform dialogue today, as were those of Confucius, Lao Tze, the historical Buddha, Muhammed and so on. The many possibly equally wise oral thinkers whose discources were not written down are no longer part of the dialogue. Without writing the concept of a universal dialogue of humanity is not possible, with writing it becomes inevitable.

Writing is a technology and it always takes a specific material form which shapes cultures. Harold Innis, the Toronto based communication theorist who inspired Marshall McLuhan, draws attention to the requirement of empires to have portable written communications. He locates the development of the technology of writing in the struggle of empires to impose a uniform written law. Writing enabled empires since the very idea of empire is to be able to write the law code at the centre and spread the same law uniformly out to all the provinces.[14] The first written law code, that of Hammurabi (2123–2081 BC), served the purpose of centralizing power. Innis's detailed accounts show how communications' technologies such as paper and print, even horses and ships carrying papyrus scrolls, were all essential to empires and shaped the nature of those empires.

While empires could unite many oral language groups under the rule of one central authority through the use of writing as an elite craft activity, the emergence of nations required printing presses and mass literacy. Benedict Anderson looked in some detail at the origins of nationalism and argued that the sense of communal identity found within nations was not possible before the Gutenberg press and was a product of what he called 'print capitalism'. Capitalist entrepreneurs printed their books in popular local languages in order to sell more copies. Previously, before Gutenberg, writing had been dominated by Latin in Europe, which provided a shared language for scholars. Because of print-capitalism readers speaking various local dialects were able to understand each other, and forge a common sense of identity within each new print-language area. The first European nation-states were formed around what Benedict called the 'imagined communities' which emerged out of these new national print-languages.[15]

In small-scale oral societies decisions are commonly taken by all the people gathered together. Face-to-face dialogue as the only medium of communication affords an egalitatrion and participatory ethic. The empires of writing before print affords the authority of the written word of the lawmaker(s) at the centre of the empire. Print was in some ways seen as a liberation towards more participation in religion and in civil life. In Europe the presses were associated with people actually being able to read the Christian bible in their own languages instead of always having it interpreted for them by priests. However, although print can of course sustain some social dialogue at a distance through pamphlets and newspapers, the participatory nature of that dialogue is circumscribed by the medium and access to the kind of education required to master it. The medium of print, by its nature, is one-to-many. Whoever controls the printing press tends to control the message. Law codes and text books are printed at the centre of the empire or nation-state and distributed to the periphery.

3) The Internet and global participation?

Television and radio, although electronic media, share the same one-to-many nature of print media. They extend the embodiment of global communication through the added dimensions of sound and vision but do not challenge the authoritative and monological regime of thought established by writing and sustained by print. The Internet is radically different from all preceding mass media because of its affordance for participation. It can support the same kind of two-way or multi-way dialogue found in the face-to-face talk of small-scale societies and at the same time it also supports the global reach of writing.

If orality and literacy impacted on identity and on ideas of citizenship then what impact is the Internet having? It is early days yet but there are already some pointers. As introduced in Chapter 5 Mark Poster argues that the Internet and related technologies challenge the way of thinking characteristic of modernism, particular the ideal of an autonomous rational self:

> A post-structuralist understanding of new communications technologies raises the possibility of a post-modern culture amid society that threatens authority as the definition of reality by the author.[16]

The claim that new communications technology will usher in a post-modern or post-structuralist reality of fragmented and multiple identities sounds a bit negative at first reading. When things are changing it is always easier to see what we are losing than to see what we might gain because the positive often takes time to emerge. The positive other side of the break-down of the authority of the 'author' as Poster puts it, is that individuals might become more open to dialogue with others and with otherness.

Of course the forgoing account is a very brief summary of vast historical changes with many specific details and peculiarities glossed over in the attempt to make a simple claim: communications technology impacts on ways of thinking that include identity, ethics and concepts of 'citizenship'.

One lesson that can clearly be learnt from the more detailed literature about how this impact happens in practice is that technology does not determine mentality in any simple way. In Chapter 5, for example, I described how one way of writing and reading can cement communal solidarity, the reading aloud of a manuscript such as the bible which was common in the middle ages, whilst another way of writing and reading, silent and solitary writing and reading of books, can support the formation of a separate autonomous inner self able to stand back from the culture around it.[17]

Just as the previously dominant media of communication, oracy and literacy, can be a part of cultural practices that have quite different effects on identity, so can the Internet. Some have argued, for example, that the Internet can be used in a way that increases the strength of narrow cultural identities because it enables individuals to spend all their time online with others in their particular cultural group, whether that is a group of Neo-Nazis or stamp collectors.[18] The argument cannot be made that the Internet determines anything in a directly causal way but it is possible to state that the Internet offers a potential for global dialogue that was not available before.

Whether or not the Internet will be a driver for global dialogue and world peace or a driver for fragmentation and tribal conflict is not simply an empirical question. We do not need to sit back and wait to see what happens. While other social sciences often seem content to describe reality, the role of education is to change it. The very idea of education, a word taken from Latin roots meaning 'to lead out' (ex + ducere), implies to actively intervene in order to bring out potential and shape the future. In this case it is perhaps up to all of us as educators to realize the potential for global dialogue implicit in the technology of the Internet.

Deconstruction and the Internet

If our ways of thinking, sustained and shaped by educational systems, have been deeply informed by writing and print then this might make it difficult to understand a new way thinking appropriate to the Internet as the still emerging next dominant mode of communication. Being a citizen of the Internet, for example, is not simply the same being a citizen of France only expanded to include all Internet users. This is because, unlike France, the Internet has no border and no boundary.

The political scientist Mark Bevir brings out the implications of Derrida's writing for our understanding of why global citizenship must avoid the error of simply universalizing the 'liberal' enlightenment ideas (ideas which I would argue are affordances of print). Bevir argues that we are in danger of associating spirit with the mission of the Enlightenment and the metaphysical idea of universal human rights. In the context of Derrida's deconstruction of Heiddeger's unfortunate association of 'spirit' with the mission of the German people, Bevir argues that liberals might be making a similar error in the promotion of universal human rights and values:

> biological racism has uncomfortable similarities with a spiritual racism associated with a form of metaphysical thinking found not only in Heidegger but also in liberal universalism. While we are still compelled to defend a 'cosmopolitan' position, we should be careful all the while to remember, always to remember, our responsibility to the Other.[19]

In defending the relevance of Derrida, Bevir points to the ethical basis of deconstruction:

> The philosophy of deconstruction points to an ethical moment of responsibility to the Other that is prior to ontology, and this moment informs the type of non-metaphysical thinking found in Derrida's textual practice.[20]

Poster and Ulmer use Derrida's approach to the 'deconstruction' of textual meaning as a kind of metaphor for the way in which 'electronic writing' or 'electracy'[21] undermines the stability, authority and certainty previously associated with print texts. Bevir also uses deconstruction but appeals beyond this to an ethical position that he claims underlies it. This ethical position of responsibility for the other comes through Derrida from his one-time teacher and long-time friend Levinas. Deconstruction is not just about play with words and meanings as some seem to think, but is about questioning our claims to 'understand' in order to project us beyond the text into a certain openness to Otherness.[22] This philosophical issue relates closely to the tension I have outlined between monologic print-based culture and dialogic oracy-based culture. Does Levinas's ethics of infinite responsibility for the other have something to teach us about the ethics and the kinds of citizenship appropriate to the dawning Internet age?

Levinas and infinite responsibility for the Other

Levinas described the western tradition of philosophy as 'egology'.[23] It is, he claimed, about building systems to 'represent otherness' rather than to relate to otherness. When others are represented as signs in our system we think we 'understand' them and so we can control them and treat them inhumanely. Only the engagement of relationship leads to humanity, he argued. That is because, for Levinas, there is something about the face of the other that calls us to account and outstrips our capacity to understand and to control. The face of the other is a singularity that breaks out of any totalizing system of thinking to speak of a reality beyond it that is infinite. Levinas's account of the difference between totality and infinity relates in some ways to the difference drawn by Bakhtin between monologic (single-voiced) communication and dialogic (multiple-voiced) communication.[24]

Both monologic thinking and totality thinking reduce the otherness of the other to a sign that is understood within a system that can be controlled. By contrast both dialogic thinking and infinity thinking remain open, seeing every 'other' as a sign of that otherness which transcends the ability to grasp and control.

Both Bakhtin and Levinas follow Socrates in contrasting living words with dead words, where living words are 'internal' to a dialogic relation and carry infinite potential for making new meaning while dead words are external to the dialogue and have become sedimented into things with fixed meaning.[25] However, whereas Socrates, an oral thinker, appears to identify these living words with the warm breath of face-to-face speech (breath is a translation of the Greek word pneuma which can also be translated as 'spirit') both Bakhtin and Levinas locate the source of meaning not in the words themselves so much as in the particular kind of difference that characterizes dialogic relations. The point that meaning requires the gap of difference between self and other, which I brought out in Chapters 2 and 4, is summed up by an often repeated claim from Volosinov, a close collaborator of Bakhtin in the 1920s: 'meaning is like an electric spark that occurs only when two different terminals are hooked together'.[26]

It is this focus on the dialogic relation as a kind of difference rather than a kind of identity that most clearly distinguishes the metaphor of thinking as dialogue across difference from Socrates' original version of thinking as face-to-face dialogue.

Understanding dialogic meaning as more like a spark across difference than like a tool in a social context makes it possible to understand the positive role of technology in educational dialogues. Bakhtin, for example, went beyond face-to-face dialogue to explore dialogue between texts arguing that it is the difference between texts which opens up 'bottomless' depths of 'contextual meaning' and leads to sparks of 'inter-illumination'. He gives the example of how, for him, reading the texts of ancient Greece, gave him an extra perspective from which to see his situation in twentieth-century Russia in a way that opened up the possibilities of thought in general.[27]

Levinas directly relates this valuing of difference to valuing the affordances of new technology. He takes on Heidegger's criticism of modern technology as enframing our thoughts and alienating us from 'being', claiming, by contrast, that Heidegger's mystical association of being with place leads directly to the horrors of Nazism (Heidegger's association of spirit with Germany, the German language and the German people) and that it is the role of technology to liberate us from the 'perpetual warfare' implied by such place-based identity by taking us out of our home space and bringing us into relationship with the others. He writes in an article in praise of the achievement of Gagarin that:

> Technology wrenches us out of the Heideggerian world and the superstitions regarding *place*. From this point on, an opportunity appears to us: to perceive men outside the situation in which they are placed, and let the human face shine in all its nudity. Socrates prefers the town in which one meets people to the countryside and the trees.[28]

Dialogic identity as infinite responsibility for the Other

Levinas stressed the infinity implicit in the dialogic difference. What makes each person truly unique and, in his language, 'singularities', is precisely what makes us all the same, that we resist all attempts to be located and situated. This speaks to Levinas of the infinity of an outside of any meaning system and it is this transcendence and infinity of the 'naked face of the other' that calls us out and gives us a direction.

Bakhtin, from within a very different tradition of thought, appears to articulate a point of view with some similarities. He points out that 'in order to understand, it is immensely important for the person who understands to be located outside the object of his or her creative understanding – in time, in space, in culture'. He was dismayed by the narrow frame of reference within with most people 'fuss about' and writes that we need to think always in the 'great time' that unites all cultures. He echoes the infinity that Levinas refers to when he claims that the meaning of any utterance is found in the whole dialogue but that this whole dialogue has no end. His notion of 'great time' was of the place of meeting between all voices from every time and place. Education on the dialogic model stimulated by Bakhtin is then about drawing students from narrow concerns to the more universal thinking of 'great time'.

Bakhtin's dialogism was developed without the influence of post-structuralism. The benefit of reading Bakhtin augmented by Derrida is to realize that master notions such as 'Great Time' or even, Levinas's version of the 'Infinite Other' are not things that we can actually grasp or pin down or become in any way but are a sort of opening towards an otherness of a kind that cannot be conceptualized.[29] This openness to otherness that cannot be conceptualized is the unnamed groundless ground implied by deconstruction. Although Derrida would of course resist saying such a thing, the implication I take from his writing is that such deconstruction can be lived beyond all words and the living of it is the essence of creative intelligence.[30]

How does collective thinking work?

There is a long tradition in psychology of studying thinking only in individuals and imagining it only as an individual phenomenon limited to individual brains. The 'Thinking Together' programme of research described in Chapter 4 offers some clear evidence of collective thinking through the simple expedient of asking children to solve reasoning test problems by talking together with only one answer sheet. This series of experimental studies demonstrated that children simply asked to work together did not do better than a child would alone but that after an educational intervention designed to promote more dialogic talk, they performed much better at group thinking.[31]

In fact it is fairly obvious that some groups think together better than others and some societies think together better than others. But collective thinking is not sufficiently studied and not sufficiently taught perhaps because it is hard for many people to conceptualize. Due to the dominant monological and physicalist view of reality maintained by print-based education, especially school science education, it seems easier for most people to imagine thinking as something material that happens within brains than as something that happens in invisible relationships. The question of how to picture collective thinking is an important question if we want to educate the planet to think better together.

The 'Thinking Together' programme demonstrated collective thinking in groups of students who were collocated and using face-to-face dialogue. Gerry Stahl has conducted numerous studies of collective thinking with students who are physically dispersed and interacting only online. He operates with an environment that supports the collaborative learning of maths. In the environment students can visually represent the problems, question each other via text chat and develop answers together. He concludes that the answer to the apparent puzzle of collective thinking is not so much individuals sharing 'common ground', the notion that they must understand things in a similar way, but that individuals learn to share a world together. His detailed discourse analyses of the communications and moves made by learners working together online shows how they construct a shared world together and use this to orient themselves and each other in order to understand by seeing things from different perspectives. Stahl writes that 'Shared understanding is not a matter of shared representations but of experiencing a shared world'.[32]

This is interesting because it confirms something that was found in the 'Thinking Together' research. As I mentioned earlier, a key difference between less successful groups and more successful groups was that the more successful groups had a more dialogic orientation and style of talk, evidenced in shared pauses that were not uncomfortable, in changing minds, in asking each other for help and even in the way that one person would start an utterance and another finish it as if this was quite normal. However, in addition there was a difference in the way that they pointed things out to each other. In the less successful groups (usually our pre-tests before we taught them how to talk together more dialogically) the use of 'because' was collocated with deictic pointing to the physical space such as 'Cos look ...'. In more successful groups (usually in the post-tests after our intervention programme) the use of 'because' was collated with longer utterances constructing shared verbal context such as:

> Because, look, on that they've taken the circle out, yes? So on that, you are going to take the circle out because they have taken the circle out of that one. (See example in Chapter 4.)

In other words the group had learnt to construct a virtual world together full of invisible processes like 'taking the circle out' that could be pointed to.

The chiasm structure of consciousness helps us to understand how 'Thinking Together' and learning together are possible. An archetypal perceptual chiasm is formed when I stand up in a landscape and experience a horizon forming around me. I am conscious of myself looking out towards the horizon but at the same time I experience myself as located at the centre of the horizon as if unseen eyes were looking at me. If another person, let us assume a woman, then walks into view, I see her within my horizon. I realize that I myself am seen by her and located within her horizon. While our consciously focused perception might be very different because looking from different perspectives we can orient ourselves towards each other because our horizons overlap. The visual world of trees and rocks and grass is as much part of my consciousness as of hers. In a similar way the virtual mathematical objects in the 'VirtualMath' online environment are shared by all the participants of that world.

While inhabiting a shared space is a necessary condition for shared cognition, alone it is not sufficient. For the objects in the shared space to become symbols that we can think with together we need to take them up from their inert background status and foreground them as shared meanings. To think together in a shared world, that shared background world needs to become a dialogic space in which everything is seen not only from my point of view but also from your point of view.

Planetary creative intelligence

Google recently announced that they are offering a prize of 30 million dollars to any team who can land on the moon and send back photos. http://www.Googlelunarxprize.org/. This is one of the eight or more 'Xprizes' which motivate effort and resources towards solving global challenges by highlighting the challenges with prizes for anyone solving them. It is an example of how the Internet can be used to support global creative intelligence. The way in which this works is rather similar to the functional architecture proposed for the Global Workspace Theory of consciousness. Lots of people and groups are aware of the challenge of space travel but perhaps not doing very much about it. By highlighting it not only with a web site but with a big prize Google generated lots of publicity for the challenge. This was carried not only by traditional media but also by millions of individuals on their blogs, social-networking sites and micro-blogging sites such as Twitter. In this way a problem that was in the background of collective consciousness has been brought to the foreground of collective consciousness. As a result extra resources are brought to bear to solve the problem. If and when a team solve the problem there will be a big award and lots of noise again on the Internet. This works as collective thinking to the extent that many of the billions of people connected to the Internet, are aware of this as shared background even while the foreground focus of their consciousness might be more specific and more individual.

Prizes have been around for a long time as a way of supporting collective creativity. The Internet has merely boosted this mechanism. But other new ways of supporting collective consciousness that are specific to the affordances of the Internet emerge each year. A recent social awareness movement called Avaaz appears to be an experiment in the kind of communications technology that might move us towards what Derrida refers to elliptically as the 'democracy that is to come'. Launched five years ago Avaaz now has fourteen million members participating in and sharing campaigns of global concern. They organize petitions on global issues such as threats to freedom, deforestation, and corruption in specific countries. The website contains stories of how this raising of awareness has had impacts making governments and businesses think twice and change their policies. On their website we read:

> Each year, Avaaz sets overall priorities through all-member polls (See 2010 poll results here), and campaign ideas are polled and tested weekly to 10,000-member random samples—and only initiatives that find a strong response are taken to scale. Campaigns that do reach the full membership are then super-charged by, often, hundreds of thousands of Avaaz members taking part within days or even hours.

In other words there is no single person or group sitting in the centre of the organization with a bureaucracy deciding how they will focus their resources. Instead issues to focus on emerge upwards from the concerns of members and when they reach critical mass through having enough links attached to them, they are broadcast globally around the Internet.

While the focus of conscious attention always appears individual and attached to a particular physical body the background is shared in much the same way as a common horizon is shared by figures in a landscape. We all share the same world and can orient towards each other through our issues and concerns within that world. The functional architecture of collective thinking is not essentially different from the functional architecture of individual thinking. In both cases agency or 'selfness' is not a fixed thing but an emergent property of dialogues.

Those dialogues are not just dialogues between physically embodied voices but also dialogues with cultural voices represented by icons and images and with the horizonal voice of the Infinite Other that is always calling us on from beyond our understanding. In other words mind is not individual but fractal. Collective consciousness and creative thinking at a planetary level is potentially just as much 'us' as thinking what to wear in the morning.

Internet initiatives such as Xprizes and Avaas show the potential for an emerging planetary creative intelligence. The mission of education is not only to teach individuals how to think better by drawing them into reflective dialogue. For individual intelligence to flourish it needs to be part of intelligent societies. It is becoming increasingly apparent that for intelligent societies to flourish they need to be part of a more intelligent world.

Dialogic identity and the Internet

In the first section of this chapter I looked at the ethical and identity implications of different communications' technologies to argue that:

1   Face-to-face dialogue supports a participatory sense of self as part of
     a community yet this tends to universal warfare because this dialogue
     community has physical limits in space and time.
2   Writing overcomes some of the spatial and temporal limits of oral dialogue
     but only at the expense of becoming disembedded from context. It has an
     affordance for monologism and tends to support empires governed from a
     centre as well as turning 'truth' into a 'representation' – i.e. the sort of thing
     that can be found in a book.
3   The Internet combines features of dialogue (everyone can participate and have
     a voice) with features of writing (it transcends location) hence potentially
     enabling a participatory self that is for the first time global rather than local.

Of course the Internet remains largely a written medium. However the way in
which writing is used locates it within participatory dialogues. The Internet is not
a giant encyclopaedia but more a vast number of voices all broadcasting at once and
many contradicting each other. Many of the signs on the Internet are 'epiphantic'
signs, like avatars, that take us to the presence of others or of alternative ways of
being.[33] The 'affordances' for self-identity and for social identity of the Internet
and associated technologies combine some affordances of oral dialogic with the
affordances of print but there is also something new. A key new element is that
the dialogue on the Internet, unlike oral dialogue, is not tied to location and so
has no fixed boundaries.

To help understand the new kind of dialogic identity that the Internet 'affords'
I turned to broadly 'dialogic' theorists Bakhtin and Derrida. These writers were
more concerned with dialogic relationships between texts than with spoken
dialogues in face-to-face settings. Derrida, in particular, leads us away from the
'logos' part of the Greek word 'dialogos' and towards a focus on the 'dia' part of
the word where dia refers to a critical difference. It is the difference between self
and other that defines dialogic, not the warm breath of the words themselves nor
the 'logic', always written down after the event of thinking, that came to define
modern accounts of reasoning.

Thinking about the importance of the 'dia' in 'dialogic' leads in turn to the
oxymoronic, but productive, idea of identification with the non-identity of the
dialogic relation (elaborated more in Chapters 2 and 3). This is identification not with
a bounded ego-identity nor with a bounded community but with the perpetually
emergent event of openness to the other. Responsibility is about our response to the
call of others so Levinas is quite correct to refer to this new ethics as infinite (in the
everyday sense of not-finite or unbounded) responsibility to Otherness. This infinite
responsibility and infinite openness is the best way we have at the moment to characterize the possibility of a new kind of citizenship that the Internet affords us. The
Internet itself is without boundaries so to identify with it as if it was a 'community' is
to identify beyond all possible limits. The responsibility that arises from participation
in a community without boundaries has to be characterized by openness rather than
by the closure of a specific imagined self or imagined community.

Education for the democracy to come

The phrase 'the democracy to come' suggests an orientation rather than a worked out political philosophy. Derrida uses this phrase to refer not to any real or known or knowable state of affairs but more to a kind of endlessly deferred promise that nonetheless guides us.[34]

The argument that different ethics emerge in the context of the affordances of communications technology has clear and striking implications for education for citizenship at the dawn of the Internet Age. The first is that education for citizenship now needs to be global in the sense of 'glocal', that is to say linking the local to global dialogues and applying global dialogues in local contexts.[35] But the second is that most current approaches to education for global citizenship are misguided because based on print-based ways of thinking. Global citizenship education is bound up with the discourse of Universal Human Rights, however this only makes sense from the point of view of print and carries with it the trace of the monologic authority of print-based law codes.

Somewhere in the centre of the empire of liberal good sense, perhaps in Paris or in New York, assemblies hammer out law codes. In the peripheries, perhaps hiding in caves in Afghanistan, or living in a traditional way in the forests of Papua New Guinea, those who do not agree are pronounced 'beyond dialogue' because they will not sign up to the new universal law of all right-thinking people. From a dialogic point of view there are no universal unsituated truths so rights must be negotiated within dialogues and within contexts. The ethic of openness to the other is not a 'universal truth' or law or 'right' since it has no propositional content. It is more a bearing witness to the context of communication, which is an open relationship with unpindownable infinite Otherness.

The model of citizenship implied by the global participatory democracy that we need to create in the future is very different from the model required for good citizenship within a bounded nation state. Instead of the focus being on identification with, and submission to, a written rational constitution the new focus will need to be on a living relationship with others and with otherness. The ideal implied by the inner logic of the Internet is a shift from universal rights, print based ethics, towards infinite responsibility, or dialogic ethics in an unbounded community.

However, as we have seen, the dialogic account of development is normally a story of augmentation rather than one of linear progress and replacement. The Internet does not replace print but incorporates and contextualizes it within a global multi-dimensional dialogue. In a similar way the voice of the democracy to come is not opposed to the idea of universal human rights nor does it seek to remove them – it seeks rather to locate them within a living dialogue characterized by openness to the other and openness to the undermining voice of the infinite other.

Education technology for global dialogue

For education it is never enough just to describe reality or to theorize about it: it is necessary also to participate in creating it. The role of new communications technology in education for global citizenship will not become clear simply by reflecting on the history of communications or on ethical theory. It is also necessary to build educational designs on the basis of provisional theories and to test them out in practice in order to evaluate and develop these theories. Just as Wikipedia gives a particular practical form to the Internet Age theory of knowledge as infinite dialogue so we need to find ways to instantiate a theory of education for citizenship as drawing learners into relationships of infinite responsibility with others and with otherness in general. I end this chapter therefore by outlining a provisional framework for educational design for citizenship education in the Internet age with a few illustrations.

A dialogic foundation for the design of education technology for global citizenship

Education for participation in global dialogue is more about the process of teaching and learning than about specific content areas. Education can be addressed in ways which open up learners to think for themselves in responding to others and to otherness. What is required is not a specific subject in the curriculum called 'civics' or 'citizenship' but rather a dialogic approach to education in general. As described in Chapter 5, dialogic education can be further described in terms of the moves of opening, widening, deepening and resourcing dialogic space. Below I take each of these terms in turn to help outline a coherent overall approach to education for Internet citizenship.

1) Opening dialogic spaces

A singular affordance of new media technologies is the possibility of supporting new dialogic spaces anywhere and everywhere, from interactive blogs under exhibits in museums to texted exchanges between pupils in different classrooms. But the technological support alone does not make a dialogic space.

One of the key findings from my own research with Neil Mercer, Lyn Dawes, Karen Littleton and others on collaborative learning around computers in classrooms is that for effective shared thinking it is not enough just to place people in groups or to give them stimulating resources to think about but they need to be prepared for 'Thinking Together' with others beforehand.[36] The expectations (or 'ground rules') of dialogic talk (or 'Exploratory Talk') promote learning and 'Thinking Together' with others. Educational approaches that improve face-to-face dialogue such as 'Thinking Together' or Philosophy for Children are important as a preparation for thinking and learning together with others on the Internet.

The focus of dialogic education in face-to-face groups needs to be on asking fruitful questions and listening with care to others and to otherness. Such skills embedded in habits and dispositions are essential for forming a dialogic identity able to participate in the global democracy of the future.

There are many spaces for possible collective dialogue on the Internet. The quality of the collective thinking in the debates that spontaneously occur under news blogs and YouTube videos could be improved if children and young people were explicitly prepared for thinking and learning together. In one EC funded study, for example, 'Philosophy Hotel', similar Philosophy for Children pedagogy in different classrooms in several European countries was extended successfully to Internet mediated 'philosophy' discussions.[37]

2) Deepening dialogic space

Deepening refers to increasing the degree of reflection on assumptions and grounds. With the right pedagogy the broadening potential of Internet dialogues also becomes a deepening as students are led to reflect on the assumptions that they carry with them into dialogues.

Talk in face-to-face dialogues exists only momentarily and only for those immediately present. Technologies that support drawing and writing can thus be thought of as a way of deepening dialogues, by turning transitory talk and thoughts into external objects that are available to learners for discussion and shared reflection.[38] However, as discussed in the first part of this paper, this can lead to the reification of knowledge into object–form as truths to be learnt of the kind found in school text books. Electronic writing affords multiplicity, flexibility, and provisionality, and so goes further than literacy in providing support for the deepening of dialogues. Often deepening follows from widening where exposure to other ways of seeing things can lead one to question one's own framing assumptions. Deepening can be understood as a form of 'deconstruction' insofar as this means consciously exploring the key distinctions that frame constructions of meaning in order to become aware of how things might be otherwise and to bear witness to the larger context.[39]

A specific form of deepening is to reflect on the process of dialogue and shared enquiry in order to become more aware of it and to refine it. Awareness tools to support collaborative learning online showing who is talking to whom and how much and what sort of things they are saying could serve this function. The most powerful example I have seen is the filming of groups of children talking together and then showing this back to them to support a discussion about how they relate to each other and the impact that their behaviour has on group thinking.

3) Widening dialogic spaces

Widening the space of dialogue means roughly increasing the degree of difference between perspectives while maintaining the creative relationship. Widening can be done through the use of the Internet to engage in real dialogues about global issues. A good example of pedagogical use of the potential of the Internet to support dialogue across difference can be seen in the development education site: http://www.throughothereyes.org.uk/ where different groups of young people around the world provide their own accounts of what is important in their lives. Web quests offer one way of scaffolding dialogic encounters between voices. Email links between geographically distant groups are another.

An example of widening dialogic space

Inter-faith dialogue provides a very interesting model for dialogic education. This is because the aim of the 'learning' is clearly not to change one's mind or to persuade the other person and yet learning takes place. There are many reports from those who have participated in inter-faith dialogue of a sense of very worth-while progress in a direction of learning that they value. Since the Catholics do not learn to be Muslims nor the Muslims learn to be Catholics what form does this learning take?

Understanding the answer to this question is understanding the vertical or growth direction in dialogic education that I referred to in Chapter 3. The outcome of Interfaith dialogue is often described in terms of participants deepening their understanding of their own faith through engaging in a dialogue with those of other faiths. There is also a sense of greater awareness of, and respect for, others and otherness in general.

In the E-Bridges project primary children in schools in Leicester, UK were twinned with children in schools in East Sussex.[40] Each child was paired with 'an email friend of a contrasting religious and/or cultural background from the partner school' and they had timetabled exchanges weekly throughout the school year as well as some residential visits.

The aim was partly to counter fracturing of Leicester along racial, cultural and religious grounds. It was located within the Citizenship curriculum goal of 'under-standing and appreciating cultural and religious difference, thinking about the lives of other people with different values and customs, seeing things from others' points of view'. There were four stages of dialogue:

1   Introduction: In this stage the email partners got to know each other as people with particular hobbies, likes and dislikes, friends and family. Questions asked included: What do you like doing in your spare time? and What are you especially good at?
2   Sharing experiences: The children compared and contrasted their experiences of celebrations, special places and practices. The kind of questions explored at this stage were: Are there any times of year that are particularly special to you?, Why are they special? and How do you celebrate them?
3   Ethical debates: These included discussions around such questions as: Is it ever alright to kill a living creature? Do you think that human beings should eat meat? Could it ever be a good thing to use violence? If you had one message that could send to the whole of humankind what would it be?

4   Questions of faith: Questions have included: What do you think happens to
you when you die? Do you think someone who has been bad will go to hell?
Do you believe in angels. If not, why not, and if so, what are they for?

In face-to-face class or group discussions there is a danger of a few children
dominating. In email dialogue, all the children have an equal chance to make their
views known and all are required to think in order to respond. Though it may be
difficult to match the quick-fire pace of spoken dialogue in electronic communication, it does provide the benefit (particularly to younger dialogue partners)
of thinking time. As a child initiates an exchange, there is time to think carefully
about how to express views or frame questions. Children receiving emails have
opportunities to think carefully about what has been said and what their responses
might be before making their contributions to the discussions.

Resourcing the space of learning

Avatars, icons and other signs on the Internet could be seen as conceptual tools
but sometimes it is more fruitful to see them as voices augmenting a dialogue.
David Shaffer's epistemic games that I referred to in Chapter 5 offer young people
the chance to learn ways of seeing and thinking that are appropriate to different
professions. They do this by taking an Avatar form and role-playing a professional.
What kind of voices do such avatars represent? They are not specific individuals
but generalized bio-scientists or journalists. They are therefore super-addressee
voices representing the generalized other of a specific community. This use of
icons to incarnate super-addressee images so as to be able to interact with them
and even to become them, is a technique that goes back a long way in education
traditions in every major religion. It has considerable potential for Internet based
education.

Embodying the affective dimensions of dialogue

In Chapter 5, I described how some of the icons we designed for the Metafora
project to help children learn how to learn together were voices in this sense.
The attitude icons we designed to help them reflect upon the role of attitudes in
learning together were inspired by the success of Edward de Bono's six Thinking
Hats[41] but were independently derived from consideration of the affective dimensions of dialogic spaces.

To do this we built on the the UK social cognition in classrooms ('types of
talk') research tradition initiated by Douglas Barnes in the 1970s and continued
by Neil Mercer. Disputational and cumulative, names Mercer gave to types of
talk, seem to be fundamental intersubjective orientations, the tendency to say 'yes'
to everything or the tendency to say 'no'.[42] Exploratory talk, the kind of talk we
ended up teaching in classrooms, is more complex as it encourages challenges
and competition between ideas within the context of agreement or co-operation.

Using evidence from classrooms and Ron Carter's research on a large corpus of spoken talk I have argued that 'playfulness' is also a fundamental intersubjective orientation.[43]

1   First of all, the cumulative orientation is founded on empathy, understanding and being accountable to the other. This orientation lies behind a) openness to the other and to the new and communicative discourse that simply seeks to understand the other, b) ethical reasoning (responsibility for consequences), c) feeling talk, intuitive responses based on intuitions.
2   Secondly, the disputational orientation is found within dialogue combined with a more original communicative attitude to produce explicit reasoning seeking to critically analyse and select. Explicit reasoning subdivides into two types of dialogue, a) analysis focusing on the quality of evidence and b) generating counter arguments and finding fault.
3   Thirdly, the playful orientation reappears in dialogue as creativity in two forms, a) lateral thinking finding unusual analogies or connections and in combination with other orientations and tasks as b) fashioning original solutions to problems.
4   Finally, reflection within dialogue on the process of dialogue itself generates a secondary type of dialogue as 'dialogue about dialogue', often a role traditionally taken by moderators.

Interestingly these eight types of dialogue correspond loosely to all of the six Thinking Hats of Edward de Bono that have proven value in business and education. In addition they suggest an ethical orientation or concern with the consequences of actions, which is now generally acknowledged to be quite important in business and in science but was missed out by the more intuitive approach of de Bono. The other additional orientation suggested by this analysis is that of 'openness' which is the context and foundation for all the other types of dialogue.[44]

These types of dialogue can appear as 'roles' when an individual just uses one or other of the orientations, for instance when someone always 'nitpicks' or finds fault or comes up with wacky ideas. However they represent a range of types of dialogue characterized by orientations within dialogue, all of which have value in different tasks and in different stages of more complex tasks. Therefore they might be put forward as a repertoire of types of dialogue that need to be personally engaged with and appropriated if students are to learn to be expert at learning to learn together.

In the Metafora project, these eight intersubjective orientations within dialogues were implemented as icons with appropriate colours and images and used to help children and young people reflect on their Internet mediated learning together. As signs they are signs for voices or ways of thinking the world.

Dr Math

The use of superaddressee voices seems increasingly common in Internet based education. In South Africa school students who have text phones but no access to the Internet via computers are able to text Dr Math with their homework problems. Learners have access to a group of volunteer tutors who are online on computers and able to respond to their requests for advice. As far as the students are concerned they are interacting with 'Dr Math', the incarnation of Mathematics.[45]

Summary and conclusion

I began this chapter by rehearsing some of the arguments in the literature that the dominant communication technology in a culture has an impact on people's sense of self-identity and of citizenship. The way in which a dominant means of communication impacts on identity and citizenship depends on the ways in which it is used in context. However, the evidence is clear that communications technologies can serve to afford some ways of being and to constrain others.

This raises the question of what is it that the Internet, and related media, will afford and what is it that they will constrain? In contrast to print based forms of communication the Internet has the potential to support dialogic thinking, allowing many to participate in real-time enquiries. This dialogism is different from the original dialogism of small-scale oral societies. The key difference is that the Internet affords global dialogue without spatial location or necessary limits. I argued that this has the potential to afford forms of self-identity and citizenship characterized by openness to the other. I used Levinas to link the new dialogic self of the Internet Age to the idea of infinite responsibility. However, the Internet can be used in many ways. My rather optimistic vision of a dialogic self, responsive to others and to otherness, is not a necessary outcome of using the Internet, just one of the possibilities that it affords. The point of educational research is not simply to describe reality but to learn through changing reality. In the final section of this chapter I proposed a design framework for education for a global participatory democracy of the future. I gave some examples of how new communications technology and the Internet could be used as a medium for education drawing children into global dialogues.

8

EDUCATION INTO DIALOGUE

This chapter summarizes the main strands of the book and brings them together into an overall theory of dialogic education for the Internet Age. This theory augments existing approaches to dialogic education with the addition of an understanding of the dialogic relationship between figure and horizon which underlies new ways of learning with the Internet. Dialogic education has always been about drawing learners into dialogue. In the Internet Age dialogic education is about drawing the world into dialogue through turning the potential of the Internet to support an unbounded dialogic space into a reality.

Expanding dialogic theory

Unpacking and expanding the meaning of dialogic has been one of the central themes of this book. Dialogic began as adjective for dialogue referring to anything that had the form of a dialogue but since Bakhtin's way of using the term it has referred to a distinctive way of seeing and thinking the world. Dialogic as a technical term originates with the simple insight that the meaning of an utterance should not be read in isolation from its context in a dialogue.

It is hard to dispute that what most words mean depends upon the way in which they are used in a context. If we follow through all the implications of this simple insight it has the potential to unravel the fabric of one reality and leave us in another. The meaning of an utterance does not only need to be read in relation to utterances that precede it and utterances that succeed it but also in relation to the cultural and historical context of the dialogue. We cannot fix the meaning of any utterance because the dialogue is ongoing since another interpretation of what was said is always possible. This same dialogic logic applies to all signs in so far as they can be read as either a response to a question or a kind of call requiring a response. And just as we can never fix the final meaning of an utterance in a dialogue so we can never fix the meaning of the context and make it stable and objective since what is relevant context depends on the focus of attention and forms around that focus like a horizon that appears to have limits for the observer but actually is unbounded.

If we take these points seriously they must move us from the relatively simple and closed monological view of the world assumed by print-based school-systems everywhere, into a more complex and open-ended dialogical view of the world. The advent of the Internet is leading to experiences which no longer make sense in the old monological world and are driving a shift to a new dialogical world.

Previous accounts of dialogic education from Socrates through to Robin Alexander, have been very influenced by the image of face to face dialogue. In this book I have expanded dialogic theory in ways that respond to the experience of dialogic learning with the Internet. In the next four sub-sections I describe four expansions of dialogic education theory to include the notion of learning as expanding dialogic space, the importance of dialogue with the Infinite Other as well as with specific others, the way in which dialogue between an inside perspective and outside horizon drives dialogic learning and finally insights from neuroscience on the multi-modal nature of dialogic relations and how these relate to consciousness.

Learning as expanding dialogic space

Dialogic theory connects with classroom pedagogy through the concept of dialogic space. The first step in understanding dialogic space is to note that dialogues have an outside, this might be people talking in physical space, and an inside, the world of meaning that they share inside the dialogue. In physical space two objects cannot occupy the same position. In dialogic space there is an overlapping of perspectives in which selves interpenetrate in order to be able to share and persuade. If there were not a space in which selves to some extent surrendered their autonomy and merged with others then education would not be possible because education involves this surrender and the possibility of change that results from it.

Vygotsky's concept of a 'Zone of Proximal Development' has been read by many as a dialogic space type of concept because it requires the mutual attunement of teacher and student. For learning to occur in the 'zone' the teacher has to be able to take on the perspective of the student to some extent and the student has to be able to take on the perspective of the teacher to some extent. Any such dialogue between perspectives must generate a shared space of possible perspectives including the original perspective of the teacher, let us call this, T1, and the initial perspective of the student, let us call this S1, and then all the possible perspectives of their negotiation in which they perhaps approximate each other's perspectives but never quite achieve them, T2, T3, Tn and so on as well as S2, S3, Sn and so on.

Vygotsky presented the ZPD as a kind of pedagogical tool to facilitate the grafting of new shoots onto the existing vine of the culture represented by the teacher. Whatever the steps of negotiation, the end result of the ZPD was to be that Sn = T1 or that the student ended up learning from the teacher and sharing their perspective and not the other way around.

My concern in this book has not been to criticize the ZPD but to develop it. My argument has been that the space of possible perspectives that opens up when two people meet has properties that make it difficult to simply use as a tool. For a start the kind of learning that goes on is not only one way. The teacher has to learn about the student's point of view in order to persuade the student to take on the teacher's point of view. This implies at the very least learning in the sense of an expanded awareness of possible points of view. What is being learnt in such expansion of awareness of possible perspectives is the dialogic space itself rather than a position within that space.

The clearest example of people learning dialogic space itself rather than positions within dialogic space occurs in interfaith dialogue groups. There are many such groups and a great deal has been written about them.[1] Most of these accounts stress that learning occurs. This learning is not the changing of faith positions, the Catholics remain Catholics and the Muslims remain Muslims and so on as one would expect. If a researcher were to give participants a questionnaire about their religious beliefs before interfaith dialogue sessions and again at the end of a series of sessions there would be little if any change. And yet many report a profound deepening of their understanding of their own faith as well as a widening of their appreciation and understanding of other faith positions. Something is being learnt through interfaith dialogue but what it is that is being learnt cannot be expressed easily in terms of positions or content or even skills. In this kind of education dialogic space is not only the means of education but also one of the most important ends or goals of education.

The learning that occurs through interfaith dialogue can perhaps only be understood as the widening and the deepening of a dialogic space. This space is not just a property of the group when they are sitting together but it is also something that each individual can take away with them. This property of dialogic space as being both individual and collective is perhaps difficult to make sense of within a monological and physicalist way of thinking. But of course dialogues are always both individual and social and can never be either one or the other. In fact selves are not physical entities but only exist within dialogues in which they are always in relation to others and also always in relation, whether they are aware of this or not, with the ultimate horizon of otherness for them which I am referring to as the Infinite Other. This idea that one of the goals of education should be the widening and deepening of dialogic space is perhaps the most distinctive contribution of dialogic education theory.

Interfaith dialogue is one kind of education that we need for the Internet Age. This should be Internet mediated dialogue that is not only for those signed up to explicit faith positions but for everyone to discuss and explore the sources of meaning and value in our lives so that we can open, widen and deepen a collective unbounded dialogic space. However interfaith dialogue of this kind was not the main focus of this book. Expanding dialogic space is also useful for understanding education into thinking and creativity. In Chapter 4, 'Educating creativity', I argued that the best way to understand teaching for creative thinking is in terms of teaching dialogic space. This is because the dialogic space that opens up between different perspectives held together in the tension of a dialogue is precisely the space of 'possibility thinking' that needs to be engaged if creativity is to be increased.[2]

It is easy to experience dialogic space. It is even possible to feel the space opening, widening, deepening, and closing down; each shift often a direct consequence of things that people say and the way that they say them. Dialogic space is a useful practical concept for pedagogy. However, it can be quite hard to understand what kind of a thing dialogic space is in theory. On the inside, I think that all dialogues are united by the singular opening of the dialogic gap. This opening on the inside of dialogues means that all dialogues have the potential for making new meaning. On the other hand every actual dialogue is different and bounded by a context in which some things are up for dialogue and others not. This apparent combination of unity and difference is quite paradoxical.

One way to help understand this paradox might be to look at spaces were people are in dialogue on the Internet. Whereas once upon a time we could imagine dialogues as bounded by physical spaces and times, this is less obvious on the Internet. Each dialogue is different and many have a specific purpose and yet they all interconnect as they can all be found by a search engine and linked to from other dialogues with a click or two. The Internet therefore supports both a multiplicity of dialogues and the potential for a single unbounded dialogic space. The combination of unity and difference on the Internet mirrors on the outside, the inner combination of unity and difference of all actual dialogues.

While all dialogue has always had this potential for infinite openness at its heart, contexts and modes of communication have managed to limit it and to disguise it. Oracy tends to afford dialogic thinking but always in contexts bounded by space and time. Writing and print overcame the spatial and temporal limitations of oracy to support an emergent dialogue of humanity. However, the one-to-many nature of print has made it prey to monologic authority relations or what Foucault has aptly termed 'regimes of truth'.[3] To identify with the space of the Internet, or to identify with the space of dialogue, is not to identify with any image of a bounded thing. This space cannot be measured in terms of a finite totality of fibre-optic cables and servers or a finite totality of voices in dialogue represented perhaps by physical bodies or by usernames and computers addresses. To paraphrase Nicholas of Cusa's definition of God, the Internet is a sphere whose centre is everywhere and whose circumference is nowhere.[4]

It follows that to identify with dialogue on the Internet is the undermining of all bounded identifications and so best understood as a form of openness rather than as a closed identity. But is it possible to have an identity with no boundary defined only by openness? Perhaps this is not so much a possible identity as a perpetual orientation towards an impossible identity? Some things that are real and important are hard to describe clearly. I think that this is the case with the concept of a dialogic identity. The best answer here, as elsewhere, might be to try it and not just to talk about it. Another way of putting this is that sometimes you just have to 'suck it and see'.

The Infinite Other

Bakhtin argued that a word spoken in a dialogue between two people has at least two meanings. Each person will inevitably interpret the word differently because of the different horizons of context that they bring to bear. In Chapter 3 I argued that we need to expand this basic notion that dialogicality implies at least two voices in dialogue together to realize that dialogicality always implies an infinite number of voices. My argument was one of infinite regress. To observe two voices in dialogue implies a third position or the witness or superaddressee. For example, if I am aware that I am talking to you then that awareness itself becomes a third voice who listens to the words to see if they make sense and I might find that my words are addressed as much to this witness as they are to you. But then if I try to pin down the witness and call it something like 'the voice of reason' and characterize it in some way in order to engage in dialogue with it, a new third voice or witness position necessarily arises out of that new dialogue.

This infinite regress is more than just word play or an intellectual game. George Herbert Mead convincingly argued that when learning to reason, a child enters into a relationship with someone Mead called the Generalized Other. The Generalized Other embodies the norms of good reasoning in a community.[5] The child cannot tell just from their interlocutor if their reasoning is good or bad but has to assess it in relation to the Generalized Other to whom they are accountable. Each community will have its own Generalized Other. The community of physicists for instance will have a different set of rules of good thinking from the community of dramatists. If you want to know if your new quantum theory is sensible you need to be able to incarnate the Generalized Other of the physicists community and not that of the dramatists. But what if our community is wrong? What if you are growing up in Nazi Germany and your Generalized Other who incarnates good thinking is always blond and blue-eyed? Or what if you suspect that the norms of scientific method are all wrong?

Good thinking does not just mean thinking with the norms of your community. Good thinking also means questioning those norms. This is why we need a concept of the Infinite Other that goes beyond the Generalized Other. The Infinite Other is the voice that does not fit into the system, the voice of the outside.

Since the Infinite Other is a process of questioning it might seem odd to describe this as a voice in a dialogue or to refer to it in the singular. In fact of course it is not really singular but infinite. We might equally refer to the infinite others as to the Infinite Other. The singularity here is perhaps like that of a horizon, more apparent than real. Odd as it may sound it is possible to feel called outwards by a horizon just as you can feel situated within a horizon as if the horizon was looking at you and locating you just as you are looking out at it.[6]

To have properties such as being singular or plural or up or down or male or female you have to be located inside a meaning system or conceptual space. The idea of the Infinite Other, as articulated by Levinas, is neither singular nor plural any more than it is male or female because it is the idea of the outside of the meaning system. However, in contrast to an abstract rationalist notion of the outside of a meaning system, this outside is not simply a nothing but it is a force that has an impact inside the meaning system. Specifically it can call to us as if it had a voice and we can enter into relationship with it albeit a rather one-sided relationship.[7] In a sense this call is always an undermining of the system and always a call to radical openness.

The chiasm between inside and outside

Expanding Bakhtin's understanding of dialogic with Levinas's idea of the Infinite Other is an important addition that turns out to be very significant for rethinking education into 'rationality'. This was the argument of Chapter 3 in which I put forward a new theory of cognitive development based on the motivating call of specific others, generalized others and the Infinite Other. For understanding education into creativity, which was the focus of Chapter 4, it proved useful to expand Bakhtin's dialogic with Merleau-Ponty's idea of the chiasm.

Analysing a simple example of creative thinking in the classroom, how a group of children came up with the solution to a Raven's reasoning test, indicated that creative thinking in dialogues was not always verbal but involved embodied thinking and perceptual thinking. Merleau-Ponty's chiasm is the idea of the mutual envelopment of an inside perspective (the sentient) and an outside perspective (the sensed) in perception. This is a dialogic idea that can help us to expand our understanding of what is actually happening in dialogues. Although dialogues often appear to be between two people, say me and my friend, in fact they are also always a dialogue between an inside perspective and an outside perspective.

In any dialogue the other or addressee appears as an outside perspective that includes me within it even as I see them within my field of vision. To enter into dialogue, even pantomiming physical dialogue, requires that I see myself from their perspective and that they see themselves from mine. In other words the dialogic relation is a chiasmic relation in Merleau-Ponty's terms. It is never just two people in dialogue it is always also an inside perspective and an outside perspective held together in dialogic tension.

Bringing in Merleau-Ponty's chiasm idea proved useful to understanding what creativity is and where it comes from. Merleau-Ponty's phenomenological account of how the unit of perceptual meaning is a chiasm between figure and ground explains why every part of the world can become a total part that reflects back upon and signifies the whole. In other words the chiasm in each act of awareness between a foreground focus and an unbounded background world explains the universal metaphoricity of perceptual meaning that is the ground of creativity.

Social creativity, creativity defined as not only surprising and original but also as useful and valued, is a combination of two kinds of thinking. On the one hand verbal dialogues set agendas, direct consciousness to problems and apply criteria to determine when those problems are solved. On the other hand the metaphorical mind generates solutions below the threshold of self-consciousness. Creativity can be understood as requiring the chiasm of both conscious and unconscious minds. This manifests in the experience of 'flow' or linked chains of 'Aha!' insights where the difference between inside and outside perspectives becomes blurred and it feels as if we are pulled by the world just as much as we are pushing the world. In other words creativity is a dialogue between the so-called conscious and unconscious minds understanding that the unconscious mind is collective as well as individual.

The neuroscience of consciousness

Christine Howe found that verbal dialogue about issues in science did not help students understand them any better at the time of the dialogue but did help them understand them better than control groups when tested two weeks later.[8] This finding illustrates why dialogic education needs to take brain processes into account as well as social processes. The 'delayed learning from dialogues' effect is best explained by the well-attested phenomenon of incubation whereby ideas mature slowly in the 'unconscious' background of the mind before popping into the foreground in 'Aha' experiences. In Howe's experiments it seems that dialogues about science issues raised the students' consciousness of these issues and led them to ask questions. These questions then triggered slower generative processes that eventually provided responses to those questions and increased their understanding. Howe's finding supports the importance of dialogue in education but tells us that dialogic theory has to be extended to account for processes that cannot all be seen and heard in the immediate context of a face-to-face dialogue.

Neuroscience-based theories of how conscious thinking functions remain speculative but currently appear to fit quite well with the expanded dialogic theory of creative thinking as a chiasm between conscious and unconscious minds that I outlined above. The Global Workspace Theory (GWT) of consciousness put forward by Baars, which has gained wide support, uses a theatre metaphor.[9] This model implies two levels of mind, a background audience of many neural processes murmuring away together in the dark and a foreground stage occasionally broadcasting to that audience. A neural process becomes conscious when it attains enough neural links to move from background to foreground. At this point the amount of electrical energy associated with the process increases five-fold indicating that it is no longer a background murmuring kind of process but is now being broadcast to large areas of the brain. The attentional blink effect, whereby we are not able to be aware of even a strong stimulus for a period of time when another stimulus occupies awareness, provides supporting evidence for GWT.

The attentional blink effect was found using stimulation with visual images on a screen. A slower attentional blink type effect has been found with studies of creative problem solving. This is burst of alpha band electrical activity just before problems are solved in an 'Aha' moment.[10] Alpha-band activity is associated with states of relaxation. The researchers involved refer to this as a 'brain blink' and speculate that it indicates turning the gaze inwards away from more powerful external visual stimuli in order to allow the less strongly broadcast signal of the emerging insight take to the stage.

Kant's notion of the transcendental, referring to things that are precondition of experience rather than objects of experience, can help us understand why an aspect of creative thinking can never be fully observed or measured. The act of conscious attention that produces a figure on a ground perception implies a background process that is not visible. In a sense, when things move from being at the background of the mind to the centre stage they move from the transcendental sphere to the empirical sphere. Dehaene and other neuroscientists often appear very naïve about this and imagine that the mental mechanisms that they are discovering are all physical and potentially observable operations of the empirical brain. However any image they may have of mechanisms, neurons, and empirical brains are all figure on ground constructions produced by a movement of consciousness that we only know through reconstructions after the event.

GWT seems plausible to many expert commentators but it is also limited as an explanation of consciousness since it does not account for where the intention to pay attention to something comes from in the first place. The self is not reducible to the focus of attention since it is the agent which often decides beforehand where to focus the attention. Merleau-Ponty's account, based on phenomenology, of the fundamental unit of consciousness as a figure on a ground in a chiasmic relation, is relevant for understanding the real location and nature of consciousness. Consciousness is not only the lit-up stage at the centre of the theatre but includes the audience. Consciousness is not to be found on one side or the other but in the dynamic relationship between these two halves. The attentional blink effect provides empirical evidence of Merleau-Ponty's claim that there is a gap between the foreground of experience and the background. His claim was that it is because of this gap, and the reversibility of perspectives around this gap which serves as a kind of hinge, that we are able to see in the first place and, above all, to make sense of what we see.

Discussion of consciousness has often been vitiated by a lack of clear definition. Sentience, or the awareness that any organism seems to have of its environment, is the first kind of consciousness.[11] It supports metaphorical generative bottom–up thinking but has no capacity to plan or to think in an intentional way. We can call this consciousness 1. Reflective awareness or consciousness of being conscious comes in through intersubjectivity. This is the other on the inside. It is found in the form of paying attention and supports planning and analytical thinking. We can call this consciousness 2. Consciousness understood as the dialogue uniting consciousness 1 and consciousness 2 we can call consciousness 3. This is actually what we mean by terms such as 'thinking' or by terms such as 'intelligence' especially creative thinking and creative intelligence.

The so-called 'unconscious' is not simply the opposite of consciousness. There is a great deal that we know even though we do not know that we know it. Thinking has to operate not only with what can be grasped and pinned down but also with trust and with faith in unknown interlocutors. This is how we think individually when we raise problems and then decide to 'sleep on them', trusting that our mind will solve them overnight. This is also how we think when we cast out questions on the Internet and wait for a response. Consciousness cannot be limited to the little circle of light that seems to be cast around the first person perspective. This apparent circle of light is just an effect of a larger dialogic flow or circuit uniting it to the darkness of the unbounded background horizon.

Once we have understood consciousness to be the whole flow uniting the visible foreground (empirical) with the invisible background (transcendental) we can see that the expansion of consciousness is not about expanding the little circle of light but is about increasing our capacity to listen to and to learn from the voices that speak to us from beyond and behind that circle of light. Becoming more creative is about increasing trust in the background voices because those voices become more reliable, it is not about increasing self-conscious control.

Phylogeny and ontogeny of conscious thought

In Chaper 4 I investigated how a creative insight arose, tracing back its route of origin at three levels: a) micro-genetically, in terms of the talk of the children and the background neural activity, b) ontogentically looking at the birth of creative and conscious thinking in early childhood and c) phylogenetically, exploring new theories of how consciousness arose historically and is still developing in symbiosis with communications technology.

In evolution new properties usually have to have a function in order to survive. The main function of consciousness 2 or self-conscious paying attention to things appears to be educational. Broadcasting a problem or issue or just a bit of experience brings extra resources to bear trying to make sense of it through multimodal pattern matching and the generation of multiple alternative perspectives or ways of seeing it.

Donald speculates that our capacity to pay attention to things at will evolved as a mechanism to speed up learning when life became so complex for our ape ancestors that relying on automatic 'instinctive' brain processes was no longer sufficient. There is some empirical archeological evidence to support his speculation that the trigger for the step up in the type of consciousness was an increase in group size leading to greater social complexity.[12]

Studies of the ontogeny of consciousness 2 also suggest that it begins as a social effect and only later becomes an apparently individual property. Children are first drawn to pay attention by others who point things out to them. Pointing things out is the most fundamental form of teaching. The evidence supports Vygotsky's claim that learning 'higher mental functions' like thinking, moves from the social plane to the individual plane. It is only after first having things pointed out to them that children learn to point things out for themselves.

The finding of this investigation into the origin and nature of creative thought is that it is dialogic. The dialogic origin and nature of creative thinking can be seen when we look at this emerging moment by moment, emerging in the life of the individual and also at how it has emerged in the life of the species. This analysis is meant as a corrective not only to the individualism of classic cognitive psychology but also to the social behaviourism that has been put forward as an alternative under the guise of situated learning theory and some forms of socio-cultural theory. To say that thinking is dialogic is to say that it is neither individual nor social but both and more because it is rooted in a dialogic space that is not reducible to any kind of physical space nor to any externally definable cultural practice.

Collective thinking and technology

All of this theory helping us to rethink what we mean by thinking is necessary to understand how technology supports collective thinking and so how collective thinking is changing as we move into the Internet Age. Collective thinking is possible because thinking is not simply a product of the foreground mind but of the dialogic chiasm between foreground and background minds described above. Individual thinking is a flow uniting questions and answers in a dialogue where the answers do not only come from specific voices but from the background field as a whole.

Although individual thinkers always experience themselves as isolated first person perspectives, actually they are voices participating in a larger dialogue. Collective thinking is possible because we share worlds with others and orient ourselves together within those worlds. This is another way of saying that while conscious thinking appears to be isolated from others the background sentient field within which such consciousness operates is a field that is shared with others or at least overlapping in the way that horizons overlap.

Communications technology, a sign painted on a cave wall for example, exists within the phenomenal field that is part of the shared mind of the communication community using the technology. The sharing of thinking through embodying it in a sign in this way leads to an expanded shared background of thinking. Turning a feature of the physical environment into a sign moves it into the shared cultural working memory that is dialogic space. This shared background of thinking is then implicated behind every conscious individual foreground act of thinking.

In oral cultures shared thinking and shared sense of self-as-thinker was inevitably limited to the face-to-face dialogue community. All might be able to see the sign on the cave wall but only those initiated into the dialogue of the community could use it as a voice to think with. One result of this was internal dialogic understanding within thousands of small language groups each referring to themselves as 'the people' or 'humanity'. This produced dialogic internal ethical codes coupled with endemic warfare between dialogue-groups.

Writing things down brought the possibility of sharing beyond the community of those in face-to-face contact. Although Oakeshott refers to the 'conversation of mankind' beginning in the 'primeval forests' this could only become a global dialogue after thoughts and feeling were written down in a form that could be shared. The shared dialogue of culture was made possible by writing but depended on a symbiosis between the technology of writing and cultural practices of education. Collective thinking was limited by induction into reading and writing and the shared dialogue depended on everyone reading the same books.

The technology of writing in conjunction with education has tremendous affordances for shared thinking in relation to oracy alone but it also has some limitations. One of these limitations is the way in which print-capitalism led to and continues to reinforce the creation of an imagined community of those who share the same national language. This print-based imagined community in conjunction with national mass education has led to and continues to sustain shared dialogues within nations and warfare between nations.

The effect of print in supporting nationalism pointed to by Anderson[13] is still very much a living problem for education and can be seen especially in debates about what books children have to read in their history classes. In 2005, for example, there were anti-Japanese demonstrations in China and Korea sparked by the content of a new history book for use in the secondary curriculum in Japan. A second very similar effect of writing is the creation of shared mutually incompatible religious identities based around different books treated as authoritative. This again tends to lead to warfare between print-based imagined communities. The limitation of print which I most focused upon in Chapter 1 and Chapter 5 of this book is related to this problem but it is more general. This is the alienation from meaning which comes from a misguided monologic interpretation of truth that arises from print-based education systems. The main problem of print can be simply summed up as tending to locate meaning and truth over there within books on the shelf of the library rather than right here in the moment where meaning and truth arise within relationships.

The obvious potential danger of monologism, arising from the technology of writing, was flagged up by Socrates at the very dawn of writing in Europe. He pointed out that instead of meaning being experienced as a property of living dialogue between voices it was now being seen as something that one could find written down in a scroll. Mass education systems have tended to impose this monological misunderstanding of meaning. Modernity can be defined by the way in which reasoning came to be seen as a matter of propositions in proofs that were either right or wrong rather than as voices in dialogue together.

Print-based education and scientism

Scientism is significant to the argument of this book because it is often the bottom line supporting the continuing dominance of monologic thinking. Scientism is a pejorative term for the widespread ideology that there is only one true reality, the tangible physical or material reality studied by the physical sciences, and only one true method to ascertain what is true, the 'scientific method' usually defined as experimental method. This world view refers for its authoritative statements to written laws such as 'the laws of physics' or the 'laws of nature' found in books, usually school text books.

The living dialogue of real science has long since discovered that the visible and tangible physical world we inhabit is an always fallible joint construction. Neils Bohr, the originator of quantum physics, was quite clear that the physical world as we perceive it is not a reality in itself but a construction from the way in which we interact with reality.[14] This was 100 years ago so why does scientism persist? *Because* it is taught in school science. This teaching takes the form of the transmission of *true* representations of reality in the written form of the science text books, received *from* the distant high priests of science. Apart from being a serious misrepresentation *of things* this scientistic approach to teaching science as if it was a collection of facts *rather than* an open enquiry is no longer effective in the Internet Age as I explained in *Chapter* 6.

It is not true, as scientism tends to *maintain* that we are each imprisoned in separate physical bodies determined in our actions *by laws* of nature. This is ironic as real science is a product of global dialogue. *Consciousness* is a part of nature. In globally connecting many spaces and many times the *Internet is* building on a potential that has always already existed. The real life message that *contemporary* physics tends towards was nicely summed up by Einstein in a letter to a friend *who* had recently lost his son:

> A human being is a part of the whole, called by us 'Universe', a part limited in time and space. He experiences himself, his thoughts and feelings as something separated from the rest — a kind of optical delusion of his consciousness. The striving to free oneself from this delusion is the one issue of true religion. Not to nourish the delusion but to try to overcome it is the way to reach the attainable measure of peace of mind.[15]

The most recent physics and mathematics points to the extent to which everything is already intertwined and intertangled. That includes issues of consciousness and matter, inside and outside, as I argued in Chapter 4. It follows that no longer teaching scientism but teaching engagement in real science is necessary if we are to realize the potential of the Internet Age to support a more effective collective consciousness.

Internet mediated thinking

Dialogic thinking is never purely individual because the meaning is emergent between voices in relationship. However there is always what Linell refers to as a double dialogic relation between each voice and its context.[16] Thinking is never only a chain of questions and answers between discrete voices but always also a chain of questions and answers between a unique voice and its cultural context. The cultural context is not a fixed world of stable things but more like a horizon cast by a gaze.

With previous dominant modes of communication, oracy and literacy, these contexts could be imagined as bounded and people could easily imagine that their thinking was limited to their community. The voice of the cultural context entered into dialogues imagined as a Generalized Other. With the Internet it is no longer possible to draw discrete boundaries about bits of culture and close them off from dialogic space. The self-as-thinker can no longer be a circumscribed identity but becomes, at least potentially, less of an identity and more of an openness.

Of course many thinking tasks require bounded dialogic spaces with rules as to what counts as relevant context, what voices can speak, and what sort of things they are allowed to say. But none of these bounded dialogues and bounded spaces can any longer claim to be a master space. All now have to participate in a larger open and unbounded space of dialogue in which they are subject to being called into question from other perspectives in an infinite process that cannot be closed down.

The ideal of an open unbounded dialogic space has always haunted dialogues occurring in apparently bounded spaces. Bakhtin referred to it as 'Great Time', the chronotope (space-time) in which all voices could dialogue together. The Internet has begun to give some practical flesh to that haunting ideal.

The pedagogical affordances of the Internet

Although print has sustained living global dialogues in the sciences and the arts, it has an affordance for the representation of reality and this affordance has been taken up and amplified by education systems. Although print can be used to support community dialogue through pamphlets and local newspapers it has an affordance for the authoritative voice and again this affordance has been taken up and amplified by education systems. The Internet was designed precisely as a way of supporting multiple voices and refusing the authority of any one single voice. Instead of representing the views of others it is possible to relate directly to them, see their videos and ask questions on their Facebook page. The Internet has an affordance for participation in dialogue and the creative anarchic proliferation of voices which print does not have. Through this it has an affordance for supporting peer-to-peer learning networks that print does not have.

Dialogic theories of education and approaches to education have been articulated before the advent of the Internet. While dialogic education, implicit or explicitly theorized, has had a big impact in some contexts these contexts have normally been face-to-face, perhaps the tutorial system at some universities, or adult education in evening classes or small group work in classrooms. Oracy affords dialogic pedagogy but it is inevitably limited in scope by its physical situation. Mass education continues to be based on the logic of print and continues to provide the framework within which small outbreaks of dialogic education are sometimes tolerated.

Theories of education articulated in the context of face-to-face oracy can be transferred to education for the Internet Age to some extent. Dialogic education approaches that promote learning through asking good questions in small groups in classrooms are an important part of the education that is needed.

However the affordances of the Internet mean that we can no longer rely on theories of education that originated with oral dialogue. The Internet can afford small group learning at a distance but it also affords a dialogic form of education that is quite new: mass peer-to-peer learning. To understand how this kind of learning works we need to expand dialogic theory from dialogue in groups and induction into bounded 'communities of practice' to understanding learning in unbounded communities.

The way in which the Internet supports collective education is remarkably similar to the functional architecture proposed as a model of how consciousness works in the embodied mind. Global Workspace Theory proposes that we think of the embodied mind as a vast number of voices in dialogue together only a few of which ever rise above the general background murmur to broadcast to the whole arena because they are selected as having something interesting to say. One evolutionary function of this collective broadcasting mechanism seems to be to motivate extra resources to solving problems that cannot be solved by automatic processes. Learning with the Internet involves a similar chiasm between a vast field of voices and resources and a central focus of attention.

At the simplest level a search on the Internet using a search engine such as Google asks a question and receives multiple answers based on pattern matching which might or might not lead to a refinement of the question or to a rephrasing and even a rethinking of the question. The resulting dialogue is a chain of questions and answers but this dialogue is not between two voices but between a central project or question and a background field.

Nicholas Carr argued that such searching is superficial because it off-loads the business of memory onto the Internet in a way that is dangerous for slow long-term creativity.[17] In embodied minds (by which I mean brains viewed from the inside) the response to questions does not take the form of instant pattern matching but can be generative and slow. Neurons seem to join together to fashion complex responses in competition with other groups of neurons until one solution is selected and popped up into the field of consciousness as a response to the question.

However, in refutation of Carr's argument, precisely this kind of creative education through chains of question and response can also be seen spontaneously emerging on the Internet. In many peer-to-peer support communities members work hard to construct good responses to questions sometime calling on the expertise of other members while doing so. Technical support forums and medical condition support forums work by mobilizing a large anonymous community to respond to questions and to support individual members with problems. This is also how successful intentionally designed educational communities like 'Scratch' work to induct young people into peer-to-peer learning dialogues. Some of the same longer term creative learning effects can be seen in the new Massive Open Online Courses (MOOCs) being run by Stanford and spin-off companies. In such courses resources which contribute to the course learning are generated by the members of courses.

Education for the Internet Age

The Internet's ready affordance for informal education puts the existing education system into question. How should we teach? What should we teach? Why should we teach? Paradoxically perhaps the answer to all these questions might be a version of the challenge, that is to say: 'education into dialogue'.

In Chapter 2 I offered a critical literature review of dialogic education approaches and theories and outlined a preliminary dialogic theory of education. In each of the chapters that followed I have applied and augmented this theory. In Chapter 3 I added the importance of dialogue with the Infinite Other implicit in every dialogue as a dialogic way of understanding how we can educate into reason and rationality. In Chapter 4 I added the importance of understanding the inside-outside dialogic relation (or chiasm). This augmentation was required for understanding creativity and the role of the perceptual body/world in creative thinking. I also introduced the essentially dialogic nature of consciousness through a review of some recent neuroscience research. Chapter 5 examined the first education technology to argue that in dialogism signs are no longer just tools for thinking but become voices in dialogic relation with other voices. This focus on signs as voices helps in the design of supports for widening and deepening and resourcing dialogic spaces on the Internet. Chapter 6 looked at the dialogic nature of science and how we could structure induction into science dialogues. Chapter 7 added the global dimension of thinking supported by the Internet and the role of education in preparing the way for the democracy that is to come. The implication of this chapter is that the mind is fractal and can be found as much in Internet mediated thinking as in small group orally mediated thinking and individual neuro-system mediated thinking. Finally, in this concluding chapter, Chapter 8, some of the new features and implications of the theory of dialogic education for the Internet Age that has emerged from the various investigations in the rest of the book, have been summarized and made more explicit.

What should we teach?

The Internet has the potential to become an unbounded dialogic space supporting global creative intelligence. One aim of education in the Internet Age should be to realize this potential through opening, widening, and deepening dialogic space(s). In Chapters 3 and 4, I illustrated ways in which opening, widening and deepening dialogic spaces in classrooms can be an effective way of teaching for creative thinking both at the individual level and at the group level. In Chapters 5, 6 and 7, I offered illustrations of ways in which this same approach to teaching for creative thinking could be expanded to larger groups mediated by the internet.

Another way of answering the question: 'What should we teach?' that follows from a dialogic theory of education for the Internet Age is to say that we should teach for participation in educational dialogue. An educational dialogue is any dialogue in which participants are learning and teaching each other. This implies teaching how to be an effective teacher as well as an effective learner.

In Chapter 5, I introduced the complex competence of learning how to learn together with others using the Internet (L2L2). L2L2 combines knowing how to structure shared inquiries in different subject areas with knowing how to work effectively with others, knowing how to engage, how to listen, when to be creative, when to be analytical etc. L2L2 is what is needed to prepare for working in interdisciplinary teams mediated by Internet tools to solve problems and build understanding in any and every area of work and life.

Dialogic education theory tends to emphasize progress by augmentation rather than by supersession. Teaching L2L2 is meant to augment rather than replace other existing educational goals for as long as existing educational goals are needed. Of course we also need to teach children how to read, write, and use mathematical symbols. But it should be recognized that these are historically contingent technologies that may not last forever. These kinds of skills and others like them need to taught as early and as effectively as possible. But in teaching discrete skills we should not forget that we are teaching them to enable thoughtful engagement in dialogue and not as ends in themselves. The so-called 4 Cs of the 21st Century Skills movement, collaboration, critical thinking, communication and creativity, are all crucial components of the more complex competence of L2L2.

Approaches that focus on teaching oral dialogue like 'Thinking Together' and Philosophy for Children have proved effective in teaching critical thinking, creative thinking, collaboration, and communication from nursery age onward. In such approaches the role of the teacher is crucial but not as a content transmitter but as a guide to the thinking together and learning to learn together process. The aim of L2L2 is that all learn how to facilitate their own learning and moderate the learning dialogues that they become involved in.

In Chapter 5, I described an alternative Internet-based education model that seems to be emerging. This is one of teaching basic communication skills and learning competences as early as possible followed by the opening of multiple trajectories of learning in which students can learn for themselves together with others. This possible new approach to education was illustrated by the thousands of Community Learning Centres in Mexico (Centros Comunitarios de Apprendizaje) where there are computers, access to Internet educational resources, and a learning guide. But to be able to take advantage of this emerging model of education skills and competences such as L2L2 need to be taught.

How should we teach?

Just as you cannot teach swimming without diving into the water, you cannot teach dialogue without engaging in dialogue. Subjects like Religious Education and Citizenship could be replaced by a new educational version of social-networking in which people all over the world share and discuss that which is of most meaning in their lives. To be able to do this constructively preparation is needed which is why teaching the complex competence of L2L2 is so important.

Chapter 6 gave detailed suggestions on how to structure a dialogic approach to teaching in a subject area within a school. The chapter was about science but is broadly relevant for any knowledge-rich subject area. The shift from print based educational thinking to Internet-based educational thinking involves a shift from subject divisions to interdisciplinary project based education. This is because the learning comes as a response to questions and it is not possible to determine in advance where that response will come from. I gave an example at the end of Chapter 6 of education through trying to respond to a real challenge, the pollution of the river Segre. Like any real world challenge based learning the investigation conducted by the students had to stray over disciplinary lines, combining chemistry, biology, physics, economic and social anthropology amongst other disciplines.

Outside of traditional school contexts the pedagogy of MOOCs is developing fast. This uses peer assessment and student generated resources along with more traditional computer-feedback devices. Although this approach is currently only being used for Higher Education there is no intrinsic reason why the same method could not be effective for education at every level.

How we should teach should be subject to the findings of continuous design-based research in which teachers play a central role. Dialogic theory of education for the Internet Age has arisen from practice to provide an orienting framework for more detailed practice-based research. If this research suggests that the most effective way to teach reading is through phonics then of course we should use phonics or whatever technique works best. Using effective techniques to teach skills does not take away from the bigger picture of teaching through engagement in motivating relationships and dialogues. The dialogic education principle is to first engage learners in the dialogic relationships that draw them out and motivate them and then remediate with the detailed skills that they need to participate more completely.

Dialogic education is potentially just as conservative as it is progressive because dialogue only progresses by listening to and building on from the voices of the past. Fortunately the voices of the past are increasingly found in accessible form on the Internet and can be consulted when needed. The depth of the engagement depends on the needs of the project. If key concepts are relevant to understanding and participating in current dialogues then they have to be taught. The account of dialogic mastery based learning in Chapter 6 gave a suggestion about how to do this in a practical way while incorporating the teaching into the larger dialogic approach.

The kind of education that the Internet supports is contingently responsive to challenges in the context of a vast background of resources and voices. This does not mean that the learning needs to be superficial, it just means that it always needs to be relevant to an issue of current concern.

Why should we teach like this?

It is common to say that in order to thrive in the new knowledge economy children will need these dialogic 'learning to learn together' type skills. That is perfectly true but it is reactive. The more proactive response to the question of why we should teach dialogic orientations is that education has a crucial role to play in bringing about a better future. The Internet affords the vision of a future global democracy – the democracy that is to come – but this vision will not draw closer to reality without education.

Unless students are open-minded and critical and responsive they cannot learn from participation in the Internet. Unless people are able to engage effectively in learning to learn together on the Internet we will not be able to confront the many global challenges that face us. In Chapter 7, Educating the planet, I presented arguments that suggest that education into dialogue as an end in itself is a way of participating in an emerging global consciousness that is the attractor state on the horizon of our current transition. I could be wrong but I think that story fits the evidence and is certainly worth investigating further.

In a very real sense the Internet has given a concrete form to Oakeshott's abstraction 'the conversation of mankind'. The most influential works of culture from all over the world are now being digitized and made available online in many ongoing projects. Many thinkers from the last fifty years are available in video form explaining and defending their ideas. Leading practitioners of every kind of profession and vocation are also available. Education as induction into participation in the dialogue of humanity no longer takes place only through face-to-face conversations in elite universities or in the long-time cycle of book or article writing and publishing but now the dialogue of humanity can be engaged in live through multiple media via the Internet.

The Internet obviously offers the opportunity for education into global dialogue. More than that, the Internet Age, has created a necessity for such education. A global space of interaction in which there are multiple voices and no certainties is already the reality of life for everyone linked by the Internet. Not all are comfortable with this and there have been reactionary responses as people retreat from the challenge of global dialogue into local certainties. Education for the Internet Age has a crucial role if people are to be able to thrive not only economically but also psychologically in this new context. The Internet makes global dialogue a possibility, but it is the job of education to make this a reality.

NOTES

1 The challenge

1 Kaiser Family Trust (2010). Generation M2: Media in the Lives of 8- to 18-Year-Olds. http://www.kff.org/entmedia/8010.cfm.
2 Collins, A. and Halverson, R. (2009). *Rethinking Education in the Age of Technology: The Digital Revolution and the Schools*. New York: Teachers College Press. This provides a good history of the current global model of schooling and its links to print technology.
3 Bereiter, C. (2002). Education and mind in the knowledge age. Mahwah, NJ: Lawrence Erlbaum Associates.
4 Lave, J. and Wenger, E. (1991). *Situated Learning: Legitimate Peripheral Participation*. Cambridge: Cambridge University Press.
5 Siemens, G. (2005). Connectivism: A learning theory for the digital age, International Journal of Instructional Technology and Distance Learning 2 (10), 2005.
   Goodyear, P. Banks, S. Hodgson, V. and McConnell, D. (eds) (2004). Advances in Research on Networked Learning. London: Kluwer Academic Publishers. In an important study Margaret Archer reports research findings suggesting it is inner dialogues that enable people to exercise agency and change the social structures around them. Archer M. (2003). *Structure, Agency and the Internal Conversation*. Cambridge: Cambridge University Press.
6 Carr, N. (2010). *The Shallows: What the Internet is Doing to Our Brains*. New York, NY: W. W. Norton & Co.
7 http://www.guardian.co.uk/uk/2009/feb/24/social-networking-site-changing-childrens-brains. See also, Greenfield, S. (2008). Modern technology is Changing the Way the Brain Works Says Neuro-Scientist. Daily Mail, 21/05/2008 Retrieved on 27 August 2008 from http://www.dailymail.co.uk/sciencetech/article-565207/Modern-technology-changing-way-brains-work-says-neuroscientist.html.
8 Plato (380 BCE/2006). *Phaedrus* (B. Jowett, trans.). Available online at: http://ebooks. adelaide. edu.au/p/plato/p71phs/ (accessed 1 December 2011). It is worth pointing out that in the Republic Plato has Socrates say very different things which appear to privilege the clarity and rigour of written ways of thinking over the more emotive and messy ways of thinking found in the oral tradition of poetry. I choose to imagine that the *Phaedrus* reports Socrates' words as an oral thinker and the Republic is more Plato's voice.

9 Toulmin, S. (1990). *Cosmopolis: the hidden agenda of modernity.* New York: Free Press.

10 Howard-Jones, P. A. (2010). *Introducing neuroeducational research: Neuroscience, education and the brain from contexts to practice.* Abingdon: Routledge.

11 García-Sierra, A., Rivera-Gaxiola, M., Percaccio, C. R., Conboy, B. T., Romo, H., Klarman, L., Ortiz, S. and Kuhl, P. T. (2011). 'Bilingual language learning: An ERP study relating early brain responses to speech, language input, and later word production'. *Journal of Phonetics,* 39,4, 546–557. doi:10.1016/j.wocn.2011.07.002

12 Ibid.

13 Thomas, M. S. C. (in press, to be published in 2012). 'Brain plasticity and education'. *British Journal of Educational Psychology* [Special Issue on Educational Neuroscience].

14 Dehaene, S. (2009). *Reading in the brain.* New York: Penguin Viking.

15 Dehaene, S., Pegado, F., Braga, L. W., Ventura, P., Nunes Filho, C., Jobert, A., Dehaene-Lambertz, G., Kolinsky, R., Morais, J. and Cohen, L. (2010). 'How learning to read changes the cortical networks for vision and language'. *Science.* 2010, Dec 3: 330 (6009), 1359–64.

16 References can be found in Olson, D. (1994). *The World on Paper.* Cambridge: Cambridge University Press.

17 Bakhtin, M. M. (1981). 'Discourse in the novel', in M. M. Bakhtin, *The Dialogic Imagination: four essays by M. M. Bakhtin.* Austin, TX: University of Texas Press: 343.

18 Giles, J. (2005). Special Report Internet encyclopaedias go head to head. *Nature,* 438, 900–1 (15 December 2005). doi:10.1038/438900a. Published online 14 December 2005 (retrieved 1 December 2011 from: http://www.nature.com/nature/journal/v438/n7070/full/438900a.html).

19 See for example, Hirsch, E. D. (1987). *Cultural Literacy: What every American Should Know,* Boston: Houghton Mifflin.

20 Eric Whitacre's Virtual Choir – Lux Aurumque. http://www.youtube.com/watch?v=D7o7BrlbaDs

21 There are many such games but the one I am most familiar with is Team Fortress 2 http://www.tf2.com/. Quite fun but dangerously addictive for 12-year-old boys apparently.

22 YouthNet (2009). Life support: young people's needs in the digital age. http://www.youthnet.org/wp-content/uploads/2011/05/Life-Support-Report.pdf (accessed 23 June 2012). This recent survey in the UK of over 900 13- to 17-year-olds found that 38 per cent had friends they had never met face to face, 45 per cent spent their happiest times of the day online and 75 per cent claimed that they 'could not live' without the Internet.

23 This point is made particularly well by one of the leading researchers in the field of consciousness studies, Max Velmans. See for example, Velmans, M. (2000). *Understanding Consciousness.* London: Routledge.

24 Boswell, James (1791/1986). Hibbert, Christopher (ed). *The Life of Samuel Johnson.* New York: Penguin Classics or Gutenberg ebooks http://www.gutenberg.org/ebooks/1564.

25 Krunic, V. and Han, R. (2008). Towards Cyber-Physical Holodeck Systems Via Physically Rendered Environments (PREs). Distributed Computing Systems Workshops, 2008. doi: 10.1109/ICDCS Workshops.2008.31.

26 Many introductions to quantum theory say this but a recent good example of the genre is Cox, B. and Forshaw, J. (2011), *The Quantum Universe: Everything that can happen does happen.* London: Allen Lane. The nature of the link between a dialogic theory of education and quantum theory is brought out well by Karen Barad in Barad, K. (2007). *Meeting the Universe Halfway.* Durham, N.C: Duke University Press.

27 Kaiser Family Trust (2010). Generation M2: Media in the Lives of 8- to 18-Year-Olds. http://www.kff.org/entmedia/8010.cfm.

28 The question arises here: is there one dialogic space or many? The nature of dialogue, which I explore in the next chapter, suggests that, like the Internet, all dialogic spaces interconnect in a radically intertextual kind of way so it is not possible to have

completely closed-off dialogic spaces. This is why we can talk as Oakeshott does, about the dialogue of humanity ('the conversation of mankind') in the singular while acknowledging that this dialogue contains many different zones and dimensions.

2 Educating dialogue

1   Alexander, R. (2000). *Culture and Pedagogy*. Oxford: Blackwell.
2   Alexander, R. (2006). *Towards Dialogic Teaching: Rethinking classroom talk*. Third Edition. Cambridge: Dialogos.
3   Wolfe S. (2006). Teaching and learning through dialogue in primary classrooms in England. Unpublished PhD thesis, University of Cambridge: 258–9; see also her paper in Beyond Current Horizons: http://www.beyondcurrenthorizons. org.uk.
4   Gordon Wells combines Bakhtin, Vygotsky and Dewey's communities of enquiry with his dialogic enquiry approach, see Wells, G. (1999). *Dialogic inquiry: Towards a sociocultural practice and theory of education*. New York: Cambridge University Press; and Wells, G. (ed.) (2001). *Action, Talk and Text: Learning and Teaching Through Inquiry*. New York: Teachers College Press.
5   Wegerif, R. and Scrimshaw, P. (eds) (1998). *Computers and Talk in the Primary Classroom*. Clevedon, UK: Multilingual Matters Ltd. This book contains five chapters drawn from my PhD thesis on the same topic conducted with Neil Mercer at the Open University. See also Wegerif, R. (1996). Collaborative learning and directive software. *Journal of Computer Assisted Learning*, 12 (1): 22–32. ISSN 0266-4909.
    Wegerif, R. (1996). Using computers to help coach exploratory talk across the curriculum. *Computers and Education*, 26 (1–3): 51-60. ISSN: 0360-1315.
    Wegerif, R., Mercer, N. and L. Dawes (1998). Software Design to Support Discussion in the Primary Classroom. *Journal of Computer Assisted Learning*, 14 (3): 199–211. ISSN 0266-4909.
6   This approach was influenced by Grice's concept of implicature or the set of cooperative assumptions required for shared meaning-making in dialogues. However rather than describe these implicit assumptions and assume that they were universal, as Grice appears to, we set out to actively shape them, using awareness of the impact that different assumptions have on group thinking as an educational means to improve group thinking by making productive assumptions explicit and then practicing them until they became implicit. See Grice, H. P. (1975). Logic and conversation, in *Syntax and Semantics, 3: Speech Acts* (P. Cole and J. Morgan eds). New York: Academic Press; and Wegerif, R. (2002). Walking or dancing? Images of thinking and learning to think in the classroom. *Journal of Interactive Learning Research*, 13 (1). 51–70.
7   Wegerif, R. and Dawes, L. (2004). *Thinking and learning with ICT: raising achievement in primary classrooms*. London: Routledge: and Wegerif. R. (2007). *Dialogic, Educational and Technology: Expanding the Space of Learning*. New York: Springer-Verlag.
8   Wegerif, R., Linares, J., Rojas-Drummond, S., Mercer, N. and Velez, M. (2005). 'Thinking Together' in the UK and Mexico: transfer of an educational innovation. *Journal of Classroom Interaction*, 40(1), 40–7.
    Mercer, N., Dawes, L., Wegerif, R. and Sams, C. (2004). Reasoning as a scientist: ways of helping children to use language to learn science. *British Educational Research Journal*, 30(3), 359–77.
    Mercer, N. and Littleton, K. (2007). *Dialogue and the Development of Children's Thinking: A Sociocultural Approach* (New Edition.). London: Routledge.
    Rajala, A., Hilppö, J. and Lipponen, L. (2011). The Emergence of Inclusive Exploratory Talk in Primary Students' Peer Interaction. *International Journal of Educational Research*. doi: 10.1016/j.ijer.2011.12.011 (Finland).
    Webb, P. and Treagust, D. (2006). Using exploratory talk to enhance problem-solving and reasoning skills in grade-7 science classrooms. *Research in Science Education*. 36(4), 381–401 (South Africa).

9 Mercer, N. (2000). *Words and Minds*. London: Routledge: Wegerif, R., Mercer, N. and Dawes, L. (1999). From social interaction to individual reasoning: an empirical investigation of a possible socio-cultural model of cognitive development. *Learning and Instruction*. 9 (5): 493–516.

10 Wegerif, R. (2008). Dialogic or Dialectic? The significance of ontological assumptions in research on Educational Dialogue. *British Educational Research Journal*, 34(3), 347–61.

11 The rationale for this shift in terms is given in Wegerif, R. (2007). *Dialogic Education and Technology: Expanding the space of learning*. New Jersey: Springer.

12 Yang, Y. and Wegerif, R. (in preparation). Learning to Learn Together in a Chinese Classroom: The Importance of Group Roles.

13 Nystrand, M. (1997). *Opening dialogue: Understanding the dynamics of language and learning in the English classroom*. New York: Teachers College Press.

14 Wells, G. (1999), op. cit.

15 Matusov, E. (2009). *Journey into dialogic pedagogy*. Hauppauge, NY: Nova Publishers.

16 There are many references to Socrates in Bakhtin, M. (1984). *Problems of Dostoevsky's poetics* (C. Emerson, ed. and trans.). Minneapolis: University of Minnesota Press.

17 Plato (360 BCE/2006) *Phaedrus* (B. Jowett, trans.). Available online at: http://ebooks. adelaide. edu.au/p/plato/p71phs/ (accessed 1 December 2011).

18 Ibid.

19 Dehaene, S. (2009). *Reading in the Brain*. London: Penguin.

20 In oral societies voices are not only given to physically embodied people but also to the rest of reality or what literate societies tend to describe either as things or as abstractions in the language, ghosts, supernatural beings, concepts, ancestors and so on. Socrates engaged in dialogue of a sort with the oracle at Delphi and also with his own 'daemon', a kind of personal spirit, and some sources describe him entering into trance states in order to talk to other spirit voices.

21 Montaigne, M. (1595). On education, in *Les Essais*.) Available online at: http://www. lib.uchicago.edu/ efts/ARTFL/projects/montaigne/ (accessed 1 December 2011).

22 Toulmin, S. (1990). *Cosmopolis: the hidden agenda of modernity*. New York: Free Press.

23 Bakhtin, M. (1986). *Speech genres and other late essays*. Austin: University of Texas: 162.

24 Plato, op. cit.

25 Matusov, E. (2009). *Journey into dialogic pedagogy*. Hauppauge, NY: Nova Publishers: 46.

26 Nikulin, D. (2010). *Dialectic and Dialogue*. Stanford: Stanford University Press. Kindle Edition.

27 Bakhtin M. (1986), op. cit., 147, 162.

28 Ibid., p. 162.

29 Nikulin, D. op. cit.

30 Plato, *Phaedrus*, op. cit. Incidentally the Greek word for 'breath', pneuma, can also be translated as 'spirit'. This suggests that the spirit is to do with the meanings on the inside of relationships rather than, as seems to be the dominant image now in our print-based reality, a supernatural being floating in its own independent supernatural space.

31 New Testament, 2 Cor. 3:6 New International Version http://www.biblegateway. com/ (accessed 22 June 2012).

32 Buber, M. (1958). *I and Thou* (Second Edition, R. Gregory Smith, trans.). Edinburgh: T & T Clark; New Testament, op. cit.

33 Buber, M. op. cit., 29.

34 Merleau-Ponty, M. (2005). *Phenomenology of Perception* (Colin Smith, trans.). London: Routledge.

35 Wegerif, R. and Mercer, N. (1997). A dialogical framework for researching peer talk, in R. Wegerif and P. Scrimshaw (eds.). *Computers and talk in the primary classroom*. Clevedon: Multilingual Matters Ltd: 49–65.

   Wegerif, R. (2005). Reason and Creativity in Classroom Dialogues. *Language and Education*, 19(3), 223–38.

36 Buber, Martin (1947). *Tales of the Hasidim: Early Masters* (O. Marx, trans.). Schocken: New York (pp. 104, 116). Referred to in Smith, M. K. (2000, 2009), Martin Buber on education. *The encyclopaedia of informal education*, http://www.infed.org/thinkers/et-buber.htm.
37 Buber M., in Hodes, A. (1972). *Encounter with Martin Buber*. London: Allen Lane/Penguin. (Also published 1971, as *Martin Buber: An Intimate Portrait*. Viking Press: New York). Referred to by Smith, M. K. (2000, 2009). 'Martin Buber on education'. *The encyclopaedia of informal education*. http://www.infed.org/thinkers/et-buber.htm.
38 Bakhtin, M. (1981). *The dialogic imagination*. Austin: University of Texas Press: 43.
39 Wegerif, R. (2011). From dialectic to dialogic: A response to Wertsch and Kazak, in T. Koschmann (ed.), *Theories of learning and studies of instructional practice*. NJ: Springer.
40 Vygotsky, L. (1986). *Thought and language* (A. Kozulin, trans.). Cambridge MA: MIT. Press; Vygotsky, L. S. (1978). *Mind in society: The development of higher psychological processes*. Cambridge, MA: Harvard University Press.
41 Rommetveit, R. (1992). Outlines of a dialogically based social-cognitive approach to human cognition and communication, in A. Wold (ed.). *The dialogical alternative: towards a theory of language and mind* . Oslo: Scandanavian Press: 19–45.
42 Mercer, N. (2000). *Words and Minds: how we use language to think together*. London: Routledge.
43 Vygotsky L. (1986), op. cit.
44 Freire, P. (1971). *Pedagogy of the oppressed*. New York: Seabury Press: 69.
45 Smith, M. K. (1997, 2002). Paulo Freire and informal education. *The encyclopaedia of informal education*. [www.infed.org/thinkers/et-freir.htm. Last update: 1 December 2011].
46 Matusov, E. (2009), op. cit., 109.
47 Oakeshott, M. (1989). *The Voice of Liberal Learning: Michael Oakeshott on Education* (T. Fuller, ed.). New Haven and London: Yale University Press.
48 Oakeshott, M. (1962). *The Voice of Poetry in the Conversation of Mankind, Rationalism in Politics and Other Essays*. London: Methuen: 197–247.
49 Oakeshott, M. (1989), op. cit., 133.
50 Linell, P. (2009). *Rethinking language, mind and world dialogically: Interactional and contextual theories of human sense-making*. Charlotte, NC: Information Age Publishing.
51 Bakhtin, M. (1986), op. cit., 7.
52 Bakhtin, M. (1986), op. cit., 192.
53 Wegerif, R. and Mercer, N. (1997). Using computer-based text analysis to integrate quantitative and qualitative methods in the investigation of collaborative learning. *Language and Education*, 11, 3, 23–29.
54 Einstein, A. (1949). *The World As I See It*. New York: Philosophical Library.
55 Thanks are due to Neil Mercer for giving me this example.
56 Austin, J. (2009). *Mini weapons of mass destruction: Build implements of spitball warfare*. Chicago: Chicago Review Press.
57 Rommetveit (1992), op. cit.; Linell (2009), op. cit.
58 Merleau-Ponty, M. (1964). *Le Visible et L'Invisible*. Paris: Gallimard: 29, 159.
    Merleau-Ponty, M. (1968). *The Visible and the Invisible* (Claude Lefort, ed. and Alphonso Lingis, trans.). Evanston, Il: Northwestern University: 15, 113.
59 Bakhtin, M. (1986), op. cit., 126.
60 Wells G. (1999), op. cit.; Linell P. (2009), op. cit.
61 This ontological view of dialogic is partly inspired by ontological interpretations of quantum physics particularly that of Karen Barad. Barad, K. (2007), *Meeting the Universe Halfway*. Durham, NC: Duke University Press.
62 The idea that a way of being in the world is ontological derives from the Heidegger of Being and Time. Being dialogic is not just about being in an already constituted world (i.e. ontic) but is a way of constituting the world (i.e. ontological).

63 See also Matusov, E. (2009), op. cit. and Sidorkin, A. M. (1999). *Beyond discourse: Education, the self and dialogue*. New York: State University of New York Press, for ontological interpretations of dialogic in education.

64 This concept is related to Biesta's account of education as subjectification, or the bringing into being of new voices, which implies a pedagogy of interruption. Biesta, G. *Good Education in an Age of Measurement: Ethics, Politics, Democracy*. New York: Paradigm: 91.

65 Hermans, H. J. M. (2001). The dialogical self: Toward a theory of personal and cultural positioning. *Culture & Psychology*. [Special Issue. Culture and the Dialogical Self: Theory, Method and Practice, 7, 243–81.]

3 Educating reason

1 http://www.youtube.com/watch?v=k2YdkQ1G5QI Meltzoff, A. N. and Moore, M, K. (1977). Imitation of facial and manual gestures by human neonates. *Science*, 198:75–8.

2 I am drawing considerably in this section on talks and papers by Sean Gallagher, see for example: Gallagher, S. 2007. Neurophilosophy and neurophenomenology, in L. Embree and T. Nenon (eds), *Phenomenology 2005* Vol. 5 (293–316). Bucharest: Zeta Press.

3 Blakemore, S-J., Bristow, D., Bird, G., Frith, C. and Ward, J. (2005). Somatosensory activations during the observation of touch and a case of vision-touch synesthesia. *Brain*, 128, 1571–83. doi:10.1093/brain/awh500ý.

4 Vygotsky, L. S. (1978). *Mind in society: The development of higher psychological processes*. Cambridge, MA: Harvard University Press: 86.

5 Vygotsky, L. (1986). *Thought and language* (A. Kozulin, trans.). Cambridge MA: MIT Press: 160–1.

6 Wertsch, J. V. (1985). *Vygotsky and the social formation of mind*. Cambridge MA: Harvard University Press: p. 64; Wertsch, J. V. (1998). *Mind as action*. New York: Oxford University Press: 133.

7 Baron-Cohen, S. (1994). The Mindreading System: new directions for research. Current Psychology of Cognition, 13, 724–50. See also extensive discussion of pointing in Tomasello, M. (2008). *Origins of Human Communication*. Cambridge MA: MIT Press.

8 Hobson, R. P. (1998). The intersubjective foundations of thought, in S. Braten (ed.). *Intersubjective Communication and Emotion in Ontogeny*. Cambridge: Cambridge University Press: 283–96;

   Hobson, R. P. (2002). *The cradle of thought : exploring the origins of thinking*. London: Macmillan.

9 Vygotsky, L. S. (1987). *The collected works of L. S. Vygotsky. Vol. 1. Problems of general psychology. Including the Volume Thinking and Speech*. (N. Minick, ed. and trans.). New York: Plenum: 287.

10 Marx, K. (1977). *Selected writings* (David McLellan, ed, and trans.). Oxford: OUP.

11 Tomasello, M., Carpenter, M., Call, J., Behne, T. and Moll, H. (2005). Understanding and sharing intentions: the origins of cultural cognition. *Behaviour and Brain Science*. 28(5), 675–91.

12 Weinberg, K. M. and Tronick, E. Z. (1996). Infants' affective reactions to the resumption of maternal interaction after the still-face. *Child Development*, 67, 905–14.

13 Trevarthen, C. (1979). Communication and cooperation in early infancy: a description of primary intersubjectivity, in M. Bullowya (ed.), *Before speech. The beginning of interpersonal communication*. Cambridge: Cambridge University Press: 321–7.

14 Ibid.

15 Gallagher, S. (2011). Strong Interaction and Self-Agency. *Humana.Mente: Journal of Philosophical Studies*, 15, 55–77.

16 Ibid.

17 Wegerif, R. (2007). *Dialogic, Education and Technology: Expanding the Space of Learning*, Chapter 2. NY and Berlin: Springer.

18 This gets to the philosophical nub of the problem with Vygotsky's argument. It assumed Marx's materialist dialectic. The dialogic alternative begins with the reality of relationships and explores how objects are constructed within relationships. Some of Habermas's later work shows how this could be seen not as opposed to Marxist dialectic but an important development of it.

19 This is probably related to the phenomenon of autopoeisis explored in systems theory. De Jaegher, H., Di Paolo, E. A. and Gallagher, S. (2010). Can social interaction constitute social cognition? *Trends in Cognitive Sciences*, 14(10), 441–7.

20 More context and qualifications are provided in, Adolph, K. E. and Kretch, K. S. (2012). Infants on the edge: Beyond the visual cliff, in A. Slater and P. Quinn (eds). *Developmental psychology: revisiting the classic studies*. London: SAGE Publications.

21 Baron-Cohen, S. (2011). *Zero Degrees of Empathy: A new theory of human cruelty*. London: Penguin/Allen Lane.

22 This repeats a thought experiment conducted by William James. William James (1950). *The Principles of Psychology*, Two Volumes (called "Principles"). New York: Dover.

23 See also Wegerif (2007), op. cit.

24 Heidegger, M. (1978). *Basic Writings*. London: Routledge: 369.

25 Ibid., p. 390.

26 'Le mot *Je* signifie *me voici*, répondant de tout et de tous'. Levinas, E. (1978). Autrement qu'être ou au-dela de l'essence. Paris: Le Livre de Poche: 180.

27 Van der Veer, R. and Valsiner, J. (1991). *Understanding Vygotsky: a quest for synthesis*. Oxford: Blackwells; Wegerif, R. (1999). Two models of reason in education. *The School Field*. 9 (3–4): 77–107. ISSN 0353-6807; Matusov, E. (2011). 'Irreconcilable differences in Vygotsky's and Bakhtin's approaches to the social and the individual: An educational perspective'. *Culture & Psychology*, 17 (1), 99–119.

28 Rogoff, B. Gauvain, G. and Ellis, C. (1991). Development viewed in its cultural context, in P. Light, A. Sheldon and B. Woodhead (eds). *Learning to think*. London: Routledge.

29 Lave, J. and Wenger, E. (1991). *Situated Learning: Legitimate Peripheral Participation*. Cambridge, UK: Cambridge University Press.

30 Wegerif, R. (2004). Towards an Account of Teaching General Thinking Skills That is Compatible with the Assumptions of Sociocultural Theory. *Educational Theory and Research*, 2(2). 143–59.

31 Bakhtin, M. (1986). *Speech genres and other late essays*. Austin: University of Texas: 126–7.

32 Mead, G., H. (1934). *Mind, Self and Society* (Charles W. Morris, ed.). Chicago: University of Chicago Press.

33 This argument is influenced by Biesta's criticism of situated learning in Biesta, G. J. J. (2004). The community of those who have nothing in common. Education and the language of responsibility. *Interchange* 35 (3), 307–24.

34 Lave and Wenger (1991), op. cit.

35 Lave and Wenger (1991), op. cit.; Wenger, E. (1999). *Communities of practice. learning, meaning and identity*. Cambridge: Cambridge University Press.

36 Wenger (1999), op. cit. p. 153.

37 Cobb, P., Gresalfi, M. and Hodge, L. L. (2009). An interpretive scheme for analysing the identities that students develop in mathematics classrooms. Journal for Research in Mathematics Education, 40, 40–68.

38 Mercer, N. (2000). *Words and Minds: how we use language to think together*. London: Routledge.

39 Mercer, N. (1995). *The guided construction of knowledge: Talk amongst teachers and learners*. Clevedon: Multilingual Matters. Mercer, N. and Littleton, K. (2007). *Dialogue and the Development of Children's Thinking: A Sociocultural Approach* (New Edition.). London: Routledge.

40 Rojas, S., Drummond, M., Fernandez, N., Mazon, R. and Wegerif, R. (2006). Explicit reasoning, creativity and co-construction in primary school children's collaborative activities. *Thinking Skills and Creativity*, 1(2), 84–94.

41 Wegerif, R. (2005). Reason and Creativity in Classroom Dialogues. *Language and Education*, 19(3). 223–38.
42 Wegerif, R. and Mercer, N. (1997). A dialogical framework for researching peer talk, in R. Wegerif and P. Scrimshaw (eds). *Computers and talk in the primary classroom*. Clevedon: Multilingual Matters: 49–65.
43 Karen Barad challenges the static implications of the image of reflection suggesting instead the more creative image of diffraction as in the complex overlapping patterns that form when waves going in different directions cross each other. She is right but diffraction as a metaphor for creative dialogue is less recognized than reflection. Barad, K. (2007). *Meeting the Universe Halfway*. Durham, NC: Duke University Press.
44 Wegerif, R. (2002). Walking or dancing? Images of thinking and learning to think in the classroom. *Journal of Interactive Learning Research*. 13 (1), 51–70.
45 The data was from the work of Richard Lehrer and Leona Schnauble to whom much thanks. This analysis is reported in more detail in Koschmann, T. (ed.). *Theories of learning and studies of instructional practice*. NJ: Springer.
46 Karmiloff-Smith, A. (1992, reprinted 1995). *Beyond Modularity: A Developmental Perspective on Cognitive Science*. Cambridge, MA: MIT Press/Bradford Books.
47 Bakhtin (1986), op. cit.
48 Mercer, N. (1995). The guided construction of knowledge: talk amongst teachers and learners. Clevedon: Multilingual Matters.
49 Ibid.
50 Linell, P. (2009). *Rethinking language, mind and world dialogically: Interactional and contextual theories of human sense-making*. Charlotte, NC: Information Age Publishing.
51 Bakhtin, 1986, op. cit.
52 More examples can be found in, Wegerif, R. (2010). *Mindexpanding: Teaching for thinking and creativity in primary education*. Buckingham: Open University Press.
53 Bruner, J. (1996). Celebrating Piaget and Vygotsky: An exercise in dialectic. Paper presented at the Second Conference for Socio-Cultural Research, Geneva.
54 Damasio, A. R. (1994). *Damasio, Descartes' error: Emotion, reason, and the human brain*. New York: Putnam.
   Gallagher, S. (2012). Neurons, neonates and narrative: From embodied resonance to empathic understanding, in Ad Foolen, Ulrike Lüdtke, Jordan Zlatev and Tim Racine (eds), *Moving ourselves: Bodily motion and emotion in the making of intersubjectivity and consciousness*. Amsterdam: John Benjamins.
55 Tomasello, M, *et al.* (2005). op. cit.
   Fernyhough, C. (1996). The dialogic mind: a dialogic approach to the higher mental functions. *New Ideas in Psychology*, 14, 47–62.

4 Educating creativity

1 Where ZPD is defined as: 'the distance between the actual developmental level as determined by independent problem solving and the level of potential development as determined through problem solving under adult guidance, or in collaboration with more capable peers'. Vygotsky, L. S. (1978). *Mind in society: The development of higher psychological processes*. Cambridge, MA: Harvard University Press: 86.
2 Vygotsky, (1986). *Thought and language* (A. Kozulin, trans.). Cambridge, MA: MIT Press. p. 236.
3 Wegerif, R. (2011). From dialectic to dialogic: A response to Wertsch and Kazak, in T. Koschmann (ed.), *Theories of learning and studies of instructional practice*. NJ: Springer.
4 Daniels, H., 2001. *Vygotsky and Pedagogy*. London: Routledge.
5 Langer, E. (1997). *The power of mindful learning*. Reading, MA: Addison-Wesley.
6 See Matusov, E. (2009). *Journey into dialogic pedagogy*. Hauppauge, NY: Nova Publishers.
7 Howe, C. (2010). *Peer groups and children's development*. Oxford: Blackwell.

8 There is also the factor that John Raven, not unreasonably, does not allow the use of Raven's reasoning test puzzles in publications but kindly produced for me an alternative version of the puzzle at the centre of this episode which enables me to use it.

9 Dawes, L., Mercer, N. and Wegerif, R. (2004, Second Edition). 'Thinking Together': A programme of activities for developing speaking, listening and thinking skills for children aged 8–11. Birmingham: Imaginative Minds Ltd.

10 Kounios, J., and Beeman, M. (2009). The Aha! moment: The cognitive neuroscience of insight. *Current Directions in Psychological Science*, 18, 210–16.

11 Howe, C. (2010), op. cit.

12 Sheth, Bhavin R., Sandkühler, Simone and Bhattacharya, Joydeep (2009). Posterior Beta and Anterior Gamma Oscillations Predict Cognitive Insight. *Journal of Cognitive Neuroscience*, 21(7), 1269–79.

13 Deacon, T. (1997). *The symbolic species: The co-evolution of language and the human brain*. London: Penguin.

14 The role of metaphoricity as fundamental thinking is brought out by Lakoff, G. and Johnson, M. (1980). *Metaphors We Live By*. Chicago: University of Chicago Press. My larger argument is taken from Merleau-Ponty especially Merleau-Ponty, M. (2005). *Phenomenology of Perception* (Colin Smith, trans.). London: Routledge.

15 Tomasello, M. (2008). *Origins of Human Communication*. Cambridge MA: MIT Press.

16 Donald, M. (2001). *A mind so rare: The evolution of human consciousness*. New York: W. W. Norton & Co.

17 Dennett, D. (1991). *Consciousness Explained*. London: Allen Lane.

18 DeHaene, S. and Naccache, L. (2001). Toward a cognitive neuroscience of consciousness: basic evidence and a workspace framework. Cognition, 79, 1–3: 1.

19 Donald, M., op. cit., p. 174.

20 Baars, B. J. (1997). *In the Theater of Consciousness*. New York, NY: Oxford University Press.

21 Dehaene and Naccache (2001) op. cit.

22 Varela, F. J. and Shear, J. (eds) (1999). The View From Within: First-Person Approaches to the Study of Consciousness. A special issue of the *Journal of Consciousness Studies*.

23 Thagard, P. and Stewart, T. C. (2011). The AHA! Experience: Creativity Through Emergent Binding in Neural Networks. *Cognitive Science*, 35: 1–33.

24 Kounios, J. and Beeman, M., op. cit.

25 Karmiloff-Smith, A. (1992, reprinted 1995). *Beyond Modularity: A Developmental Perspective on Cognitive Science*. Cambridge, MA: MIT Press/Bradford Books.

26 Lakoff and Johnson, op. cit.

27 Donald, M., op. cit.

28 Libet, B. (2004). *Mind time: The temporal factor in consciousness, Perspectives in Cognitive Neuroscience*. Harvard University Press.

29 Sheth, Bhavin R., Sandkuhler, Simone and Bhattacharya, Joydeep (2009). Posterior Beta and Anterior Gamma Oscillations Predict Cognitive Insight. *Journal of Cognitive Neuroscience*, 21(7), 1269–79.

30 Claxton, G. (2006) Thinking at the edge: developing soft creativity. *Cambridge Journal of Education*, 36(3), 351–62.

31 'I entitle transcendental all knowledge which is occupied not so much with objects as with the mode of our knowledge of objects in so far as this mode of knowledge is to be possible a priori'. Kant, I., (1781/1929). *Critique of Pure Reason* (Norman Kemp Smith, trans.). London: Macmillan Press: 59.

32 Penrose, R. (1994). *Shadows of the mind: a search for the missing science of consciousness*. Oxford: Oxford University Press.

33 Velmans, M. (2000). *Understanding Consciousness*. London: Routledge.

34 Merleau-Ponty op. cit.

35 Heidegger, M. (1978). *Basic Writings*. London: Routledge: 369.

36 Merleau-Ponty, M. (1964). *Le Visible et l'Invisible*. Paris: Gallimard.

Merleau-Ponty, M. (1968). *The Visible and the Invisible* (Claude Lefort, notes trans. and ed.).

37 Deleuze, G. (1994) *Difference and Repetition* (Paul Patton, trans.). New York: Columbia University Press.

38 Deridda, J. (1968). La Différance, in *Théorie d'ensemble*. Paris: Éditions de Seuil.
Derrida, J. (1973). Différance, in *Derrida, J., Speech and Phenomena: and other essays on Husserl's Theory of Sign* Evanston: Northwestern University Press.

39 Leibniz, G. (1973). *Leibniz. Philosophical Writings* (Parkinson, G., ed.; Morris, M. and Parkinson, G., trans.). London: Dent and Sons.

40 Mallarmé, S. (1998). *Poésies et autres textes.* Paris: Le Livre de Poche.

41 Bhaskar, R. A. (1997). *A Realist Theory of Science.* London: Verso.

42 Geirland, John (1996). Go With The Flow. *Wired magazine*, September, Issue 4.09. http://www.wired.com/magazine.

43 Csikszentmihalyi, M. (1996). *Creativity: flow and the psychology of discovery and invention.* New York: Harper Perennial.

44 Ibid., p. 119.

45 Ibid., p. 103.

46 Sawyer, K. (2007). *Group genius: The creative power of collaboration.* New York: Basic Books: 42.

47 Rojas Drummond, S. Fernandez, M. Mazon, N. and Wegerif, R. (2006). Collaborative talk and creativity. *Teaching Thinking and Creativity*, 1(2). 84–94.

48 Langer, E. J. and Piper, A. I. (1987). The prevention of mindlessness. *Journal of Personality and Social Psychology*, 53, 280–7.

49 Langer, E., Hatem, M., Joss, J. and Howell, M. (1989). Conditional teaching and mindful learning: The role of uncertainty in education. *Creativity Research Journal*, 2, 139–50.

50 Langer, E. and Moldoveanu, M. (2000). The construct of mindfulness. *Journal of Social Issues*, 56 (1), 1–9.

51 Craft, A., Cremin, T., Burnard, P., Dragovic, T. and Chappell, K. (2012). Possibility Thinking: Culminative Studies Of An Evidence-Based Concept Driving Creativity?, *Education 3–13: International Journal Of Primary, Elementary And Early Years Education.* doi:10.1080/03004279.2012.656671 Link: Http://Dx.Doi.Org/10.1080/03004279.20 12.656671.

52 Craft, A., McConnon, L. and Matthews, A. (2012). Creativity and child-initiated play: fostering possibility thinking in four-year-olds. *Thinking Skills and Creativity* 7(1), 48–61.

5 Educating technology

1 Lewis-Williams, D. J. (2002). *The Mind In The Cave: Consciousness And The Origins Of Art.* London: Thames & Hudson.

2 Lewis-Williams, J. D. and Pearce, D. G. (2004). *San Spirituality: Roots, Expressions and Social Consequences.* Walnut Creek: Altamira Press.

3 Leimann, M. (2002). Toward semiotic dialogism: the role of sign mediation in the dialogical self. *Theory and Psychology*, 12(2): 221–35.

4 By oral peoples I mean societies which have no writing. Although it may sound odd to be possessed by signs, in reality this is how signs normally work. Consider the experience of reading a novel. The difference I am making here between oral and literate is not so much in the way that signs actually work but in the dominant way of thinking about how signs work.

5 Claxton, G. (2008). *What is the Point of School?* London: Oneworld Publications. Claxton quotes surveys that show how boring most students find schoolwork.

6 Dehaene, S. (2009). *Reading in the Brain.* New York: The Viking Press. Dehaene S., Pegado F., Braga, L. W., Ventura P., Nunes Filho, G., Jobert A., Dehaene-Lambertz G., Kolinsky R., Morais J. and Cohen L. (2010). How learning to read changes the cortical networks for vision and language. *Science*, 330 (6009): 1359–64.

7 http://www.hearing-voices.org/ contains some research on this.
8 A. J. Ayer, a fiercely anti-metaphysical philosopher, was overwhelmed by mysterious light accompanied with a feeling of joy and freedom. After a while he attributed this experience to a temporary effect of a chemical imbalance in his brain, perhaps a shortage of oxygen, and he thought little more of it. The difference between an experience which transforms someone's life and one which is dismissed, does not lie only in the experience but in the interpretation of that experience. This selectivity of the attention can be influenced by education. There are two sources for this account of Ayer's incident: What I Saw When I Was Dead. *National Review* 40, 20, 8–40; Postscript to a Postmortem. *Spectator* 261, 8362, 12–14. Both are referred to in Lee W. Bailey (1996). *The Near-Death Experience. A Reader.* London: Routledge.
9 Rommetveit, R. (1992). Outlines of a dialogically based social-cognitive approach to human cognition and communication, in A. Wold (ed.). *The dialogical alternative: towards a theory of language and mind.* Oslo: Scandinavian Press: 19–45.
10 Olson, D. (1994). *The World on Paper.* Cambridge: Cambridge University Press.
    Ong, W. J. (1982). *Orality and Literacy: The Technologizing of The Word.* London: Methuen.
11 Goody, J. (1977). *The domestication of the savage mind.* Cambridge: Cambridge University Press.
12 Plato (360 BCE/2006). *Phaedrus* (B. Jowett, trans.). Available online at: http://ebooks.adelaide. edu.au/p/plato/p71phs/ (accessed 1 December 2011).
13 New Testament, New International Edition (2011). Available online at http://www.devotions.net/bible/00new.htm Accessed 18.06.11. Revelation 22:18–9.
14 Toulmin, S. (1990). *Cosmopolis: the hidden agenda of modernity.* New York: Free Press: 30.
15 Ibid., 31.
16 Salomon, G. (1992). New information technologies in education, in M. C. Alkin (ed.). *Encyclopaedia of educational research* (Sixth edition). New York: Macmillan: 892–903.
17 Carr, N. (2010). *The Shallows: What the Internet is Doing to Our Brains.* New York, NY: W. W. Norton & Co.
18 Poster, M. (1995). *The Second Media Age.* Oxford: Blackwell: 398.
19 Thomas, D. and Brown, J. S. (2011). *A new culture of learning: Cultivating the Imagination for a World of Constant Change.* New York: Createspace.
20 Ong, W. J., op. cit., 117.
21 Ong, W. J., op. cit., 129.
22 Goody, J., op. cit.
23 Alexander, R. (2000). *Culture and Pedagogy.* Oxford: Blackwell.
24 Davidson, C. (2011). How the Brain Science of Attention Will Transform the Way We Live, Work, and Learn. New York: Viking: 13.
25 Saul, J. R. (1992). *Voltaire's Bastards: The Dictatorship of Reason in the West.* Toronto: Penguin Books.
26 Collins, A. and Halverson, R. (2009). *Rethinking education in the age of technology: The digital revolution and schooling in America.* New York: Teachers College Press.
27 Thomas, D. and Brown, J. S., op. cit.
28 Ibid., 23.
29 Gee, J. P. (2003). *What video games have to teach us about learning and literacy.* New York: Palgrave/Macmillan.
30 Shaffer, D. W. (2007). *How Computer Games Help Children Learn.* New York: Palgrave.
31 Mackness, J., Mak, S. F. J., and Williams, R. (2010). The Ideals and Reality of Participating in a MOOC. Proceedings of the 7th International Conference on Networked Learning.
32 http://www.ted.com/talks/daphne_koller_what_we_re_learning_from_online_education.html
33 Ramírez, M. S. y Burgos, J. V. (2010) (coords.). Recursos educativos abiertos en ambientes enriquecidos con tecnología: Innovación en la práctica educativa. México: Instituto Tecnológico y de Estudios Superiores de Monterrey. Disponible en:http://www.lulu.com.

34 http://www.centroscomunitariosdeaprendizaje.org.mx/

35 Anderson, B. R. (1991). Imagined communities: reflections on the origin and spread of nationalism. London: Verso: 224.

36 www.elgg.com. We called our version of ELGG 'The Hive'. Using Facebook directly would equally have worked but ELGG provided a university-owned environment that we could control more easily.

37 Amal Al'Ibrahim. The pedagogical affordances of social network technology: A study in an undergraduate course in Exeter University. The 4th Saudi International Conference, Manchester University, July 2010.

38 Maarten de Laat helped with the formulation of this account of L2L2 used in the Metafora project. The idea of L2L2 was partly inspired by his account of social meta-cognition in De Laat, M. (2006) Networked Learning. Apeldoorn: Politie Academy. I would also like to acknowledge here the contribution of all the Metafora team, especially the members of the pedagogical team who have helped with this analysis, Reuma de Groot, Chronis Kynigos and Nikoleta Yiannoutsou as well as Ivan and Matteo of Testaluna who designed the icons.

39 Bereiter, C. (1994). Implications of Postmodernism for Science, or, Science as Progressive Discourse. *Educational Psychologist*, 29(1) 3–12.

40 To see applications of this dialogic approach to understanding educational technology: Pifarré, M. and Kleine Staarman, J. (2011). Wiki-supported collaborative learning in 'Primary Education: How a "dialogic space" is created for 'Thinking Together'. International Journal of Computer-Supported collaborative Learning. Hennessey, S. (2011) The role of digital artefacts on the interactive whiteboard in supporting classroom dialogue. Journal of Computer Assisted Learning.

6 Educating science

1 This chapter is adapted from Wegerif, R., Postlethwaite, K., Skinner, N., Mansour, N., Morgan, A. and Hetherington, L. (2013). Dialogic science education for diversity, in Mansour, N. and Wegerif, R. (eds) (2013). *Science Education for Diversity*. New Jersey: Springer.

I would particularly like to acknowledge the important contribution of Keith Postlethwaite. It draws on research funded by the EC Framework 7 Programme, specifically the Science Education for Diversity Project (244717). The members of the Exeter University team who helped with the writing of this chapter included Nasser Mansour, Keith Postlethwaite, Lindsay Letherington, Nigel Skinner, Alun Morgan and Andy Dean. The larger team included Professor Helen Haste (Harvard), Professor Saouma BouJaoude, Dr. Rola Khishfe, Dr. Dian Sarieddine, Dr. Sahar Alameh, Dr. Nesreen Ghaddar (American University of Beirut, Lebanon), Professor Huseyin Bag, Dr. Ayse Savran Gencer (Pamukkale University, Turkey), Assistant Professor Michiel van Eijck, Dr. Ralf Griethuijsen (Eindhoven University of Technology), Dr. Ng Swee Chin, Dr. Oo Pou San (Tunku Abdul Rahman College, Malaysia), Dr. Sugra Chunawala, Dr. Chitra Natarajan, Dr. Beena Choksi (Tata Institute of Fundamental Research, India).

2 European Commission. (2004). Europe needs More Scientists: Report by the High Level Group on Increasing Human Resources for Science and Technology. Brussels: European Commission.

3 Sjøberg, S. and Schreiner, C. (2007). Perceptions and images of science and science education, in *Communicating European Research 2005*. Claessens, M. (ed). Heidelberg, Germany: Springer.

Osborne, J. and Dillon. J. (2008). *Science Education in Europe: Critical Reflections*. London: Nuffield Foundation.

4 Ibid.

5 SED WP3 (2011) SEDWP3D1: Survey Research Synthesis Report. Available on: http://www.marchmont.ac.uk/Documents/Projects/sed/201106_wp3.pdf.

6 Kang, S., Scharmann, L. C. and Noh, T. (2005). Examining students' views on the nature of science: Results from Korean 6th, 8th, and 10th graders. *Science Education*, 89, 314–34.
    Kawasaki. K. (1996). The concepts of science in Japanese and Western education. *Science and Education*, 5 (1) 1–20.
7 Alters, B. J. (1997). Whose nature of science? *Journal of Research in Science Teaching*, 34: 39–55.
8 Smith, M. U., Lederman, N. G., Bell, R. L., McComas, W. F. and Clough, M. P. (1997). How great is the disagreement about the nature of science: A response to Alters. *Journal of Research in Science Teaching*, 34, 1101–3.
9 Osborne, J., Simon, S. and Collins S. (2003). Attitudes towards science: A review of the literature and its implications. *International Journal of Science Education*, 25:9, 1049–79.
10 McComas, W. F. and J. K. Olson (1998). The nature of science in international standards documents, in *The Nature of Science in Science Education: Rationales and Strategies* (W. F. McComas, ed.), 41–52. Dordrecht, The Netherlands: Kluwer Academic Publisher.
11 Rudolph, J. L. (2000). Reconsidering the 'nature of science' as a curriculum component. *Journal of Curriculum Studies*. 32(3) 403–19
12 Dupré J. (1993). *The Disorder of Things: Metaphysical Foundations of the Disunity of Science*. Cambridge, MA: Harvard University Press.
    Dupré, J. (2001). *Human Nature and the Limits of Science*. Oxford: Oxford University Press.
13 Dupré, J. 1993, op. cit., 18.
14 Habermas, J. (1984). *The Theory of Communicative Action*, Vol. 1. Cambridge: Polity Press.
    Rorty, R. (1991). *Objectivity, Relativism, and Truth: Philosophical Papers*, Vol. 1. Cambridge: Cambridge University Press.
15 Dunbar, K. (1997). How scientists think: on-line creativity and conceptual change in science, in T. B. Ward, S. M. Smith and J. Vaid (eds). *Creative Thought: An Investigation of Conceptual Structures and Processes*. Washington, DC: American Psychological Association: 13. I am influenced here by K. Sawyer (2006). *Explaining Creativity: The science of human innovation*. New York: Oxford University Press, and K. Sawyer (2007). *Group Genius: The creative power of collaboration*. New York: Basic Books.
16 Gillies, D (1998). The Duhem Thesis and the Quine Thesis, in M. Curd and J. A. Cover (eds) (1998). *Philosophy of Science: The Central Issues*. New York: W. W. Norton & Co: 302–19.
17 Bakhtin, M. M. (1984). *Problems of Dostoevsky's poetics* (C. Emerson, ed. and trans.). Minneapolis: University of Minnesota Press.
18 Bakhtin, M. M. (1986). *Speech Genres and Other Late Essays*, Austin, TX: University of Texas Press: 114.
19 Ibid., p. 168.
20 Bakhtin, M. M. (1981). Discourse in the novel, in M. M. Bakhtin, *The Dialogic Imagination: four essays by M. M. Bakhtin*. Austin, TX: University of Texas Press: 343.
21 See also Roth, M. (2009). *Dialogism: A Bakhtinian Perspective on Science Language and Learning*. Rotterdam: Sense Publishers.
22 Sjøberg and Schreiner (2007), op. cit.
23 Osborne and Dillon (2008), op. cit.
24 Sjøberg, S. and Schreiner, C. (2005). How do learners in different cultures relate to science and technology? *Asia-Pacific Forum on Science Learning and Teaching*, 6(2).
25 Giddens, Anthony (2000). *Runaway World*. London: Routledge.
26 SED WP3, op. cit.
27 SED WP2 (2011) SEDWP2D1: Documentary Analysis Synthesis Report. Available on: http://www.marchmont.ac.uk/Documents/Projects/sed/wp2_final_report.pdf. (accessed 21 Feb 2012).
28 Nanda, M. (1997). The science wars in India. *Dissent*, 44(1), 79–80.
29 Carter, L. 2004. Thinking Differently About Cultural Diversity: Using Postcolonial Theory to (Re)read Science Education. *Science Education*, 88: 819–36.

30 Hermans, H. J. M. (2001). The dialogical self: Toward a theory of personal and cultural positioning. *Culture & Psychology*. Special Issue: Culture and the Dialogical Self: Theory, Method and Practice, 7, 243–81.

31 Haste, H. (2004). Science in my Future: A study of values and beliefs in relation to science and technology amongst 11–21 year olds. London: Nestlé Social Research Programme. A report available at www.spreckley.co.uk/nestle/science-in-my-future-full.pdf.

32 Sjoberg and Schreiner (2005), op. cit.

33 Sjøberg and Schreiner (2007), op. cit.

34 Rocard M. *et al.* (2007). *Science Education Now: a renewed pedagogy for the future of Europe.* Luxembourg: Office for Official Publications of the European Communities: 2.

35 Minner, D., Levy, A. and Century, J. (2010). Inquiry-Based Science Instruction—What Is It and Does It Matter? Results from a Research Synthesis Years 1984 to 2002. *Journal of Research in Science Teaching*, 47, 4, 474–96.

   CILASS (2008) Inquiry-based learning: a conceptual framework. Available at http://www.shef.ac.uk/cilass/resources (last accessed 22 Sept 2011).

36 Minner *et al.* (2010), op. cit., p. 493.

37 Rogoff, B. (1994). Developing understanding of the idea of communities of learners. *Mind, Culture, and Activity*, 1 (4), 209–29.

   Brown, A. L. (1992). Design experiments: Theoretical and methodological challenges in creating complex interventions in classroom settings. *Journal of the Learning Sciences*, 2(2), 141–78.

38 Polman, J. L. and Pea, R. D. (2001). Transformative communication as a cultural tool for guiding inquiry science. *Science Education*, 85: 223–38.

39 Sprod. T. (2011). *Discussions in Science: Promoting Conceptual Understanding in the Middle School Years.* Melbourne: Australian Council Educational Research (ACER).

40 Mercer, N., Dawes, L., Wegerif, R. and Sams, C. (2004). Reasoning as a scientist: Ways of helping children to use language to learn science. *British Educational Research Journal* 30(3), 359–77.

   Webb, P. and Treagust, D. (2006). Using exploratory talk to enhance problem-solving and reasoning skills in grade-7 science classrooms. *Research in Science Education,* 36(4), 381–401.

41 Oakeshott, M. (1989) *The Voice of Liberal Learning: Michael Oakeshott on Education* (T. Fuller, ed.). New Haven and London: Yale University Press.

42 Millar, R. and Osborne, J. F. (eds.) (1998). *Beyond 2000: Science education for the future.* London: King's College London.

   Driver, R., Newton, P. and Osborne, J. (2000). Establishing the norms of scientific argumentation in classrooms. *Science Education*, 84(3), 287–312.

   Millar, R. (2006). Twenty First Century Science: insights from the design and implementation of a scientific literacy approach in school science. *International Journal of Science Education,* 28(13), 1499–1521.

43 Osborne, J., Erduran, S. and Simon, S. (2004). Enhancing the quality of argument in school science. *Journal of Research in Science Teaching*, 41(10), 994–1020.

44 Mercer, N., Dawes, L., Wegerif, R. and Sams, C. (2004). Reasoning as a scientist: Ways of helping children to use language to learn science. *British Educational Research Journal,* 30(3), 359–77.

   Lemke, J. L. (1990). *Talking science: Language, learning and values.* Norwood, NJ: Ablex Publishing.

   Mortimer, E. F. Scott. P. H. (2003). *Meaning making in secondary science classrooms.* Maidenhead: Open University Press.

45 Lemke, 1990, op. cit.

46 Mercer *et al.* (2004), op. cit.; Osborne (2007) op. cit.; Osborne *et al.* (2004), op. cit.

47 Seddon, K., Skinner NC. and Postlethwaite K. C. (2008). Creating a model to examine motivation for sustained engagement in online communities. Education and Information Technologies, Vol. 13, Number 1: 17–34.

48 Parmesan, C., Ryrholm, N., Stefanescu C. *et al.* (1999). Poleward shifts in geographical ranges of butterfly species associated with regional warming. *Nature,* 399, 579–83.

7 Educating the planet

 1 Adapted and expanded considerably from a keynote talk given at the 'Civitas Educationis: Interrogazioni e sfide pedagogiche' conference held in Naples in November 2009 and published as Wegerif, R. (2011). Civitas Educationis, Tecnologie della comunicazione ed Infinita Responsabilità, in Frauenfelder, E., De Sanctis, O., Corbi, E. (eds). Civitas Educationis: Interrogazioni e sfide pedagogiche. Napoli: Liguori.
 2 Linell, P. (2009). *Rethinking language, mind and world dialogically: Interactional and contextual theories of human sense-making.* Charlotte, NC: Information Age Publishing.
 3 Rommetveit, R. (1992). Outlines of a dialogically based social-cognitive approach to human cognition and communication, in A. Wold (ed.), *The dialogical alternative: towards a theory of language and mind:* 19–45. Oslo: Scandanavian Press.
 4 In the Analects of Confucius we can read: "Zi Gong asked, saying, 'Is there one word that may serve as a rule of practice for all one's life?' The Master said, 'Is not RECIPROCITY such a word?' and also 'Never impose on others what you would not choose for yourself'. Confucius, *Analects* (James Legge, trans.) http://ctext.org/analects (accessed 23 June 2012).
 5 Matthew 7:12; see also Luke 6:31. New Testament, New International Edition (2011). Available online at http://www.devotions.net/bible/00new.htm (accessed 18.06.11).
 6 Kitab al-Kafi, Vol. 2: 146 (Muhammad Sarwar, trans.). http://gadir.free.fr/eng/books/ Kafi/html/eng/books/hadith/al-kafi/index.htm (accessed 23 June 2012).
 7 Blackburn, S. (2001). *Ethics: A Very Short Introduction.* Oxford: Oxford University Press: 101.
 8 Luria, A. (1976). *Cognitive Development Its Cultural and Social Foundations.* Cambridge, MA: Harvard University Press.
 9 Wattles, J. (1996). *The Golden Rule.* New York: Oxford University Press.
10 Pinker, S. (2011). *The Better Angels of our Nature.* New York: Viking.
11 I suspect that this is a deficit model of the thinking of orality. See Price-Williams, D. (1999). In Search of Mythopoetic Thought. *Ethos,* 27: 25–32.
12 Olson, D. (1994). *The World on Paper.* Cambridge: Cambridge University Press.
      Ong, W. J. (1982). *Orality and Literacy: The Technologizing of The Word.* Methuen, London.
      Goody, J. (1977). *The domestication of the savage mind.* Cambridge: Cambridge University Press.
13 Price-Williams, D., op. cit.
14 Innis, H. (1950). *Empire and Communications.* Oxford: Clarendon Press: 30.
15 Anderson, B. (1983) Imagined Communities: Reflections on the Origin and Spread of Nationalism. London: Verso.
16 Poster, M. (1995). *The Second Media Age.* Oxford: Blackwell.
17 Ong, W., op. cit.,129.
18 This effect is discussed in Castells, M. (2002). *The Internet galaxy: Reflections on the Internet, business, and society.* New York: Oxford University Press.
19 Bevir, M. (2001). Derrida and Heidegger Controversy: Global Friendship against Racism, in S. Caney and P. Jones (eds), *Human Rights and Global Diversity.* London and Portland: Frank Cass.
20 Ibid. p. 135.
21 Ulmer, G. L. (2003). *Internet Invention: From Literacy to Electracy.* New York: Longman.
22 While of course for Derrida this is an Otherness and a responsibility that cannot and should not be named without falling into a contradiction this does not mean that he does not take responsibility for the Other seriously. See Derrida, J. (1992). *The Gift of Death* (David Wills, trans.). Chicago: University of Chicago Press.
23 Levinas, E. (1961). *Totalité et Infini: essai sur l'extériorité.* Paris: Le Livre de Poche.

24 Bakhtin, M. (1986). *Speech genres and other late essays*. Austin: University of Texas.
25 Bakhtin, M. (1981). Discourse in the novel, in M. M. Bakhtin (ed.), *The dialogic Imagination. Four essays by M. M. Bakhtin*. Austin: University of Texas Press: 276. Lévinas, E. (1978), Autrement qu'être ou au-dela de l'essence. Paris: Livre de Poche: 239. Of course there is a difference between them in Levinas's according of asymmetry to this relation arguing that the face of the other is above me and not a call to reciprocity. This means that my calling Levinas a dialogic thinker is open to challenge. However, I am not focusing here on the asymmetry to symmetry distinction in dialogue but on some insights from Levinas that expand dialogic theory.
26 Volosinov, V. N. (1986). Marxism and the philosophy of language. Cambridge, MA: Harvard University Press: 102–3. Bakhtin op. cit. and one to Levians, E. (1990) Heidegger, Gagarin and Us, in *Difficult Freedom: Essays on Judaism*, (SeaÅLn Hand, trans.). Baltimore: Johns Hopkins Press: 231–4.
27 Bakhtin, op. cit page 7.
28 Levinas, E. (1990). Heidegger, Gagarin and Us, in *Difficult Freedom: Essays on Judaism*, (Sean Hand, trans.). Baltimore: Johns Hopkins Press: 231–4.
29 In *The Gift of Death*, op. cit. Derrida brings out some problems with the concept of the 'Infinite Other' describing how responsibility to one other involves not responding to all the other others each one of whom is also an Infinite Other. This is just reminding us that the Infinity in the Infinite Other concept should not be read as an abstract universal concept or even in the singular but more as a constant undermining of all grounds that is as plural as it is singular in the way that a horizon is singular yet has many, infinitely many, points of view.
30 I am here reading Derrida's différance notion, against Derrida, as a version of Merleau-Ponty's écart between sentient and sensed and so reading Derrida's deconstruction as functionally equivalent to Merleau-Ponty's 'hyper-reflection' which remains in the gap between sentient and sensed. There is some support for this move in the literature for example, Reynolds, J. (2004). *Merleau-Ponty and Derrida: Intertwining Embodiment and Alterity*. Athens: Ohio University Press.
31 Wegerif, R., Mercer, N. and Dawes, L. (1999). From social interaction to individual reasoning: an empirical investigation of a possible socio-cultural model of cognitive development. *Learning and Instruction,* 9 (5).
32 Stahl, G., Zhou, N., Cakir, M. P. and Sarmiento-Klapper, J. W. (2011). Seeing what we mean: Co-experiencing a shared virtual world. Paper presented at the international conference on Computer Support for Collaborative Learning (CSCL 2011). Hong Kong, China. Proceedings: 534–41. Web: http://GerryStahl.net/pub/cscl2011.pdf, http://GerryStahl.net/pub/cscl2011.ppt.pdf,http://youtu.be/HC6eLNNIvCk.
33 Leimann, M. (2002). Toward semiotic dialogism: the role of sign mediation in the dialogical self. *Theory and Psychology* 12(2): 221–35.
34 Fritsch, M. (2002) Derrida's Democracy To Come. *Constellations: An International Journal of Critical and Democratic Theory,* 9:4: 574–97.
35 Brooks, J., Normore, A. (2010). Educational Leadership and Globalization: Literacy for a Glocal Perspective. *Educational Policy* 24 (1): 52–82.
36 Wegerif, R. and Dawes, L. (2004). *Thinking and Learning with ICT: raising achievement in primary classrooms*. London: Routledge.
37 A study by Steve Williams and Richard Athlone described in Wegerif, R (2007). *Dialogic, Education and Technology: Expanding the Space of Learning*. NY and Berlin: Springer: 267.
38 Goody, op. cit.
39 Biesta, G. (2010). *Good Education in an Age of Measurement: Ethics, Politics, Democracy*. New York: Paradigm.
40 Ipgrave, J. (2003). Building E-Bridges. Inter-faith Dialogue by E-mail. *Teaching Thinking,* Summer, Issue 11.
41 de Bono, Edward (1985). *Six Thinking Hats: An Essential Approach to Business Management*. Little, Brown, & Company. ISBN 0-316-17791-1 (hardback) and 0316178314 (paperback).

42 See also Habermas, J. (1979). 'What is Universal Pragmatics?' in Habermas, Jürgen (1979). *Communication and the Evolution of Society* (Thomas McCarthy, trans.). Boston, MA: Beacon Press.
43 Wegerif, R. (2005) Reason and Creativity in Classroom Dialogues. *Language and Education,* 19(3). 223–38.
44 There is an analysis of the importance of openness as a foundational orientation in Higham, R, Freathy, R, Wegerif, R (2010). Developing responsible leadership through a 'pedagogy of challenge': an investigation into leadership education for teenagers. *School Leadership and Management.* 30(5), 419–34.
45 Dr. Math http://researchspace.csir.co.za/dspace/bitstream/10204/1614/1/Butgereit_2007.pdf (accessed 23 June 2012).

8 Education into dialogue

1 Smock, D. (ed) (2002). *Interfaith Dialogue and Peacebuilding.* Washington, DC: US Institute of Peace Press.
2 Craft, A., Cremin, T., Burnard, P., Dragovic, T. and Chappell, K. (2012). Possibility Thinking: Culminative Studies Of An Evidence-Based Concept Driving Creativity?, *Education 3–13: International Journal Of Primary, Elementary And Early Years Education.* doi:10.1080/03004279.2012.656671.
3 Foucault, M. (1973). *The order of things: An archaeology of the human sciences.* (Sheridan-Smith, trans). New York: Vintage.
4 De Cusa, N. (1440/2012) On Learned Ignorance. (J. Hopkins, trans.). http://my.pclink.com/~allchin/1814/retrial/cusa1.pdf. (Accessed 22 June 2012.)
5 Mead, G. H. (1934). *Mind, Self, and Society* (Charles W. Morris, ed.). Chicago: University of Chicago Press.
6 Like all metaphors this visual metaphor of a horizon is limited in many respects.
7 I feel the need to point out here that the Infinite Other is not God, at least not the interventionist God of the Abramamic religious traditions. It is more an effect of the way that consciousness works. A necessary and influential illusion one might say. For me dialogic theory is an entirely scientific approach that helps us to understand religious experience and so what is valid in religious worldviews.
8 Howe, C. (2010). *Peer groups and children's development.* Oxford: Blackwell.
9 Baars, B. J. (1997). *In the Theater of Consciousness.* New York, NY: Oxford University Press.
10 Kounios, J. and Beeman, M. (2009). The Aha! moment: The cognitive neuroscience of insight. Current Directions. *Psychological Science,* 18, 210–16.
11 Deacon, T. (1997). *The symbolic species: The co-evolution of language and the human brain.* London: Penguin: 455.
12 Donald, M. (2001). *A mind so rare: The evolution of human consciousness.* New York: W.W. Norton & Co. Ltd; Tomasello, M, Carpenter, M., Call, J., Behne, T. and Moll, H. (2005). Understanding and sharing intentions: the origins of cultural cognition. *Behaviour and Brain Science.* 28(5), 675–91.
13 Anderson, B. (1983) Imagined Communities: Reflections on the Origin and Spread of Nationalism. London: Verso.
14 Barad, K. (2007) Meeting the Universe Halfway. Durham, NC: Duke University Press.
15 A scan of the original letter from Einstein to Marcus, written February 12th 1950, can be found on http://weblog.liberatormagazine.com/2010/10/einstein-on-being-human-sayings.html.
16 Linell, P. (2009). *Rethinking language, mind and world dialogically: Interactional and contextual theories of human sense-making.* Charlotte, NC: Information Age Publishing.
17 Carr, N. (2010). *The Shallows: What the Internet is Doing to Our Brains;* New York, NY: W. W. Norton & Co. Ltd.

REFERENCES

Adolph, K. E. and Kretch, K. S. (2012). Infants on the edge: Beyond the visual cliff, in A. Slater and P. Quinn (eds). *Developmental psychology: revisiting the classic studies*. London: SAGE Publications.

Al'lbrahim., A. (2010). The pedagogical affordances of social network technology: A study in an undergraduate course in Exeter University. The 4th Saudi International Conference, Manchester University, July.

Alexander, R. (2000). *Culture and Pedagogy*. Oxford: Blackwell.

— (2006). *Towards Dialogic Teaching: Rethinking classroom talk* (Third Edition). Cambridge: Dialogos.

Alters, B. J. (1997). Whose nature of science? *Journal of Research in Science Teaching*, 34: 39–55.

Anderson, B. (1983). *Imagined Communities: Reflections on the Origin and Spread of Nationalism*. London: Verso

Archer, M. (2003). *Structure, Agency and the Internal Conversation*. Cambridge: Cambridge University Press,

Austin, J. (2009). *Mini weapons of mass destruction: Build implements of spitball warfare*. Chicago: Chicago Review Press.

Baars, B. J. (1997). *In the Theater of Consciousness*. New York: Oxford University Press.

Bakhtin, M. M. (1981). Discourse in the novel, in M. M. Bakhtin (ed.), *The dialogic Imagination. Four essays by M. M. Bakhtin*. Austin: University of Texas Press.

— (1984). *Problems of Dostoevsky's poetics* (C. Emerson, ed. and trans.). Minneapolis: University of Minnesota Press.

— (1986). *Speech genres and other late essays*. Austin: University of Texas.

Barad, K. (2007). *Meeting the Universe Halfway*. Durham, N.C: Duke University Press.

Baron-Cohen, S. (1994). The Mindreading System: new directions for research. *Current Psychology of Cognition*, 13, 724–50.

— (2011). *Zero Degrees of Empathy: A new theory of human cruelty*. London: Penguin/Allen Lane.

Bereiter, C. (1994). Implications of Postmodernism for Science, or, Science as Progressive Discourse. *Educational Psychologist*, 29(1) 3–12.

— (2002). *Education and mind in the knowledge age*. Mahwah, NJ: Lawrence Erlbaum Associates.

Bevir, M. (2001). Derrida and Heidegger Controversy: Global Friendship against Racism, in S. Caney and P. Jones (eds), *Human Rights and Global Diversity*. London and Portland: Frank Cass.

Bhaskar, R. A. (1997). *A Realist Theory of Science*. London: Verso.

Biesta, G. (2004). The community of those who have nothing in common. Education and the language of responsibility. *Interchange* 35(3), 307–24.

— (2006). *Beyond learning: Democratic education for a human future*. Boulder CO: Paradigm Press.

— (2010). *Good Education in an Age of Measurement: Ethics, Politics, Democracy*. New York: Paradigm.

Blackburn, S. (2001). *Ethics: A Very Short Introduction*. Oxford: Oxford University Press.

Blakemore, S-J., Bristow, D., Bird, G., Frith, C. and Ward, J. (2005). Somatosensory activations during the observation of touch and a case of vision-touch synesthesia. *Brain,* 128, 1571–83. doi:10.1093/brain/awh500ý

Boswell, James (1791/1986). *The Life of Samuel Johnson* (Christopher Hibbert, ed.). New York: Penguin Classics or Gutenberg ebooks http://www.gutenberg.org/ebooks/1564.

Brooks, J. and Normore, A. (2010). Educational Leadership and Globalization: Literacy for a Glocal Perspective. *Educational Policy,* 24 (1): 52–82.

Brown, A. L. (1992). Design experiments: Theoretical and methodological challenges in creating complex interventions in classroom settings. *Journal of the Learning Sciences,* 2(2), 141–78.

Bruner, J. (1996). Celebrating Piaget and Vygotsky: An exercise in dialectic. Paper presented at the Second Conference for Socio-Cultural Research, Geneva.

Buber, M. (1947). *Tales of the Hasidim: Early Masters* (0. Marx, trans.). Schocken: New York. Referred to in Smith, M. K. (2000, 2009). Martin Buber on education. *The encyclopaedia of informal education,* http://www.infed.org/thinkers/et-buber.htm.

— (1958). *I and Thou* (Second Edition) (R. Gregory Smith, trans.). Edinburgh: T & T Clark.

Carr, N. (2010). *The Shallows: What the Internet is Doing to Our Brains*. New York, W. W. Norton & Co.

Carter, L. 2004. Thinking Differently About Cultural Diversity: Using Postcolonial Theory to (Re)read Science Education. *Science Education,* 88: 819–36.

Castells, M. (1997, Second Edition, 2004). *The Power of Identity, The Information Age: Economy, Society and Culture, Volume II*. Oxford: Blackwell.

— (2002). *The Internet galaxy: Reflections on the Internet, Business, and Society*. New York: Oxford University Press.

CILASS (2008). Inquiry-based learning: a conceptual framework. Available at http://www.shef.ac.uk/cilass/resources (accessed 22 Sept 2011).

Claxton, G. (2006) Thinking at the edge: developing soft creativity. *Cambridge Journal of Education,* 36(3), 351–62.

— (2008). *What is the Point of School?* London: Oneworld Publications.

Cobb, P., Gresalfi, M. and Hodge, L. L. (2009). An interpretive scheme for analysing the identities that students develop in mathematics classrooms. *Journal for Research in Mathematics Education,* 40–68.

Collins, A. and Halverson, R. (2009). *Rethinking Education in the Age of Technology: The Digital Revolution and the Schools*. New York: Teachers College Press.

Confucius, *Analects* (J. Legge, trans.) http://ctext.org/analects (accessed 23 June 2012).

Cox, B. and Forshaw, J. (2011). *The Quantum Universe: Everything that can happen does happen*. London: Allen Lane.

Craft, A., Cremin, T., Burnard, P., Dragovic, T. and Chappell, K. (2012). Possibility Thinking: Culminative Studies Of An Evidence-Based Concept Driving Creativity?,

Education 3–13: International Journal Of Primary, Elementary And Early Years Education. doi:10.1080/03004279.2012.656671.

Craft, A., McConnon, L. and Matthews, A. (2012). Creativity and child-initiated play: fostering possibility thinking in four-year-olds. *Thinking Skills and Creativity*, 7(1) 48–61.

Csikszentmihalyi, M. (1996). *Creativity: flow and the psychology of discovery and invention.* New York: Harper Perennial.

Damasio, A. R. (1994). *Descartes' error: emotion, reason, and the human brain.* New York: Putnam.

Daniels, H., (2001). *Vygotsky and Pedagogy.* London: Routledge.

Davidson, C. (2011). How the Brain Science of Attention Will Transform the Way We Live, Work, and Learn. New York: Viking: 13.

Dawes, L., Mercer, N. and Wegerif, R. (2004). 'Thinking Together': A programme of activities for developing speaking, listening and thinking skills for children aged 8–11 (Second Edition). Birmingham: Imaginative Minds Ltd.

Deacon, T. (1997). *The symbolic species: The co-evolution of language and the human brain.* London: Penguin.

de Bono, Edward (1985). *Six Thinking Hats: An Essential Approach to Business Management.* Little, Brown, & Company.

De Cusa, N. (1440/2012) On Learned Ignorance. (J. Hopkins, trans.). http:// my.pclink. com/~allchin/1814/retrial/cusa1.pdf. (Accessed 22 June 2012.)

Dehaene, S. (2009). *Reading in the Brain.* New York: The Viking Press.

Dehaene, S. and Naccache, L. (2001) Toward a cognitive neuroscience of consciousness: basic evidence and a workspace framework. *Cognition*, 79, 1–37.

Dehaene S., Pegado F., Braga, L. W., Ventura P., Nunes Filho, G., Jobert A., Dehaene-Lambertz G., Kolinsky R., Morais J. and Cohen L. (2010). How learning to read changes the cortical networks for vision and language. *Science*, 330 (6009): 1359–64.

De Jaegher, H., Di Paolo, E. A. and Gallagher, S. (2010). Can social interaction constitute social cognition?, *Trends in Cognitive Sciences*, 14(10), 441–7.

De Laat, M. (2006) Networked Learning. Apeldoorn: Politie Academy.

Deleuze, G. (1994). *Difference and Repetition* (Paul Patton, trans.). New York: Columbia University Press.

Dennett, D. (1991). *Consciousness Explained.* London: Allen Lane.

Derrida, J. (1968). La Différance, in *'Théorie d'ensemble'*. Paris: Éditions de Seuil: 41–66.

— (1973). Differance, in Derrida, J., *Speech and Phenomena: and other essays on Husserl's Theory of Signs.* Evanston: Northwestern University Press.

— (1989). *Of Spirit: Heidegger and the Question.* Chicago: University of Chicago Press.

— (1992). *The Gift of Death* (David Wills, trans.). Chicago: University of Chicago Press.

Donald, M. (2001). *A Mind So Rare: The evolution of human consciousness.* New York: W. W. Norton & Co.

Driver, R., Newton, P. and Osborne, J. (2000). Establishing the norms of scientific argumentation in classrooms. *Science Education*, 84(3), 287–312.

Dupré J. (1993). *The Disorder of Things: Metaphysical Foundations of the Disunity of Science.* Cambridge, MA: Harvard University Press.

— (2001). *Human Nature and the Limits of Science.* Oxford University Press.

Dunbar, K. (1997). How scientists think: on-line creativity and conceptual change in science, in T. B. Ward, S. M. Smith and J. Vaid (eds). *Creative Thought: An Investigation of Conceptual Structures and Processes.* Washington, DC: American Psychological Association.

Einstein, A. (1949). The World As I See It. New York: Philosophical Library.

European Commission (2004). *Europe needs More Scientists: Report by the High Level Group on Increasing Human Resources for Science and Technology.* Brussels. European Commission.

Fernyhough, C. (1996). The dialogic mind: a dialogic approach to the higher mental functions. *New Ideas in Psychology*, 14, 47–62.

Foucault, M. (1973). *The Order of Things: An Archaeology of the Human Sciences*. (Sheridan-Smith, trans). New York: Vintage.

Freire, P. (1972). *Pedagogy of the Oppressed*. Harmondsworth: Penguin.

Fritsch, M. (2002). Derrida's Democracy To Come. *Constellations: An International Journal of Critical and Democratic Theory*, 9:4, 574–97.

Gallagher, S. (2011). Strong Interaction and Self-Agency. *Humana.Mente: Journal of Philosophical Studies*, 15, 55–77.

— (2012). Neurons, neonates and narrative: From embodied resonance to empathic understanding, in Ad Foolen, Ulrike Lüdtke, Jordan Zlatev and Tim Racine (eds), *Moving ourselves: Bodily motion and emotion in the making of intersubjectivity and consciousness*. Amsterdam: John Benjamins: 13–33.

— (2007). Neurophilosophy and neurophenomenology, in L. Embree and T. Nenon (eds), *Phenomenology 2005 Volume 5*. Bucharest: Zeta Press. 293–316.

Garcia-Sierra, A., Rivera-Gaxiola, M., Percaccio, C. R., Conboy, B. T., Romo, H., Klarman, L., Ortiz, S. and Kuhl, P. T. (2011). Bilingual language learning: An ERP study relating early brain responses to speech, language input, and later word production. *Journal of Phonetics*, 39, 4, 546–57. doi:10.1016/j.wocn.2011.07.002.

Gee, J. P. (2003). *What video games have to teach us about learning and literacy*. New York: Palgrave/Macmillan.

Geirland, John (1996). Go With The Flow. *Wired* magazine. September, Issue 4.09. Available on http://www.wired.com/wired/archive/4.09/czik_pr.html (accessed 26 August 2006).

Giddens, A. (2000). *Runaway World*. London: Routledge.

Giles, J. (2005). Special Report Internet encyclopaedias go head to head. *Nature*, 438, 900-901 (15 December 2005). doi:10.1038/438900a; published online 14 December 2005 (retrieved 1 December 2011). from: http://www.nature.com/nature/journal/v438/n7070/full/438900a.html

Gillies, D. (1998). The Duhem Thesis and the Quine Thesis, in M. Curd and J. A. Cover (eds) (1998), *Philosophy of Science: The Central Issues*. New York: W. W. Norton & Co. 302–19.

Goody, J. (1977). *The domestication of the savage mind*. Cambridge: Cambridge University Press.

Goodyear, P., Banks, S., Hodgson, V. and McConnell, D. (eds) (2004). Advances in Research on Networked Learning. London: Kluwer Academic Publishers.

Greenfield, S. (2008). Modern technology is Changing the Way the Brain Works Says Neuro-Scientist. *Daily Mail*, 21 May 2008 (retrieved 27 August 2008 from http://www.dailymail.co.uk/sciencetech/article-565207/Modern-technology-changing-way-brains-work-says-neuroscientist.html).

Grice, H. P. 1975. Logic and conversation, in *Syntax and Semantics*, 3: Speech Acts, (P. Cole and J. Morgan, eds). New York: Academic Press.

Habermas, J. (1979). What is Universal Pragmatics?, in Habermas, J. (1979), *Communication and the Evolution of Society* (Thomas McCarthy, trans.). Boston, MA: Beacon Press.

— (1984). *The Theory of Communicative Action, Volume 1*. Cambridge: Polity Press.

— (1993). *Justification and Application*. Cambridge, MA: MIT Press.

Haste, H. (2004). *Science in my Future: A study of values and beliefs in relation to science and technology amongst 11–21 year olds*. London: Nestle Social Research Programme.

Hegel, G. W. F. (1975). *The Logic of Hegel* (W. Wallace, trans.). Oxford: Clarendon Press.

Heidegger, M. (1978). *Basic Writings*. London: Routledge.

Hennessey, S. (2011). The role of digital artefacts on the interactive whiteboard in supporting classroom dialogue. Journal of Computer Assisted Learning. 27(6) 463–89.

Hermans, H. J. M. (2001). The dialogical self: Toward a theory of personal and cultural positioning. *Culture & Psychology*. [Special Issue: Culture and the Dialogical Self: Theory, Method and Practice, 7, 243–81.]

Higham, R., Freathy, R. and Wegerif, R. (2010). Developing responsible leadership through a 'pedagogy of challenge': an investigation into leadership education for teenagers. *School Leadership and Management*. 30(5), 419–34.

Hirsch, E. D. (1987). *Cultural Literacy: What every American Should Know*. Boston: Houghton Mifflin.

Hobson, R. P. (1998). The intersubjective foundations of thought, in (S. Braten, ed.). *Intersubjective Communication and Emotion in Ontogeny*. Cambridge: Cambridge University Press: 283–96.

— (2002). *The cradle of thought : exploring the origins of thinking*. London: Macmillan.

Hodes, A. (1972). *Encounter with Martin Buber*. London: Allen Lane. (Also published 1971, as *Martin Buber: An Intimate Portrait*. New York: The Viking Press.)

Howard-Jones, P. A. (2010). *Introducing neuroeducational research: Neuroscience, education and the brain from contexts to practice*. Abingdon: Routledge.

Howe, C. (2010). *Peer groups and children's development*. Oxford: Blackwell.

Innis, H. (1950). *Empire and Communications*. Oxford: Clarendon Press.

Ipgrave, J. (2003). Building E-Bridges. Inter-faith Dialogue by E-mail. *Teaching Thinking*, Summer, Issue 11.

James, W. (1950). *The Principles of Psychology*, Two Volumes (called "Principles"). New York: Dover.

Kaiser Family Trust (2010). Generation M2: Media in the Lives of 8- to 18-Year-Olds. http://www.kff.org/entmedia/8010.cfm.

Kang, S., Scharmann, L. C. and Noh, T. (2005). Examining students' views on the nature of science: Results from Korean 6th, 8th, and 10th graders. *Science Education*, 89, 314–34.

Kant, I. (1781/1929). *Critique of Pure Reason* (Norman Kemp Smith, trans.). London: Macmillan Press.

Karmiloff-Smith, A. (1992, reprinted 1995). *Beyond Modularity: A Developmental Perspective on Cognitive Science*. Cambridge, MA: MIT Press/Bradford Books.

Kawasaki. K. (1996). The concepts of science in Japanese and Western education. *Science and Education,* 5 (1), 1–20.

Koschmann, T. (ed.) (2011). *Theories of learning and studies of instructional practice*. New Jersey: Springer.

Kounios, J. and Beeman, M. (2009). The Aha! moment: The cognitive neuroscience of insight. *Current Directions in Psychological Science*, 18, 210–16.

Krunic, V. and Han, R. (2008). Towards Cyber-Physical Holodeck Systems Via Physically Rendered Environments (PREs). *Distributed Computing Systems Workshops*, 2008. doi: 10.1109/ICDCS.Workshops.2008.31.

Lakoff, G. and Johnson, M. (1980). Metaphors We Live By. Chicago: University of Chicago Press.

Langer, E. and Moldoveanu, M. (2000). The construct of mindfulness. *Journal of Social Issues*, 56 (1), 1–9.

Langer, E. J. and Piper, A. I. (1987). The prevention of mindlessness. *Journal of Personality and Social Psychology*, 53, 280–7.

Langer, E., Hatem, M., Joss, J. and Howell, M. (1989). Conditional teaching and mindful learning: The role of uncertainty in education. *Creativity Research Journal*, 2, 139–50.

Lave, J. and Wenger, E. (1991). *Situated Learning: Legitimate Peripheral Participation*. Cambridge: Cambridge University Press.

Leibniz, G. (1973), Philosophical writings. (G. H. R. Parkinson, ed., Mary Morris and G. H .R. Parkinson, trans.). London: J. M. Dent & Sons Ltd.

Leimann, M. (2002). Toward semiotic dialogism: the role of sign mediation in the dialogical self. *Theory and Psychology* 12(2): 221–35.

Lemke, J. L. (1990). *Talking science: Language, learning and values.* Norwood, NJ: Ablex Publishing.

Levinas, E. (1961). *Totalité et Infini: essai sur l'extériorité.* Paris: Le Livre de Poche.

— (1978). *Autrement qu'être ou au-dela de l'essence.* Paris: Le Livre de Poche.

— (1989) 'Substitution' (A. Lingis, trans.), in S. Hand (ed.), *The Levinas Reader.* Oxford: Blackwell: 88–125.

— (1990) Heidegger, Gagarin and Us, in *Difficult Freedom: Essays on Judaism,* (Seán Hand, trans.). Baltimore: Johns Hopkins Press: 231–4.

Lewis-Williams, D. J. (2002). *The Mind In The Cave: Consciousness And The Origins Of Art.* London: Thames & Hudson.

Lewis-Williams, J. D. and Pearce, D. G. (2004). *San Spirituality: Roots, Expressions and Social Consequences.* Walnut Creek: Altamira Press.

Libet, B. (2004). *Mind time: The temporal factor in consciousness, Perspectives in Cognitive Neuroscience.* Cambridge, MA: Harvard University Press.

Linell, P. (2009). *Rethinking language, mind and world dialogically: Interactional and contextual theories of human sense-making.* Charlotte, NC: Information Age Publishing.

Luria, A. (1976). *Cognitive Development Its Cultural and Social Foundations.* Cambridge, MA: Harvard University Press.

Mallarmé, S. (1998). *Poésies et autres texts.* Paris, Le Livre de Poche.

Mackness, J., Mak, S. F. J. and Williams, R. (2010). The Ideals and Reality of Participating in a MOOC. Proceedings of the 7th International Conference on Networked Learning.

Mansour, N. and Wegerif, R. (in press for 2012/13). *Science Education for Diversity.* New Jersey: Springer Science.

Marx, K. (1977). *Selected writings* (David McLellan, trans. and ed.). Oxford: Oxford University Press.

Matusov, E. (2009). *Journey into dialogic pedagogy.* Hauppauge, NY: Nova Publishers.

— (2011). Irreconcilable differences in Vygotsky's and Bakhtin's approaches to the social and the individual: An educational perspective. *Culture & Psychology,* 17 (1), 99–119.

McComas, W. F., and Olson. J. K. (1998). The nature of science in international standards documents, in W. F. McComas (ed.), *The Nature of Science in Science Education: Rationales and Strategies.* Dordrecht, The Netherlands: Kluwer Academic Publisher. 41–52.

Mead, G., H. (1934). *Mind, Self, and Society* (Charles W. Morris. ed.). Chicago: University of Chicago Press.

Meltzoff, A. N. and Moore, M. K. (1977). Imitation of facial and manual gestures by human neonates. *Science* 198:75–8.

Mercer, N. (1995). *The guided construction of knowledge: Talk amongst teachers and learners.* Clevedon: Multilingual Matters.

— (2000). *Words and Minds: how we use language to think together.* London: Routledge.

Mercer, N. and Littleton, K. (2007). *Dialogue and the Development of Children's Thinking: A Sociocultural Approach.* London: Routledge.

Mercer, N., Dawes, L., Wegerif, R. and Sams, C. (2004). Reasoning as a scientist: Ways of helping children to use language to learn science. *British Educational Research Journal* 30(3), 359–77.

Merleau-Ponty, M. (1964). *Le Visible et L'Invisible.* (Claude Lefort, ed.). Paris: Gallimard.

— (1968) The Visible and the Invisible. (Claude Lefort, ed., Alphonso Lingis, trans.). Evanston, Il: Northwestern University Press.

— (2005). *Phenomenology of Perception* (Colin Smith, trans.). London: Routledge.

Millar, R. (2006). Twenty First Century Science: insights from the design and implementation of a scientific literacy approach in school science. *International Journal of Science Education*, 28(13), 1499–1521.

Millar, R. and Osborne, J. F. (eds) (1998). *Beyond 2000: Science education for the future.* London: King's College London.

Minner, D., Levy, A. and Century, J. (2010) Inquiry-Based Science Instruction—What Is It and Does It Matter? Results from a Research Synthesis Years 1984 to 2002. *Journal of Research in Science Teaching*, 47, 4, 474–96.

Montaigne, M. (1595). *Les Essais.* Available online at: http://www.lib.uchicago.edu/ efts/ ARTFL/projects/montaigne/ (accessed 1 December 2011).

Mortimer, E. F. and Scott. P. H. (2003). *Meaning making in secondary science classrooms.* Maidenhead: Open University Press.

Nanda, M. (1997). The science wars in India. *Dissent*, 44(1), 79–80.

New Testament, New International Edition (2011). Available online at http://www. devotions.net/bible/00new.htm (accessed 18 June 2011).

Nikulin, D. (2010). *Dialectic and Dialogue.* Stanford: Stanford University Press. Kindle Edition.

Nystrand, M. (1997). *Opening dialogue: Understanding the dynamics of language and learning in the English classroom.* New York: Teachers College Press.

Oakeshott, M. (1962). *The Voice of Poetry in the Conversation of Mankind, Rationalism in Politics and Other Essays.* London: Methuen.

— (1989) *The Voice of Liberal Learning: Michael Oakeshott on Education* (T. Fuller, ed.). New Haven and London: Yale University Press.

Olson, D. (1994). *The World on Paper.* Cambridge: Cambridge University Press.

Ong, W. J. (1982). *Orality and Literacy: The Technologizing of The Word.* Methuen, London.

Osborne, J. (2007). Engaging young people with science: Thoughts about future direction of science education, in C. Linder, L. Östman and P. Wickman (eds). Promoting scientific literacy: science education research in transaction. Proceedings of Linnaeus Tercentenary Symposium held at Uppsala University, Uppsala, Sweden, 28–29 May 2007: 105–112.

Osborne, J. and Dillon. J. (2008). *Science Education in Europe: Critical Reflections.* London: Nuffield Foundation.

Osborne, J., Collins, S., Ratcliffe, M., Millar, R. and Duschl, R. (2003). What "ideas-about-science" should be taught in school science? A Delphi study of the expert community. *Journal of Research on Science Teaching*, (40) 7, 692–720, 2003.

Osborne, J., Erduran, S. and Simon, S. (2004). Enhancing the quality of argument in school science. *Journal of Research in Science Teaching*, 41(10), 994–1020.

Osborne, J., Simon, S and Collins, S (2003). Attitudes towards science: A review of the literature and its implications. *International Journal of Science Education*, 25:9, 1049–79.

Parmesan, C., Ryrholm, N., Stefanescu, C., *et al.* (1999). Poleward shifts in geographical ranges of butterfly species associated with regional warming. *Nature* 399, 579–83.

Penrose, R. (1989). *Emperor's new mind: Concerning computers, minds and the laws of physics.* Oxford: Oxford University Press.

— (1994). *Shadows of the mind: a search for the missing science of consciousness.* Oxford: Oxford University Press.

Pifarré, M. and Kleine Staarman, J. (2011). Wiki-supported collaborative learning in Primary Education: How a "dialogic space" is created for 'Thinking Together'. *International Journal of Computer-Supported collaborative Learning* 6(2), 187–205.

Pinker, S. (2011). *The Better Angels of our Nature.* New York: The Viking Press.

Plato (360 BCE/2006). *Phaedrus* (B. Jowett, trans.). Available online at: http://ebooks. adelaide. edu.au/p/plato/p71phs/ (accessed 1 December 2011).

— (380 BCE/2006). *Meno* (B. Jowett, trans.). Available online at: http://ebooks.adelaide. edu.au/p/plato/p71phs/ (accessed 1 December 2011).

Polman, J. L. and Pea, R. D. (2001). Transformative communication as a cultural tool for guiding inquiry science. *Science Education*, 85: 223–38.

Poster, M. (1995). *The Second Media Age*. Oxford: Blackwell.

Price-Williams, D. (1999). In Search of Mythopoetic Thought. *Ethos*, 27: 25–32.

Rajala, A., Hilppö. J. and Lipponen, L. (2011). The Emergence of Inclusive Exploratory Talk in Primary Students' Peer Interaction. *International Journal of Educational Research*. doi: 10.1016/j.ijer.2011.12.011.

Ramírez, M. S. and y Burgos, J. V. (2010) (coords.). Recursos educativos abiertos en ambientes enriquecidos con tecnología: Innovación en la práctica educativa. México: Instituto Tecnológico y de Estudios Superiores de Monterrey. Disponible en:http://www.lulu.com.

Reynolds, J. (2004), *Merleau-Ponty and Derrida: Intertwining Embodiment and Alterity*. Athens: Ohio University Press.

Rocard M. *et al.* (2007). *Science Education Now: a renewed pedagogy for the future of Europe*. Luxembourg: Office for Official Publications of the European Communities.

Rogoff, B. (1994). Developing understanding of the idea of communities of learners. *Mind, Culture, and Activity*, 1 (4), 209–29.

Rogoff, B., Gauvain, G. and Ellis, C. (1991). Development viewed in its cultural context, in P. Light, A. Sheldon and B. Woodhead (eds), *Learning to think*. London: Routledge.

Rojas-Drummond, S., Fernandez, M. Mazon, N. and Wegerif, R. (2006). Collaborative talk and creativity. *Teaching Thinking and Creativity*, 1(2). 84–94.

— (2006). Explicit reasoning, creativity and co-construction in primary school children's collaborative activities. *Thinking Skills and Creativity*, 1(2), 84–94.

Rommetveit, R. (1992). Outlines of a dialogically based social–cognitive approach to human cognition and communication, in A. Wold (ed.), *The dialogical alternative: towards a theory of language and mind*. Oslo: Scandanavian Press.

Rorty, R. (1991). *Objectivity, Relativism, and Truth: Philosophical Papers*, Volume 1. Cambridge: Cambridge University Press.

Roth, M. (2009). *Dialogism: A Bakhtinian Perspective on Science Language and Learning*. Rotterdam: Sense Publishers.

Rudolph, J. L. (2000). Reconsidering the 'nature of science' as a curriculum component. *Journal of Curriculum Studies*. 32(3) 403–19.

Salomon, G. (1992). New information technologies in education, in M. C. Alkin (ed.), *Encyclopaedia of educational research* (Sixth Edition). New York: Macmillan.

Saul, J. R. (1992). *Voltaire's Bastards: The Dictatorship of Reason in the West*. Toronto: Penguin Books.

Sawyer, K., (2006). *Explaining Creativity: The science of human innovation*. New York: Oxford University Press.

— (2007). *Group genius: The creative power of collaboration*. New York: Basic Books.

Seddon, K., Skinner, N. C. and Postlethwaite, K. C. (2008). Creating a model to examine motivation for sustained engagement in online communities. *Education and Information Technologies*, Volume 13, Number 1:17–34.

SED WP2 (2011) SEDWP2D1: Documentary Analysis Synthesis Report. Available on: http://www.marchmont.ac.uk/Documents/Projects/sed/wp2_final_report.pdf (accessed 21 Feb 2012).

SED WP3 (2011) SEDWP3D1: Survey Research Synthesis Report. Available on: http://www.marchmont.ac.uk/Documents/Projects/sed/201106_wp3.pdf.

Shaffer, D. W. (2007). *How Computer Games Help Children Learn*. New York: Palgrave.

Sheth, Bhavin R., Sandkühler, S. and Bhattacharya, Joydeep (2009). Posterior Beta and Anterior Gamma Oscillations Predict Cognitive Insight. *Journal of Cognitive Neuroscience*, 21(7): 1269–79.

Shotter, J. (2001).Toward A Third Revolution In Psychology: From Inner Mental Representations To Dialogical Social Practices, in D. Bakhurst and S. Shanker (eds), *Culture, Language, Self: the Philosophical Psychology of Jerome Bruner*. London: Sage Publications.

Sidorkin, A. M. (1999). Beyond discourse: Education, the self and dialogue. New York: State University of New York Press.

Siemens, G., Connectivism: A learning theory for the digital age. *International Journal of Instructional Technology and Distance Learning* 2 (10), 2005.

Sjøberg, S. and Schreiner, C. (2005). How do learners in different cultures relate to science and technology? *Asia-Pacific Forum on Science Learning and Teaching*, 6(2): 1–17

— (2007). Perceptions and images of science and science education, in M. Claessens (ed.), *Communicating European Research 2005*. Heidelberg, Germany: Springer.

Smith, M. K. (1997, 2002). Paulo Freire and informal education. *The encyclopaedia of informal education*. [www.infed.org/thinkers/et-freir.htm. Last update: 1 December 2011].

— (2000, 2009). Martin Buber on education. *The encyclopaedia of informal education*, http://www.infed.org/thinkers/et-buber.htm.

Smith, M. U., Lederman, N. G., Bell, R. L., McComas, W. F. and Clough, M. P. (1997). How great is the disagreement about the nature of science: A response to Alters. *Journal of Research in Science Teaching*, 34, 1101–3.

Smock, D. (ed.) (2002). *Interfaith Dialogue and Peacebuilding*. Washington, DC: US Institute of Peace Press.

Sprod. T. (2011). *Discussions in Science: Promoting Conceptual Understanding in the Middle School Years*. Melbourne: Australian Council Educational Research (ACER).

Stahl, G., Zhou, N., Cakir, M. P. and Sarmiento-Klapper, J. W. (2011). Seeing what we mean: Co-experiencing a shared virtual world. Proceedings of the International Conference on Computer Support for Collaborative Learning (CSCL 2011). Hong Kong, China. 534–41.

Tallis, R. (2011). Aping Mankind: Neuromania, Darwinitis and the Misrepresentation of Humanity. Durham: Acumen Publishing.

Thagard, P. and Stewart, T. C. (2011). The AHA! Experience: Creativity Through Emergent Binding in Neural Networks. *Cognitive Science*, 35: 1–33.

Thomas, D. and Brown, J. S. (2011). *A new culture of learning: Cultivating the Imagination for a World of Constant Change*. New York: Createspace.

Thomas, M. S. C. (in press). Brain plasticity and education. *British Journal of Educational Psychology* [Special issue on Educational Neuroscience]. To be published in 2012.

Tomasello, M. (2008). *Origins of Human Communication*. Cambridge MA: MIT Press.

Tomasello, M, Carpenter, M., Call, J., Behne, T. and Moll, H. (2005). Understanding and sharing intentions: the origins of cultural cognition. *Behaviour and Brain Science,* 28(5), 675–91.

Toulmin, S. (1990). *Cosmopolis: the hidden agenda of modernity*. New York: Free Press.

Trevarthen, C. (1979). Communication and cooperation in early infancy: a description of primary intersubjectivity, in M. Bullowa (ed.), *Before speech. The beginning of interpersonal communication*. Cambridge: Cambridge University Press.

Ulmer, G. L. (2003). *Internet Invention: From Literacy to Electracy*. New York: Longman.

Varela, F. J. and Shear, J. (eds) (1999). The View From Within: First-Person Approaches to the Study of Consciousness. A special issue of the *Journal of Consciousness Studies*.

van der Veer, R. and Valsiner, J. (1991). *Understanding Vygotsky: A quest for synthesis*. Oxford: Blackwell.

Velmans, M. (2000). *Understanding Consciousness*. London: Routledge.

Volosinov, V. N. (1986). *Marxism and the philosophy of language*. Cambridge, MA: Harvard University Press.

Vygotsky, L. S. (1978). Mind in society: *The development of higher psychological processes*. Cambridge, MA: Harvard University Press.

— (1986). *Thought and language* (A. Kozulin, trans.). Cambridge, MA: MIT Press.

— (1987). *The collected works of L. S. Vygotsky. Volume 1. Problems of general psychology. Including the Volume Thinking and speech*. (N. Minick, ed. and trans.). New York: Plenum.

— (1991). The Genesis of Higher Mental functions, in P. Light, S. Sheldon and B. Woodhead (eds), *Learning to think*. London: Routledge: 32–41.

Wattles, J. (1996). *The Golden Rule*. New York: Oxford University Press.

Webb, P. and Treagust, D. (2006). Using exploratory talk to enhance problem-solving and reasoning skills in grade-7 science classrooms. *Research in Science Education*, 36(4), 381–401.

Wegerif, R. (1996) Collaborative learning and directive software. *Journal of Computer Assisted Learning*, 12 (1): 22–32. ISSN 0266-4909.

— (1999). Two models of reason in education. *The School Field*, 9 (3–4): 77–107.

— (2002). Walking or dancing? Images of thinking and learning to think in the classroom. *Journal of Interactive Learning Research*, 13 (1). 51–70.

— (2004). Towards an account of teaching general thinking skills that is compatible with the assumptions of sociocultural theory. *Theory and Research in Education*, 2(2), 143–59.

— (2005). Reason and Creativity in Classroom Dialogues. *Language and Education*, 19(3). 223–38.

— (2007). *Dialogic, Education and Technology: Expanding the Space of Learning*. New York and Berlin: Springer.

— (2008). Dialogic or Dialectic? The significance of ontological assumptions in research on Educational Dialogue. *British Educational Research Journal*, 34(3), 347–61.

— (2010). *Mindexpanding: Teaching for thinking and creativity in primary education*. Buckingham: Open University Press.

— (2011). Civitas Educationis, Tecnologie della comunicazione ed Infinita Responsabilità, in Frauenfelder, E., De Sanctis, O., Corbi, E. (eds). Civitas Educationis: Interrogazioni e sfide pedagogiche. Napoli: Liguori.

— (2011). From dialectic to dialogic: A response to Wertsch and Kazak, in T. Koschmann (ed.), *Theories of learning and studies of instructional practice*. NJ: Springer.

Wegerif, R. and Mercer, N. (1997). A dialogical framework for researching peer talk, in Wegerif R. and Scrimshaw P. (eds), *Computers and talk in the primary classroom*. Clevedon: Multilingual Matters.

Wegerif, R. and Dawes, L. (2004). *Thinking and Learning with ICT: raising achievement in primary classrooms*. London: Routledge.

Wegerif, R. and Scrimshaw, P. (eds) (1998), *Computers and Talk in the Primary Classroom*. Clevedon: Multilingual Matters.

Wegerif, R., Mercer, N. and Dawes, L. (1999). From social interaction to individual reasoning: An empirical investigation of a possible sociocultural model of cognitive development. *Learning and Instruction*, 9(5), 493–516.

Wegerif, R., Perez Linares, J., Rojas Drummond, S., Mercer, N. and Velez, M. (2005). 'Thinking Together' in the UK and Mexico: Transfer of an educational innovation. *Journal of Classroom Interaction*, 40(1), 40–7.

Wegerif, R., Postlethwaite, K., Skinner, N., Mansour, N., Morgan, A., Hetherington, L. (2013). Dialogic science education for diversity, in Mansour, N and Wegerif, R (eds) (2013). *Science Education for Diversity*. New Jersey: Springer.

Weinberg, K. M. and Tronick, E. Z. (1996). Infants' affective reactions to the resumption of maternal interaction after the still-face. *Child Development*, 67, 905–14.

Wells, G. (1999). *Dialogic inquiry: Towards a sociocultural practice and theory of education.* Cambridge: Cambridge University Press.

Wells, G. (ed.) (2001). *Action, Talk and Text: Learning and Teaching Through Through Inquiry.* New York: Teachers College Press.

Wenger, E. (1999). *Communities of practice. Learning, meaning and identity.* Cambridge: Cambridge University Press.

Wertsch, J. V. (1985). *Vygotsky and the social formation of mind.* Cambridge, MA: Harvard University Press.

— (1991). *Voices of the Mind.* New York: Harvester.

— (1998). *Mind as Action.* New York: Oxford University Press.

Wolfe S. (2006). Teaching and learning through dialogue in primary classrooms in England. Unpublished PhD thesis, University of Cambridge.

Yang, Y and Wegerif, R. (in preparation). *Learning to Learn Together in a Chinese Classroom: The Importance of Group Roles.*

YouthNet (2009). Life support: young people's needs in the digital age. http://www. youthnet.org/wp-content/uploads/2011/05/Life-Support-Report.pdf (accessed 23 June 2012).

INDEX